JAN 17 2012

PELLISSIPPI STATE
LIBRARY SERVICES
P. O. BOX 22990
KNOXVILLE, TN 37933-0990

TASHLINESQUE

THE HOLLYWOOD COMEDIES OF FRANK TASHLIN

ETHAN DE SEIFE

WESLEYAN UNIVERSITY PRESS

Middletown, Connecticut

Wesleyan University Press
Middletown CT 06459
www.wesleyan.edu/wespress
© 2012 by Ethan de Seife
All rights reserved
Manufactured in the United States of America
Designed by Richard Hendel
Typeset in Chapparal, Meta, and Mostra types by
Tseng Information Systems, Inc.

Wesleyan University Press is a member of the Green Press Initiative.
The paper used in this book meets their minimum requirement for recycled paper.

Library of Congress Cataloging-in-Publication Data
Seife, Ethan de.
Tashlinesque: The Hollywood comedies of Frank Tashlin / Ethan de Seife.
   p. cm.
Includes bibliographical references and index.
Includes filmography.
ISBN 978-0-8195-7240-0 (cloth: alk. paper) —
ISBN 978-0-8195-7241-7 (ebook)
1. Tashlin, Frank—Criticism and influence. I. Title.
PN1998.3.T365S46 2012
791.4302′33092—dc23
                              2011047917

5 4 3 2 1

For

Lo, Lala, and Laura

and Godfrey

CONTENTS

Preface: Tashlin Resurgent / ix

Acknowledgments / xv

INTRODUCTION
The Director Who Wasn't / 1

CHAPTER ONE
Tish-Tash in Cartoonland / 16

CHAPTER TWO
Tashlin, Comedy, and the "Live-Action Cartoon" / 52

CHAPTER THREE
"Hurry up! This is impossible!": Tashlin's Early Feature Films / 69

CHAPTER FOUR
The Artist and His Model: Tashlin and Jerry Lewis in the 1950s / 94

CHAPTER FIVE
The Director and the Bombshell: Tashlin and Jayne Mansfield / 119

CHAPTER SIX
Disorderly Conduct: Tashlin in the 1960s / 145

CHAPTER SEVEN
The Man in the Middle: Tashlin, Auteurs, and Programmers / 174

CHAPTER EIGHT
Who's Minding the Store?: Tashlin's Influence / 187

Appendix: Frank Tashlin's Creative Work / 211

Notes / 219

Index / 243

PREFACE TASHLIN RESURGENT

Director Frank Tashlin has left an indelible impression on American and global film comedy. His films are some of the funniest, most visually inventive comedies ever made, and they feature landmark performances by some of the greatest comedians in American film history, a list that includes not only Bob Hope and Jerry Lewis, but Porky Pig, Daffy Duck, and Bugs Bunny. Tashlin's unusual career offers fascinating insights into the ways in which vaudeville-style comedy shaped American film comedy; the development, the flowering, and the legacy of the "Golden Age" of Hollywood animation; the complex histories of ribald sexual comedy and challenging satirical comedy within American film; the value and the power of the Auteur Theory; both the writings and the films of the French New Wave; the inner workings of the Hollywood studio system itself; and the power and indelibility of film genres.

Yet Tashlin's name is still largely unfamiliar, and his influence, though significant, is acknowledged by only a few acolytes. Even within film studies, his reputation is not as strong as it ought to be. As I argue in this book, Tashlin has been generally misunderstood for decades.

It is the goal of this volume to put the films of Frank Tashlin in their proper context, and to show how and why his films are vital, important, and worthy of scrutiny. The most important context for understanding Tashlin's films is that of comedy, the genre into which nearly all of his work must be categorized, and a major reason that his reputation is not stronger than it is.

Tashlin is rarely cited as an influence by filmmakers and, aside from a small number of scholarly articles, has been largely ignored by the critical establishment. His films have won no awards, and the path of his scattershot extracinematic career is strewn with false starts and oddities. Even the most passionate cinephiles among my undergraduate film students do not recognize the director's name. Tashlin's star does not burn brightly in the film studies firmament.

When Tashlin's decade-long partnership with Jerry Lewis ended with *The Disorderly Orderly* in 1964, the director began a slow fade into an obscurity that, save for isolated pockets of adulation composed of auteur idolators like Peter Bogdanovich, has continued to the present day. He has not yet really been reclaimed by the cognoscenti in Hollywood or academe, though several of his contemporaries have been either officially recognized (Stanley Donen and Blake Edwards have both received "lifetime achievement" Oscars; Edwards's films, at long last, are the subject of a book) or are the objects of devoted film-studies academic cults (Robert Aldrich, Anthony Mann, Nicholas Ray).

But perhaps the tide is turning. The last decade or so has witnessed something of a newfound scholarly and popular interest in the films of Frank Tashlin. When I started writing this book, I was compelled to remark on the underrepresentation on video of Tashlin's animated work. At that time, only the first two volumes of the Looney Tunes DVD sets had been released; among their 116 films is but a single Tashlin cartoon. Since then, Volumes 3, 4, 5, and 6 of this fine (if haphazardly organized) series have, by the time of this writing, made available more than two dozen Tashlin cartoons and Tashlin-oriented "bonus features" to the toon-hungry public. Online, two of the rarest of all Tashlin films have recently surfaced. *The Lady Said No* (1947; one of his few forays into stop-motion animation), served as the inaugural download at Cartoon Brew Films, a website run by animation historians/enthusiasts Jerry Beck and Amid Amidi. Even more improbably, Tashlin's incredibly obscure, church-funded, anti-nuclear animated short, *The Way of Peace* (1947), has, through the efforts of researchers into the history of the Evangelical Lutheran Church in America, been digitized and uploaded for all to see.[1]

On the feature-film front, Twentieth Century-Fox released, in August 2006, a handsome three-disc Jayne Mansfield DVD set that includes two of Tashlin's live-action masterpieces, *The Girl Can't Help It* (1956) and *Will Success Spoil Rock Hunter?* (1957); these films, too, have been "legitimized" by the inclusion of commentary tracks and suchlike. And Paramount has finally done right by the legacy of one of its most profitable and important series: the two-volume, seven-disc "Dean Martin and Jerry Lewis Collection" has, at long last, given us excellent versions of thirteen of this great duo's films, including Tashlin's pair, *Artists and Models* (1955) and *Hollywood or Bust* (1956). Tashlin's work remains underrepresented on DVD, but there exist other, more egregious omissions (e.g., nearly the entire filmographies of both Kenji Mizoguchi and Mikio Naruse, but this is not the place to complain).

Even more surprising than the occasional DVD release is the Tashlin retrospective that played at repertory cinemas such as New York's Film Forum and Chicago's Gene Siskel Film Center in 2006. Film Forum, for one, showed new 35mm prints of, among six other features, such near-forgotten films as *The Lieutenant Wore Skirts* (1956) and *Bachelor Flat* (1962).[2]

No one is more surprised—or delighted—by these developments than I am. The research for this project was, at times, challenging. The difficulty was not in finding historical documents, for the great majority of these reside in the excellently maintained Frank Tashlin Collection at the Margaret Herrick Library in Beverly Hills. The trickiest task was locating the films themselves, some of which existed only in private collections. To locate the prints for my research—and for the Tashlin retrospective that I curated at the University of Wisconsin-Madison Cinematheque in 2003—I had to plead with archivists all over North America and Europe, and relied on the generosity of private donors. More than one fellow film programmer, on learning of the series, called me to express disbelief. "How did you assemble a *Tashlin* series?" they would ask incredulously. "Those films are impossible to find!" Not impossible—just very difficult and rather out of favor. I would never have imagined that, just four years later, Tashlin retrospectives—featuring new prints!—would find audiences in major cities.

The uptick in interest in Tashlin's work would seem to be part and parcel of two recent phenomena: the escalation of interest in film comedy in general, and the prominence of animation within both media scholarship and mass media.

Regarding scholarship on film comedy, works such as Henry Jenkins's *What Made Pistachio Nuts?: Early Sound Comedy and the Vaudeville Aesthetic*, Steve Seidman's *Comedian Comedy: A Tradition in American Film*, and Steve Neale's and Frank Krutnik's *Popular Film and Television Comedy* have laid the groundwork for a blossoming of scholarly studies on film comedy over the past two decades. These books advanced the field significantly from earlier works that belong to a more anecdotal, observational tradition. Jenkins, Seidman, Neale, and Krutnik are vital figures in the effort to take comedy seriously—a task made all the more difficult by its seemingly oxymoronic nature. Such scholars focus their questions both stylistically and historically, asking how certain comic styles developed and how media industries changed (and were changed by) transformations in the styles, subject matters, and directors and performers of comedy.

These works, which seem now to belong to the "first wave" of serious comedy scholarship, have sown many seeds. The last decade alone has seen the publication of scholarly texts on such unlikely and heretofore academically "inconsequential" or *verboten* subjects as Blake Edwards, Italian popular film comedy, and even the musical comedies of Grigorii Aleksandrov; we now have on our shelves definitive texts on the history of African-American comedy, a host of new books that re-evaluate American romantic comedy, and at least three recent scholarly and/or biographical volumes on Buster Keaton alone.[3] And these are just the published books; this quick survey does not take into account such forums as scholarly articles and academic conferences, many of which have seen a concurrent, if less quantifiable, rise in good, solid comedy scholarship. Happily, this particular subfield seems wide and vigorous enough to support more esoteric excursions of a scholarly nature—one of which may be this book. Though my own interest in Tashlin's films goes back a couple of decades now, a volume such as this surely could not have been written without the laying down of extensive groundwork, and by changes in the climate of film studies that permit the publishing of a work such as this.

The second current—the explosion of animation—is harder still to quantify, but undeniable nevertheless. Perhaps traceable to the 1992 U.S. launch of Cartoon Network but certainly percolating before that time, animation's rise to ubiquity is nothing less than incredible. Of the fifty biggest-grossing films worldwide as of August, 2011, not a single one does not make use of drawn, stop-motion, and/or computer animation of some kind.[4] Even the seemingly "all natural" romantic musical comedy *Mamma Mia!* (2008), whose $600 million at the box office earns it the mere rank of fifty-fifth-biggest-grossing film, counts among its technicians dozens of compositors and digital effects artists.[5] Moreover, almost every new medium and media/entertainment-delivery device in the last two decades—cable television, satellite television, internet video, mobile phones of all stripes, every videogame platform you can name, as well as billboards, subway advertisements, Tamagotchi, and countless other bits of gimcrackery—all of these things depend on animation to deliver narratives, games, advertising, and information. In the modern, media-besotted world, animation is almost unavoidable.

A large percentage of the moving images that permeate the modern media landscape—be they measured by running time or percentage of onscreen real estate—are animated.

Tashlin fits into the animation equation by assisting in the development—as a matter of course in his job as a working animator from the 1920s through the 1940s—of the syntax and semantics of American animation. Tashlin helped to define the Golden Age of American animation, which has come to serve as *the* baseline for the style of much of the animation produced around the world in the decades since. The rules of volume, movement, shape, line, dimensionality, narration, comedy, character, expressivity, and many other facets of animation were mined, experimented upon, and codified during this remarkably fertile period of cinematic innovation, and Tashlin was right there in the thick of it. Most modern animation still derives—narratively, stylistically, volumetrically—from the principles that were put into practice during Tashlin's tenure as an animator.

All of which is to say that a study of Frank Tashlin's films—both animated and live-action, for he is one of the very few directors to bridge that gap—suggests contexts that are relevant not only to understanding the films of this long-neglected director, but that open up avenues of inquiry into wider-reaching areas of film and media study. Tashlin is an unusual director, and a historical and stylistic analysis of his work can and does encourage us to consider the intersections of comedy (and genre in general), animation, Hollywood stardom, authorship, censorship, industrial changes in Hollywood over a forty-year period, and many other important topics in film history. Frank Tashlin is ripe for rediscovery. If we are witnessing some kind of Tashlin renaissance, I am pleased to play my part.

The Handy-Dandy-Dandy Guide to the Book about Frank Tashlin

For the most part, this volume is arranged chronologically. Chapter One examines his animated work in detail. Chapter Two steps out of chronology—somewhat—to investigate the resemblance, or lack thereof, of Tashlin's short cartoons and his feature-length live-action films. Chapter Three focuses on two of Tashlin's early features, *The First Time* and *Son of Paleface*, both of interest for their demonstration of his rapidly developing live-action style. Chapter Four singles out *Artists and*

Models as one of the more consequential films in Tashlin's career: it was the first of eight films Tashlin made with Jerry Lewis, the most important of all of his comedic collaborators. This chapter also considers Tashlin's second and final Martin and Lewis picture, *Hollywood or Bust*. Chapter Five addresses the two films that represent Tashlin's artistic zenith: *The Girl Can't Help It* and *Will Success Spoil Rock Hunter?*.[6] In these films, all of the most important aspects of Tashlin's style come together to yield the richest comedic results of the director's career. The subjects of Chapter Six are several of the films of Tashlin's late feature career, with an emphasis on both the nearly forgotten *Bachelor Flat* and on *The Disorderly Orderly*, his last Jerry Lewis film.

Chapter Seven steps out of chronology to summarize and contextualize: I consider Tashlin's films alongside those of auteurs such as Howard Hawks and Billy Wilder, as well as program directors such as Norman Taurog and Hal Walker. As well, this chapter takes on, at the level of the mechanics of style and comedy, the generalization that has dominated Tashlin criticism for almost fifty years: that his cartoons anticipate his features, and that his features somehow resemble live-action cartoons. Chapter Eight reflects more fully on Tashlin's influence on a small number of modern filmmakers.

By mapping a study of the most relevant features of Tashlin's style atop a chronological study of his films, a sense of the development of the director's method emerges. Such an approach, I believe, highlights not only the generic and stylistic traditions of which Tashlin's films are part, but the elements of his style that belong peculiarly to him. The principal goal of this volume is to place the filmmaking style of Frank Tashlin in a historical context. For as long as Tashlin has been taken even somewhat seriously, his films have been studied *outside* of the contexts that are most relevant and most potentially revealing: comedy history, Hollywood history, stylistic history. The many arguments about the similarity of Tashlin's animated and live-action films are ultimately unrewarding; to learn more about this fine director, I propose a different approach. Frank Tashlin should be seen neither as a unique filmmaking talent, nor as merely a cog in the Hollywood machine. Like all creative artists working within a profit-driven system, he falls somewhere in between these extremes. Above all, Tashlin is a director of comedies, and his style is most fruitfully understood in light of the ways he uses it for the creation of humor.

ACKNOWLEDGMENTS

Without the constant support, encouragement, and advice of Lea Jacobs, this book would never have been written. Her suggestions were always excellent ones, and the finished product is far better as a result of her contributions. I also wish to thank David Bordwell, Vance Kepley, Patrick Rumble, and Ben Singer, all of whom made invaluable contributions that strengthened the project immeasurably. Kelley Conway and Malcolm Turvey offered astute comments and assistance. Special thanks to Keith Cohen, whose early criticisms and suggestions were enormously encouraging.

I owe a tremendous debt to Howard Prouty, Acquisitions Archivist at the Margaret Herrick Library in Beverly Hills, who, long before I ever embarked on this project, meticulously catalogued the contents of the Frank Tashlin Collection. Howard was extremely generous in granting me access to the entire collection, and was unfailingly friendly and helpful, to boot. Also at the Margaret Herrick Library, Barbara Hall, Jenny Romero, and Heather von Rohr helped me a great deal. Archivists all over Los Angeles were very kind in their assistance: Ned Comstock at USC's Doheny Memorial Library Cinema-Television Archive; Randi Hokett and Jennifer Prindiville at USC's Warner Bros. Archive; and Steve Ricci, Mark Quigley, and Yvonne Behrens at the UCLA Film & Television Archive. More than once, and on short notice, Schawn Belston at Twentieth Century-Fox generously provided hard-to-find research materials. At the Wisconsin Center for Film and Theatre Research, my friends Maxine Fleckner-Ducey and Dorinda Hartmann made my research fun and easy. The staffs of the University of Wisconsin-Madison's Memorial Library, Gettysburg College's Musselman Library, and Hofstra University's office of Faculty Computing Services provided valuable research and technical assistance.

Dewey McGuire contributed ideas, suggestions, articles, and many bad puns to this project. Jerry Beck and Mark Kausler, two of the greatest friends and advocates Hollywood animation will ever have, went out of their way to arrange for me to see several rare Tashlin cartoons; without their help, my work would be seriously incomplete.

Joe Dante lent me his time and shared with me his vast knowledge of Tashlin and Hollywood comedy. My interview with Tony Randall took place less than a year before his death, and I was fortunate to glean some of the insights of this great actor.

Roger Garcia shared his expert thoughts on Tashlin with me; Donald Crafton kindly sent me a copy of an unpublished article; Henry Jenkins helped me focus my thoughts on vaudeville comedy; and Christine Becker sent me a copy of her essay on Tashlin, which suggested numerous avenues of inquiry. Charlie Keil and Daniel Goldmark, in editing for publication an excerpt of the chapter on Tashlin's animation, helped me bring my arguments into focus.

My research trips would not have been anywhere near as enjoyable or successful without my group of terrific friends in Los Angeles. In particular, I want to thank, for their hospitality and support, Ed Lee; Bill Wolkoff; David Goodman, Tanya Ward Goodman, Theo Goodman, and the not-quite-born-by-that-point Sadie Goodman; Danielle Langston, Carl Grodach, and Otto Grodach; Martha Simmons and Carlos Jean; Henry Myers; Ari Chaet; and Bill Macomber.

In Madison, Andrew Yonda, Paddy Rourke, Erik Gunneson, and Kevin French lent me their technical expertise; Linda Henzl, Kim Bjarkman, Philip Sewell, Brian Block, Dave Resha, Carlee P. Ragsdale, and Lauren R. Robinson were very generous in their support.

One could not ask for a better study partner than Katherine Spring, whose intelligence is outweighed only by her kindness. Tom Yoshikami has been a great and loyal friend for years, and was always available when I needed assistance and advice. Lisa Jarvinen never failed to offer encouragement from the trenches of academic warfare. Paul Ramaeker, our man in the antipodes, has given all kinds of advice on writing, researching, and the maintenance of morale.

Though Eric Levy has since moved on from Wesleyan University Press, it was his interest in my research that brought this book about, and his unflagging enthusiasm for it that helped me to get it done. Also at Wes Press, Parker Smathers and Suzanna Tamminen provided frequent and invaluable editorial assistance. I thank Amanda Dupuis and Ann Klefstad for making the book far more readable and easier on the eyes. Jay Herman has earned the rank of Wizard of Photoshop: without his help, the images for this book, so important in discussing cinematic style, would not exist at all.

Any errors in my work are, of course, my own; but if, by some chance, it turned out well, I have Jeanine Basinger to thank. I was fortunate to study with, work with, and be inspired by her at Wesleyan University, and I owe to her any success I find as a film scholar.

My family provided all kinds of support: emotional, moral, financial, and anything else you can think of. Jane Needham, Bill Needham, Allison de Seife, Jimmy Witt, and Rita Aborn are, respectively, the best mother, stepfather, sister, uncle, and grandmother a guy could ask for, and I love them all very much.

Finally, my wife, Laura Holtan, continues to inspire me and keep me sane. None of my work would be nearly as worthwhile if she were not by my side. Like everything else I do, this book is dedicated to her.

INTRODUCTION THE DIRECTOR WHO WASN'T

Francis Fredrick von Taschlein was born on February 19, 1913, in Weehawken, New Jersey, a town whose irresistibly comical name the director employs as the putative birthplace of Patricia Crowley's character in *Hollywood or Bust*.[1] In 1927, a student publication at Junior High School 126 in Queens, New York, was "profusely illustrated" with Tashlin's cartoons.[2] Two years later, at the age of sixteen, Tashlin found a job as a cel-washer at Fleischer Animation's New York studios; this led to a job at Van Beuren, the nearly forgotten animation studio responsible for such series as the original *Tom and Jerry*, whose titular characters are neither feline nor murine, but human. At Van Beuren, Tashlin worked his way from inker to in-betweener to animator, a common career progression for a talented young man in his field. Around 1930, he started selling cartoons to a number of humor magazines, such as *Hooey*, *Slapstick*, and the marvelously named *Captain Billy's Whiz Bang*.[3]

Tashlin received his first screen credit for the Tom and Jerry film *Hook and Ladder Hokum*, released in April 1933. (For Tashlin's complete filmography, see the Appendix.) It was around this time that Tashlin met Leon Schlesinger, producer of Warner Bros.' Looney Tunes and Merrie Melodies cartoons. Tashlin accepted Schlesinger's job offer and moved to Los Angeles to join the stable of young, innovative animators at the fabled "Termite Terrace" building.

Tashlin had three separate tours of duty with Warners. The first intermission occurred in early 1934, when Tashlin's daily comic strip, "Van Boring" (a silent, hapless character modeled on Tashlin's former boss, Amedée J. Van Beuren), began its two-year run in the *Los Angeles Times*.[4] Schlesinger asked for a piece of the strip's profits; Tashlin wrote of the situation, "He wanted a cut of it, and I said go to hell. So he fired me."[5]

Tashlin found work as a gagman at Hal Roach Studios, where he worked (without receiving screen credit) on a couple of "Our Gang" shorts, a Laurel and Hardy feature,[6] and a vehicle for comedian Patsy Kelly. It is not often remembered that Tashlin had firsthand experience writing for some of Hollywood's most successful live-action slapstick series.

In his second stint at Termite Terrace (April 1936–December 1938), Tashlin's chief charge was the development of Warner Bros. animation's first star, Porky Pig. During this time, Tashlin directed twenty-one cartoons, thirteen of which featured Porky, who had debuted in Friz Freleng's *I Haven't Got a Hat* (1935). Tashlin directed about a third of Porky's films in the character's first three years of existence, and invented Porky's girlfriend, Petunia, for his 1937 film *Porky's Romance*.[7]

The years 1939–1940 were frustrating, transitional ones for Tashlin, who left Schlesinger for Disney in January 1939. Working there for two years as a story- and gagman, Tashlin received not a single screen credit. He worked on an unspecified number of cartoon shorts, and may have contributed ideas to the features *Fantasia* (1940) and *Lady and the Tramp* (1955).[8]

Just before the famous Disney animators' strike in 1941, Tashlin left the studio, having been offered a plum job as head of the story department at Screen Gems, Columbia Pictures' new animation division.[9] He soon rose to production supervisor, and hired a raft of new employees, many of them disgruntled Disney dissidents. The work Tashlin supervised at Screen Gems is regarded in animation circles as the best ever produced by that studio; one film in particular, *The Fox and the Grapes* (1941), is often cited as especially influential. It has a classic "blackout" structure: the fox tries a variety of increasingly baroque methods to steal a bunch of grapes, failing every time. Chuck Jones said that *The Fox and the Grapes* inspired his "Road Runner and Coyote" series, though the blackout-gag format itself is a remnant from variety shows, vaudeville, and other forms of episodic theatrical entertainment.[10]

In June 1942, Tashlin returned again to the Schlesinger Unit, where he oversaw fourteen cartoons that feature all of Warners' marquee characters: Bugs Bunny, Daffy Duck, Porky Pig, Elmer Fudd. He also directed four of the fascinating "Private Snafu" cartoons, which comprised the Schlesinger Unit's contribution to the war effort. The Snafu films were

Figure I.1 A risqué moment from Tashlin's Private Snafu film *Censored* (1944)

made expressly for the armed forces, and employ bawdier humor than do the theatrical cartoons.

After leaving Warner Bros. for the final time in 1944, Tashlin was hired as supervising director of United Artists' "Daffy Ditties" series. There, Tashlin supervised three films made with a stop-motion "replacement" animation process not unlike that of George Pal's "Puppetoons" films, in which, rather than manipulating a single, posable puppet, entirely new puppets were created for each of a character's many positions.[11] At around the same time, Tashlin acquired a job as a writer on *A Night in Casablanca* (1946), the Marx Brothers' penultimate feature; this position resulted in Tashlin signing a writer's contract with Paramount.[12] Tashlin contributed gags to the Bob Hope films *Monsieur Beaucaire* (1946) and *The Paleface* (1948), and wrote jokes for Eddie Bracken's radio show, among other comedy projects. In 1946, Tashlin's first children's book, *The Bear That Wasn't*, was published, to largely favorable reviews. The book is still in print.

From 1948 through 1950, Tashlin served as a hired-gun gag- and storyman for Paramount, Columbia, Universal, and United Artists. In later interviews, Tashlin expressed dissatisfaction about films such as *The Paleface*, made for Paramount in 1948. He spoke with vitriol of director Norman Z. McLeod, who, he said, "botched" the film and stripped it of its satirical content. (Tashlin's work is compared with McLeod's in Chapter Seven.) In a personal letter, Tashlin wrote, of some of the films he scripted, "See them and weep—believe me originally these were bright scripts—but when the butchers, right down to cutting, get through, you're ready to step in front of a fast freight—but, then it's too late—your name is up there—and as you know, in Hollywood the writer is always the fall guy."[13]

Previews in late 1950 for the Bob Hope comedy *The Lemon Drop Kid* were unsuccessful, so Hope and producer Robert Welch removed studio veteran Sidney Lanfield from the helm. Welch, who had worked with Tashlin on *The Paleface*, offered him the job. Tashlin, until then one of the film's writers, shot retakes and new material; though the screen credit still went to Lanfield, Tashlin directed about one-third of the finished film.[14]

Hope and Welch offered Tashlin the job as writer/director of *Son of Paleface*.[15] Reluctant to sign a contract with a single studio, Tashlin inked a one-picture deal to write and direct *The First Time* at Columbia before *Son of Paleface* got off the ground. He shot *The First Time* in the spring of 1951, and directed *Son of Paleface* later that year, signing a non-exclusive contract with Paramount as writer-director. With the success of the latter film, Tashlin was now in demand as a writer and director of comedy.

As his directorial career took off, another chapter of Tashlin's life came to a close with the 1951 publication of *The World That Isn't*, the last of his putative children's books and an unrelentingly bleak work. The world it depicts is peopled by thoughtless, irresponsible, superstitious, gluttonous, foolhardy, two-faced philistines with no concern whatsoever for their fellow man. Done in by their own stupidity, these people demolish their world with an atom bomb; only then can civilization be rebuilt, this time the right way. One shudders to think of parents reading it to their kids at bedtime.

Paramount did not exercise its option on his contract, so Tashlin, as he was apparently prone to do, meandered from studio to studio. For RKO (just a few years from folding), he made his next two features, the domestic comedy *Marry Me Again* (1953) and the very naughty *Susan*

Slept Here (1954), an adaptation of a play about a thirty-five-year-old bachelor and the eighteen-year-old girl who complicates his bachelorhood. Around this time, Tashlin wrote the illustrators' manual *How to Create Cartoons*. This now-rare document details Tashlin's "SCOTArt" system of illustration: Square, Circle, Oval, Triangle: the four basic shapes that, according to the author, underlie any successful illustrated undertaking.

In 1954, Tashlin signed a deal with Paramount's Hal Wallis Unit to direct the next Dean Martin and Jerry Lewis picture. The influential duo was on its last legs: the once-chummy Dean and Jerry were squabbling openly,[16] but managed to eke out three more films together, including Tashlin's pair, *Artists and Models* (1955) and *Hollywood or Bust* (1956), almost certainly the best of the lot.[17]

The mid-1950s represent the acme of Tashlin's career. Both of Tashlin's Martin and Lewis pictures are well-regarded, as are *The Lieutenant Wore Skirts*, *The Girl Can't Help It* (both 1956), and *Will Success Spoil Rock Hunter?* (1957), all made for Twentieth Century-Fox. These last two films are usually acknowledged as Tashlin's greatest achievements; in them, Tashlin used Jayne Mansfield as both the embodiment of luxe-padded Fifties glitz and a vivid satire thereof. Whatever reputation Tashlin has as an *auteur* is largely staked on his Mansfield films.

Tashlin's films did not occupy any special place in the estimations of mid-1950s American film critics. However, in France, where the spirited young intellectuals of *Cahiers du Cinéma* and *Positif* immersed themselves in Hollywood past and present, Tashlin was held in great esteem. *Positif* published a Frank Tashlin issue in 1958,[18] and *Cahiers du Cinéma* frequently published rave reviews of his films, often written by Jean-Luc Godard, below at his most effusive:

> Frank Tashlin has not renovated the Hollywood comedy. He has done better. There is not a difference in degree between *Hollywood or Bust* and *It Happened One Night*, between *The Girl Can't Help It* and *Design for Living*, but a difference in kind. Tashlin, in other words, has not renewed but created. And henceforth, when you talk about a comedy, don't say, "It's Chaplinesque"; say, loud and clear, "It's Tashlinesque."[19]

Following his two Mansfield pictures, Tashlin directed the first two of his six solo Jerry Lewis films: *Rock-a-Bye Baby* and *The Geisha Boy* (both

1958). These films feature a strain of sentimentalism that marks most post-1957 Jerry Lewis films. Tashlin's next film, *Say One for Me* (1959), is one of several in which Bing Crosby plays an amiable, desexualized priest. With its teeth yanked out by the Production Code Administration, which was especially sensitive about matters clerical, *Say One for Me* is probably Tashlin's least funny feature.

Tashlin directed another Lewis picture, *Cinderfella*, in 1960. If on-set reports are accurate, Lewis appears to have had more creative control over this film than over any of his other Tashlin pictures; the film's heavy sentimentality is generally seen as evidence of this situation. Nevertheless, their next pairing, *It's Only Money* (1962), is one of Lewis's zaniest.

If there is a forgotten Tashlin film, it may be *Bachelor Flat* (1962), a vehicle for British comedian Terry-Thomas that tends more toward pure farce than any other Tashlin film save *The Glass Bottom Boat* (1966). After directing *It's Only Money* for Paramount, Tashlin returned to Columbia to direct Danny Kaye in *The Man from the Diners' Club* (1963). Kaye (like Lewis, a Borscht Belt veteran) was past his prime as a comic leading man, and this was his last starring role. The final two collaborations with Jerry Lewis followed: *Who's Minding the Store?* (1963) and *The Disorderly Orderly* (1964).

Tashlin directed four more films before retiring from the business, each of which has the unmistakable air of a "one-off" picture. The director's studio-hopping continued: he made *The Alphabet Murders* (1965) and *The Glass Bottom Boat* for MGM; *Caprice* (1967) for Fox; and his final picture, the Bob Hope comedy *The Private Navy of Sgt. O'Farrell* (1968), for United Artists.

Each of Tashlin's final three films is a vehicle for a comic star who had lost much of his or her luster. Doris Day was forty-two years old in 1966, but still playing a much younger woman—a fact not lost on audience members, one of whose comment cards at a preview screening of *The Glass Bottom Boat* suggested that the studio cut the scenes "with Doris Day like a 22-year-old."[20] *The Glass Bottom Boat* is a highlight of Tashlin's late career, with its bold use of color and the CinemaScope frame, and a gentle sense of the absurd. Tashlin's second Doris Day picture is less successful: *Caprice* is a labored spoof of the then-popular mod British spy films. Tashlin fared little better with his last feature, *The Private Navy of Sgt. O'Farrell*, which reunited him with Bob Hope. Hope's popularity had faded significantly since his first collaboration with Tashlin, *The Paleface*, twenty years earlier. *The Private Navy of Sgt. O'Farrell*, like Hope himself in the late 1960s, was quite out of step with the times; it also suffers from by far the worst cinematography of any of Tashlin's films. It is interesting but not necessarily meaningful that Tashlin's feature career is bookended by Bob Hope films.

After *The Private Navy of Sgt. O'Farrell*, Tashlin made no more films, nor did he maintain any formal connections with the industry. Though he did write a few screenplays, none was published or produced. Tashlin suffered a heart attack on May 2, 1972, and died three days later at Mt. Sinai Hospital in Hollywood, not quite sixty.

Tashlin in Context

This book's final chapter considers the influence that Tashlin has had on modern filmmakers, using as examples three directors whom I have ordered according to the degrees to which their own styles have been shaped by Tashlin's: Pedro Almodóvar, Jean-Luc Godard, and Joe Dante. Dante, who has repeatedly acknowledged his debt to Tashlin and whose films offer ample evidence thereof, has remarked, on the DVD commentary track for his underrated *Gremlins 2: The New Batch* (1990),

> The whole thing with influences in movies is that . . . they're not conscious. I mean, I saw a lot of Frank Tashlin movies when I was a kid, and I saw a lot of Warner Bros. cartoons, and you don't consciously access that stuff when you're working, but it is an influence. . . . In [*Gremlins 2*] you'll see sort of *Hellzapoppin'* kind of stuff. I like that . . . Pirandellian "breaking-the-frame" stuff. That always interests me. It unfortunately interests me a lot more than it does the people who run studios.[21]

For Dante, one of the hallmarks of Tashlin's style is that his films acknowledge their own constructedness and audiences. His comments hint at an admiration for a certain type of anarchic humor, which he sees in abundance in Tashlin's films. "There wasn't anybody else who was able to do that kind of outrageous gag as successfully as [Tashlin] did," Dante has said. "He could have directed *Hellzapoppin'* had he been directing [features] in '41."[22]

Gremlins 2 brims with inside jokes and oddball antics: at one point a gremlin is transformed into a burst of electrical energy and trapped inside a videophone, where it is tortured by Muzak—as empty an emblem of modern society as exists, and one that Tashlin would have relished excoriating. In another scene, the film appears to melt and break (a gag used often by Looney Tunes animators), and the narrative comes to a halt while a bunch of gremlins thread up a 1950s nudie-cutie film; it is only when scolded by angry movie patron Hulk Hogan that the troublemakers "replace" the original film.[23] Dante believes, not unreasonably, that Tashlin would have liked *Gremlins 2*, "because it defies convention in the sense that it doesn't appear to take its narrative seriously. It doesn't mind breaking out and referring to itself."[24] *Gremlins 2* captures the spirit, sense of humor, and irreverence of the films of one of its director's principal influences. It may be the most Tashlinian film of the last thirty years, and it is arguably more Tashlinian than the last several films made by Tashlin himself.[25]

But is it sufficient to say that a film that breaks the frame and has a wild, racy sense of humor owes a debt to Tashlin? Dante provides a clue: he points to *Hellzapoppin'*, probably the least *sensible* of all studio-era comedies (save, perhaps, *Never Give a Sucker an Even Break*, also 1941), as a milestone of this type of humor, even though it was made ten years before Tashlin directed his first live-action film. Though Tashlin was skilled in frame-breaking, he is not its sole exemplar. The roots of anarchic Hollywood comedy can be traced back beyond Tashlin's entry into the motion picture business, and even before his birth, to such traditions as the slapstick comedy films of the 1910s, as well as the vaudeville stage.

Dante's remarks highlight another of the problems in studying Tashlin: his work has rarely been considered within the historical, aesthetic, and economic contexts that are most germane to it. Considering Tashlin as part of a generic tradition helps to explain the roots of his humor and visual style. How, for instance, might we compare Tashlin's style of animation to that of Tex Avery, whom Tashlin identified as an influence? How do Tashlin's comic sensibilities compare with those of the acknowledged auteurs of mid-century Hollywood comedy, such as Howard Hawks and Billy Wilder?

In the small body of literature on his work, Tashlin has long been considered unique or exceptional. To disagree with such claims is not to deny Tashlin's directorial talents, which are overdue for serious study. Rather, it is to the benefit of Tashlin's legacy to take a serious look at what it means for a film to be (as Godard put it) *Tashlinesque*.

The present volume describes and analyzes in detail Frank Tashlin's cinematic style. His visual style is of significant interest, for Tashlin was a master of *mise-en-scène*. But there are other, equally important areas of Tashlin's work that must be considered. Above all other considerations is that of the conventions of comedy, the genre to which the vast majority of his films belong. The powerful conventions of a time-tested genre (even one as capacious as comedy) offer greater explanatory power than do claims for Tashlin's uniqueness. A study of Tashlin's relationship to the norms of his chosen genre tells us a great deal about his style.

Tashlin is an important director for a number of reasons. The relationship between his animated work and his live-action work is one of the most interesting of them, but not necessarily because the one is the forerunner of and direct influence on the other, as is so often argued in the literature on Tashlin. Rather, the fact that Tashlin found success in both of these realms of filmmaking suggests that these realms themselves are more closely related than is usually acknowledged. Most of the literature on Hollywood animation does not treat it within a generic context; most of the literature on Hollywood comedy does not take into account animation.[26] The creative artists in the fields of both animated and live-action comedy drew from the same deep well: vaudeville, the music-hall tradition, comedian comedy, slapstick. Which is to say that the influences on Buster Keaton are the very influences that shaped the comedy of Tex Avery. Tashlin, as it happens, was one of the few to bridge the gap between animation and live-action. More than anything, this fact indicates the depth of the common comic heritage; that more directors did *not* make the leap from animation to live-action is more surprising than the fact that Tashlin *did*.[27] Tashlin's films provide the richest and most thorough case study of the give-and-take between animated and live-action comedy during the studio era.

As well, Tashlin's films open a window onto the mechanisms of censorship in Hollywood. Time and again, Tashlin managed to slip potentially objectionable material past the censors of the Production Code Administration. Tashlin had a predilection for risqué humor: he worked it into nearly every one of his films—a tendency that earned him no great favor in the eyes of the PCA. Nevertheless, despite the efforts of Hollywood's official censorship agency, numerous racy jokes made it into Tashlin's films. Tashlin directed most of his features during a time of great transition for Hollywood's censorship authority, and in fact may have provided some of the ammunition that eventually brought down its walls. By studying the bawdy humor in Tashlin's films, we may also study the ways that the genre of comedy changed during Tashlin's career, as well as the transitions that the PCA itself underwent.

The context of authorship is also important in assessing Tashlin's style and career. If we define an *auteur* as a filmmaker whose distinctive stylistic and/or thematic stamp is apparent in all of his films, and a *programmer* as a director who "churned out" genre pictures to fit a studio's release schedule, Tashlin splits the difference neatly, occupying a curious middle ground. He is perhaps best considered as an extremely talented program director: Tashlin's stylistic, thematic, and comic strategies are present to varying degrees in nearly all of his films, but those films are, for the most part, program comedies, a class of film that, during the studio era, neither allowed for nor rewarded stylistic consistency: no Frank Tashlin or Jerry Lewis film was ever nominated for an Academy Award.[28] The fact that Tashlin worked within a single genre is the principal reason for the auteur/programmer complication, a topic taken up in Chapter Seven.

Finally, Tashlin must be considered within the context of the Hollywood studio system. His films were, at root, devices with which various studios attempted to make money. Little scholarly work on Tashlin considers his films as the products of a particular industry, though such an approach reveals a great deal about the director, as well as about the industry itself. To place Tashlin in the historical/economic context of the Hollywood studio system is not to diminish his importance, or to somehow reduce him to a cog in a big machine. Rather, such a study affords us a deeper understanding of the ways in which Tashlin carved out for himself a particular place in studio-era Hollywood.

Key Terms and Concepts

Before making sense of Tashlin's films themselves, a summary of some of the relevant terms and concepts used herein is in order. Most fundamental is the *gag*, here used interchangeably with *joke* to mean any individual moment of comedy. A gag can be verbal, visual, sonic, or some combination of the above. In the same way that we may consider the shot to be the basic unit of filmmaking, the gag is the basic unit of the comedy. I have employed Noël Carroll's definition of *sight gag*—"A form of visual humor in which amusement is generated by the play of alternative interpretations projected by the image or image series"—and broadened it.[29] Tashlin's films make frequent use of visual comedy that does not necessarily involve a play of alternative interpretations; in his case, an unusual gesture, color, or prop can and often does serve as a gag in and of itself. "Sight gag" is used here quite generally to refer to any instance of comedy that exists solely on the visual register.

The *blackout gag* is a staple of both vaudeville and Hollywood animation: it refers to a gag that has no relationship to the gags that surround it; a quick, one-off joke followed, on the stage, by a literal blacking-out of the lights or lowering of the curtain. In film, such gags are often bracketed by dissolves, fades, or other "chapter-ending" devices.

Not quite the converse of the gag, the *non-gag*, an important dimension of Tashlin's humor, is a joke (often, in Tashlin's case, a sight gag) that aims not for guffaws but for an appreciation of its cleverness. Jacques Tati is surely the master of the non-gag, but Tashlin excels at it, as well. These shall become clear by example.

On a more global level, several oft-conflated comedy concepts must be teased apart: *satire, parody*, and *lampoon*. Margaret Rose, in her definitive work on the subject, differentiates the first two terms on several grounds. Parody, Rose argues, uses "the preformed material of its 'target' as a constituent part of its own structure," whereas satire "need not make itself dependent on [preformed material] for its own character . . . , but may simply make fun of a target external to itself."[30] There are other differences, but this is the most relevant: satire is directed outward, toward an external target; parody uses the conventions of a form to mock the form itself. *Son of Paleface* offers a clear example. The film is a parody of the Western genre, in that it stars Bob Hope as a weak-kneed cowboy; it also satirizes censorship strictures, Hollywood in general, and American sexual mores of the early 1950s. While Tashlin's films engage both of these levels of comedy, I refer to such humor, collectively, as "satire" or "satirical humor." *Lampoon* refers, more generally, to a form of comedy dependent on ridicule. Lampooning is often, but not always, performed with good-natured imitation or mockery; as a verb, its closest definition may be simply "to make fun of."[31]

Tashlin, especially at his peak, is a formidable satirist, and is at his most compelling when his films embrace a paradoxically cheery yet dire ambivalence. This study considers the satirical aspects of each of the films on which it focuses.

In analyzing Tashlin, I have found it advantageous to watch his films repeatedly and carefully, and to take note of the most relevant recurring features of visual style, comic method, thematic material, and historical context. Their recurrence, their privileged status in the films, and, most important, their potential as explanatory mechanisms select them as relevant. These topics and features are laid out below.

Sight gags and non-gags are crucial to Tashlin's style. Tashlin is a director for whom *mise-en-scène* is far more important than editing—which has much to do with his apprenticeship as an animator. His visual style relies heavily on humorous props, sets, and performances; Tashlin's many non-gags often take visual form, as well.

Performance receives special attention in the chapters that follow, for the simple reason that Tashlin's films are often comedian comedies, as defined by Steve Seidman in his influential monograph *Comedian Comedy: A Tradition in Hollywood Film*. Much of the performative comedy in Tashlin's films can be traced to the vaudeville stage. Henry Jenkins's book *What Made Pistachio Nuts?* argues for the dominance of vaudeville as an influence on early film comedy, and closes with a throwing down of the gauntlet, of sorts.

> Though the period of its greatest influence ended in 1934, the vaudeville aesthetic left a strong imprint of [sic] screen comedy.... On the margins of the studio system, in poverty row productions, short subjects, and animated cartoons, anarchistic comedy remained a viable alternative to the more integrative styles of comedy preferred by the majors. Works like *Hellzapoppin* and *Never Give a Sucker an Even Break* [both 1941] suggest the possibility of anarchistic comedy even in the face of the relative conservatism of late 1930s and early 1940s comedian comedy. The whole vocabulary of anarchistic comedy was inherited by the character cartoons of the 1940s, with Bugs Bunny's humiliation of the stodgy Elmer Fudd a pleasurable reworking of the earlier confrontations between Groucho Marx and Margaret Dumont.... By the late 1940s, Hollywood again embraced the more reflexive and performance-centered style

of comedy associated with the vaudeville aesthetic. The films of Hope and Crosby, Danny Kaye, Martin and Lewis, and others build upon the formal traditions of early sound comedy.[32]

This anarchistic, "performance-centered style of comedy" found new homes in two areas in which Tashlin worked: animation, and comedian comedies starring such figures as Hope, Crosby, Martin, Lewis, and Kaye. Subsequent chapters take up Jenkins's approach, investigating the ways in which the vaudeville aesthetic influenced Tashlin and some of his most important comic performers.

The following chapters also consider the sexual humor in Tashlin's films, a strain of comedy that, in Tashlin, often overlaps with the satirical: much of his best satire—which is to say, his most ambiguous—targets contemporary sexual mores. Not all of Tashlin's sexual comedy is satirical, however. A great deal of it, in fact, is often little more than comic displays of prurience. As nearly every writer on Tashlin has noted, a vibrant strain of blue humor runs through his films. But while Tashlin's particular method of sexual humor is his own, it is hardly the case that films were "clean" until Tashlin came along. American film, from nearly the point of its inception, is laced with sexual comedy. As well, many of the traditions from which Hollywood comedy drew (and draws)—vaudeville, the Borscht Belt—are rife with their own traditions of bawdy humor. The sexual comedy in Tashlin's films must be considered not only as an important facet of his style, but as part of a durable tradition.

An adjunct to the study of sexual humor is that of the censorship of Tashlin's films, and his response thereto. He often did battle with the Production Code Administration. The reasons for the censorship of Tashlin's films were almost always identical—"sex suggestiveness"—but his responses differ greatly, and, in fact, offer a useful index of his approach to filmmaking. Only Tashlin's last film, *The Private Navy of Sgt. O'Farrell*, was made after the PCA had lost its authority; all of his other works were subject to official censorship of some kind. A charting of the rationales behind the censorship of Tashlin's films reveals a great deal about the changes in official censorship strategy. By studying the ways in which Tashlin responded to the censorship decrees, we can understand the range of creative options available to a director whose every film came under scrutiny. Personally, I suspect that when the PCA censors spied Tashlin's name on a script, they winced and rolled up their sleeves.

The last of the major features of Tashlin's style I have considered is one that subtends all the others: the integration of gags and narrative, a somewhat contentious issue in comedy studies. The two most articulate arguments on the subject have been advanced by Donald Crafton and Tom Gunning. Summarizing, Crafton holds that gags interrupt narratives, or, at best, possess immensely reduced potential for narrative advancement. Gunning, on the other hand, argues that gags do not interrupt narrative, but are themselves a *form* of narrative, and that their principal function—the disruption of the story—is itself an essential component of conventional narrative.[33] In many ways, Tashlin's films internalize the differing approaches to this matter: they offer evidence of a great many strategies for integrating comic material with story material, ranging from full integration to near-opposition. In fact, this is the dimension of Tashlin's style that most readily lends itself to chronological study: in his earliest films, gag and narrative are often unrelated; in the films of his peak period (the mid-1950s), the humor derives almost entirely from narrative situation; in the films of his late-period decline, he reverts, in a way, to a less integrated combination of the two. Whether consciously or not, Tashlin explores a fairly wide range of narrative options available to directors of comedies; comparison with auteurs and program-film directors highlight how unusual is Tashlin's varied method.

Above all other considerations is that of comedy itself. In addition to giving us a sense of the possibilities and limitations of the genre, a study of Tashlin's work allows us to consider a number of topics relevant to comedy studies. While a great deal of good work has been done on the effects of censorship on Hollywood film, little of this work takes into consideration the effects of censorship on comedy in particular. Excellent works, such as Gregory D. Black's *The Catholic Crusade against the Movies, 1940–1975* and Nina C. Leibman's *Living Room Lectures: The Fifties Family in Film & Television*, study the effects of censorship on the more "serious" genres of drama and melodrama, to the exclusion of comedy.[34] But comedy has transgression "built in" to its genre identity, making it a potentially revelatory area of inquiry. Tashlin's films in particular, with their especially prominent transgressive content, show some of the responses to censorship available to a director of comedies.

More broadly, a study of Tashlin's films has the potential to expand and complicate our conceptions of both auteurism and genre itself. Can a director be said to be an auteur if he worked exclusively in a single genre? How does an adherence to a single, "non-serious" genre compromise the claims for a director's authorship? Tashlin may be an auteur who worked in program pictures, or he may be an unusually skilled program director; the difference is largely academic. I hope to suggest that there is room within our conception of authorship for a director whose strength was not in subverting, combining, or spanning genres, but in adhering to the conventions of one genre in particular.

1 TISH-TASH IN CARTOONLAND

One fruitful way of understanding Frank Tashlin's career is to look at his peregrinations from studio to studio. While most pronounced in his live-action career, this peripatetic tendency announced itself when he was a young (and apparently restless) animator. Tashlin's animated work organizes itself into several distinct phases: Warner Bros., 1936–1938; Screen Gems, 1941–1942; Warner Bros., 1942–1944; and an unusual one-off cartoon, funded by the Lutheran Church, from 1947. Between 1933, the date of his first cartoon as an animator, and 1945, the end of his tenure with United Artists' animation division, Tashlin animated, directed, or supervised 59 animated films, an average of about four and a half cartoons per year.[1]

At Warner Bros., the humor and general aesthetic sensibilities of the Schlesinger Unit were extremely important to Tashlin's own style. His 1930s Warners cartoons were made during a time of great experimentation for the studio, a fact that surely played a large role in his development as an animator. Tashlin's 1940s Warners cartoons were made during a time when the studio had found surer footing, a fact that, intriguingly, *also* allowed for experimentation on the part of the Warners directors.

The Looney Tunes and Merrie Melodies that Tashlin made between 1933 and 1936 were, in several ways, important models for the evolution of the Warner Bros. house style during the years 1938–1942—the period in which the Schlesinger Unit's collective style came into its own. Tashlin played a key role in determining the performative and phenotypic parameters of Warners' all-important first star, Porky Pig; the evolution of Bugs Bunny, Warner Bros.' marquee character, proceeded along similar lines. Tashlin's experimentations with visual design and sight gags (see, for instance, Figures 1.1 to 1.4, and 1.7) also seem to have been inspirational for the Warners animators of the early 1940s.

Along with Tex Avery's devil-may-care comic attitude and Friz Freleng's talent for storytelling, Tashlin's character design and visual humor are almost certainly the elements of the 1930s cartoons that were of the greatest value to Jones, Clampett, and their colleagues in the early years of the 1940s. Jones's penchant for abstract, non-comic design is, in some ways, an extension of Tashlin's experimentation with non-gags and showy animation; Clampett's mastery of character-based humor owes a great debt to Tashlin's expertise in that same field. This is not to say that intra-studio influence was a one-way street or that Tashlin was a font of all things Looney; with animators as gifted as Jones, Clampett, and Freleng in the same office, it is extremely unlikely that Tashlin did not learn from them. But it is Tashlin's style that is at issue here.

With regard to the development of Tashlin's own style, we can chart the evolution of several important tendencies from the 1930s cartoons to those of the 1940s. Tashlin made great strides in the areas of character design and performer-based humor. In such 1940s films as *Puss 'n' Booty* and *Porky Pig's Feat*, we see Tashlin making especially fine use of his talent for visual design. Among other achievements, *Puss 'n' Booty* makes humorous use of offscreen space, and *Porky Pig's Feat* uses camera movements and compositions themselves as important sources of comedy. In these regards, Tashlin stands out from Jones, Clampett, and his other Warner Bros. colleagues. Not only that, but we can identify these tendencies, among others, as key elements of Tashlin's style that would manifest themselves, in various forms, in his live-action comedies.

Though techniques such as self-reflexive and sexual humor were part and parcel of the Warner Bros. house style, Tashlin employed these devices in different ways and for different ends than did his colleagues. Tashlin was especially interested in techniques that challenged both propriety and traditional modes of viewership. While nearly all of the Warners directors employed sexual humor, Tashlin pulled it off more consistently and emphatically than his colleagues; the same is true of his gags that challenge diegetic integrity. On the whole, perhaps the thing that separates Tashlin's style from those of the other Warners animators is that he was more interested in using stylistic devices for comic ends. When Tashlin used an unusual composition, he did so for a laugh; the same is true of his shatterings of the fourth wall and of his manipulations of the gag/narrative relationship. As we will see in this and subsequent chapters, Tashlin was uncommonly single-minded in his pursuit of humor.

Warner Bros., 1936–1938

Prior to joining Warner Bros. full time in 1936, Tashlin worked on two one-off cartoons, which merit a brief look. *Hook and Ladder Hokum* (1933, Van Beuren, codirected with Vernon Stallings) is one in a series of films featuring the two uncharismatic characters Tom and Jerry, who have nothing to do with MGM's cat-and-mouse duo.[2] In this film, they are firefighters, a situation that provides various opportunities for comedy: a soot-blackened character exclaims, "Mammy!"; our heroes slide down a column of water as if it were a fireman's pole. References to Al Jolson and Ed Wynn prefigure Tashlin's career-long penchant for making comedy out of the artifacts of popular culture. The film is notable only for being a pitch-perfect exemplar of the "rubber hose" style of animation that dominated Hollywood cartoons in the early 1930s. Michael Barrier defines this style as characterized by a figure who "reaches for something and stretches his arm several times its normal length while his body remains stationary."[3] In *Hook and Ladder Hokum*, the effect is doubled: not only are the characters loose-limbed, but half of the gags actually involve hoses.

Buddy's Beer Garden (1933, Warner Bros.), for which Tashlin was an animator, is another archetypal cartoon: it is a perfect example of the style of the early 1930s Merrie Melodies. The film is an especially plain attempt to cash in on Disney's highly successful "Silly Symphonies" formula. This plotless film's characters lack personalities but are aggressively cute, and everyone sings and bobs in time to the constant light-swing score—a technique known as "Mickey Mousing." It is a workmanlike cartoon; the only hints of Tashlinian humor are the appearances of an impossibly voluptuous Mae West figure and a wisecracking parrot that morphs into Jimmy Durante. The film offers no major insight into Tashlin's style; it is more interesting as evidence of Warners' early, carbon-copy strategy of coping with the Disney monolith.

It is important to note that teasing apart Tashlin's—or Tex Avery's, or Friz Freleng's—style from what we might call the Warner Bros. "house style" of animation is difficult, especially given the working methods at the Schlesinger Unit. By the mid-1930s, the creative minds at Termite Terrace had settled into a method that capitalized on their collective talents. Writers were not assigned to a particular director; rather, they worked "in a kind of pool system": a director could enlist the services of any of the unit's skilled writers, such as Tedd Pierce, Melvin "Tubby" Millar, and Ben "Bugs" Hardaway—the men whom Leonard Maltin calls "the unsung heroes of cartoon history."[4] In addition, writers and directors held "jam sessions," in which they would help each other develop gags. Maltin quotes Chuck Jones: "We had no hesitation in adopting ideas from other [Warners directors'] pictures. If it worked for them, it would work for us. So the result was that unconsciously we were really working as a 'house,' but we were essentially separate also."[5] While this turned out to be an immensely fruitful division of labor for the Schlesinger Unit, it makes the historian's task difficult, for it is difficult to know where the director stops and the house style begins. The best we can do is to consider in detail the essential features of each director's style within the delimitations of the overall studio style.

Between 1936 and 1938, Tashlin "supervised"[6] twenty-one cartoons, thirteen of which feature Porky Pig. It is during this period that Tashlin began to develop a recognizable style, one of the hallmarks of which is a penchant for gags that depend purely on visual design. Frequently, Tashlin engages in visual play that is more clever than it is funny; these "non-gags" would become one of his signature techniques. As in the films of Jacques Tati, Tashlin's non-gags contribute to a tone of whimsy, even if they don't elicit belly laughs. Warners was keen to allow such a spirit to permeate their cartoons, as they were a no-cost way of differentiating their product from that of their greatest rival.[7]

Tashlin was an excellent animator, and he knew it: even some of his early films display a certain showiness. A few seconds into *Little Beau Porky* (1936), Tashlin depicts the morning marches of a group of legionnaires by showing their shadows as they fall upon the irregularly shaped walls of a desert outpost (Figure 1.1). This moment is not humorous—it exists solely as a display of technical virtuosity: to animate shadows on irregular surfaces is tricky. A glorious example of visual play occurs in *Porky's Railroad* (1937). In an overhead shot, Porky's train, the 15th Century Unlimited, approaches a switching yard. As a single railroad track fans out to become a dozen, each of the train's cars veers off onto a sepa-

Figure 1.1 Showy animation in *Little Beau Porky*

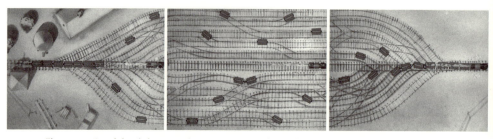

Figure 1.2 A quick, elaborate, virtuoso non-gag in *Porky's Railroad*

rate branch, only to rejoin the others, in their original order, once the tracks narrow down to one again at the far end of the yard (Figure 1.2). This is clearly the work of an animator who had mastered the use of time and space: the whole setup lasts little more than three seconds, and ends before the viewer can adequately take in the complicated mechanics of each car's path. This shot is emblematic of Tashlin's style: an elaborate visual scenario that is far cleverer than it is funny.

A persistent claim about Tashlin's animation is that he often selected "unusual" camera angles that somehow evoke live-action cinema. Representative of this argument is Greg Ford's assertion that "It is foolhardy to even approach Tashlin's feature comedies without referring back to his days at Warner Bros. Cartoons."[8] Ford writes,

> Tashlin's taste for the language of feature films was evident from the very beginning in his first stint as an animation director at Warners in 1936. Tashlin's first Warners cartoon, *Porky's Poultry Plant* (1936), contains delirious high and low angled shots (and rapid-fire editing) of a daredevil aerial dogfight with a marauding buzzard. He employs elaborate montages of bugles blown and bayoneted rifles raised high in . . . *Little Beau Porky* (1936) . . . *Little Pancho Vanilla* (1938) utilizes simulated "camera movement" that was quite unusual for animated films of the period; . . . *Wholly Smoke* (1938) opens with a fancy "tracking shot" . . . [and also] incorporates atmospheric "dissolves" that chronicle Porky's mounting cigar sickness and tobacco-bred hallucinations.[9]

It is unclear how the techniques that Ford enumerates are peculiar to the realm of live-action cinema (which is presumably what he means in referring to "feature films"), and how Tashlin's use of these techniques in his animated work is evidence that his cartoons evince a live-action-like style. There is no such thing as a monolithic "live-action film style"; the tools that Ford identifies are just that: tools. They have long been available to filmmakers in both live-action and animation.[10] Whether these techniques were unusual for animation *of the time* is an entirely different claim, the proof of which would require a great raft of supporting evidence.[11]

In fact, it is not evident that Tashlin's cartoons more regularly include "unusual" camera angles than do those of his colleagues. Tashlin made quite a few films in the 1930s in which most of the shots are frontally composed (see Figure 1.3a and 1.3b). Such compositions comprise the bulk of the shots in *Porky's Poultry Plant, Little Beau Porky, Porky in the North Woods* (all 1936), *Speaking of the Weather, Porky's Road Race, Porky's Romance* (all 1937), *Have You Got Any Castles?* (1938), and many others. Most of these films *do* contain a few strikingly composed shots that Tashlin uses precisely to break the monotony of the straight-ahead composition (an example is Figure 1.3c), but the films' images are still overwhelmingly frontally composed.

Figure 1.3

A. Receding depth in the kitchen in *Porky's Romance*
B. Frontal composition in *Porky's Road Race*
C. A dramatic high-angle shot from *Porky's Poultry Plant*
D. Proscenium composition augmented by a strong diagonal in *Porky at the Crocadero*

Occasionally, Tashlin will alter a traditional composition in a small but significant way, with the result that a straight-on shot takes on the appearance of a canted-angle shot. A key example is Figure 1.3d, which, save for the sharp diagonal that cuts through the bottom third of the frame, is actually a very conventional proscenium composition. Friz Freleng is usually considered the most "conventional" Warners animator, but Tashlin was just as likely to compose his frames for a proscenium, at least in his 1930s cartoons.

Another visual technique that Tashlin begins to develop in his 1930s cartoons is the humorous use of offscreen space. *Porky in the North*

Woods contains several such gags. In one, Porky frees an unseen animal from a trap, but before doing so he puts a clothespin on his nose; only when the camera moves back do we see that the imperiled critter is a skunk. In *Porky's Road Race*, Porky and the film's villain, "Borax Karoff," pilot their own cars as they drive into a tunnel whose interior is hidden from the camera, but emerge from it having somehow exchanged vehicles. In *Porky the Fireman* (1938), a dog rescues a fat woman from a high window by simply dropping her. Tashlin keeps his camera on the dog at the top of his ladder, as we hear the sounds of the woman falling and crash-landing on the sidewalk.

A common conception about Tashlin's work at Warners is that his cartoons are unusually rapidly cut and thus more like live-action films than are other cartoons. Influential animation historian Leonard Maltin analyzes a six-second sequence from Tashlin's film *Porky's Romance*, in which the gluttonous Petunia Pig, after having turned Porky away from her door, notices that he had brought for her a huge box of chocolates. Seeing the heart-shaped bonbon box prompts her to change her mind about her suitor, rush out the door, and whisk the delighted but confused Porky into her parlor. Maltin correctly counts ten shots in this sequence, for an Average Shot Length (ASL) of two-thirds of a second, for this sequence only. For this and other reasons, Maltin argues that Tashlin was an unusually innovative animator: "Tashlin's strongest suit was his interest in the cartoon as *film* . . . Even in his early period he toyed with the possibilities of camera angle, cutting, montage, and other cinematic devices at a time when some of his colleagues were still taking more prosaic approaches to their work."[12]

Maltin overstates the importance of this one sequence, which accounts for less than 1.5 percent of the film's running time: a burst of rapid editing does not necessarily an innovator make. In fact, the overall ASL of *Porky's Romance* is 8.77 seconds, and the average ASL for Tashlin's cartoons is 6.37 seconds, which means that this film, on the whole, is edited significantly *less* rapidly than Tashlin's norm. The clip Maltin selects is too brief and unrepresentative to support claims as strong as this one.

Maltin also errs in divorcing Tashlin's work from its generic context. In Maltin's example, for instance, Tashlin uses rapid editing for a very particular *purpose*: to enhance the humor of the scene. The gag is about the rapidity with which Petunia changes her mind about her suitor once she sees the box of sweets. The rapid-fire editing is a comic device employed to emphasize both frantic pace and female fickleness.

A study of thirty-seven Warner Bros. cartoons made between the years 1935 and 1940 reveals that Warners animators worked within a fairly wide range of ASLs. Certain of Tashlin's films tend toward the low end of the ASL spectrum, but films by other directors are cut just as quickly, or more quickly. Chuck Jones's *Sniffles Takes a Trip* (1940), for instance, has an ASL of 5.08 seconds, as well as its own brief sequence of rapid-fire editing. Tex Avery and Friz Freleng also directed rapidly cut cartoons during this period: Avery's *Daffy Duck in Hollywood* (1938) has an ASL of 5.29 seconds; Freleng's 1936 *Boulevardier from the Bronx* clocks in at 5.5 seconds.

At the other end of the spectrum, Jones, Avery, and Freleng all made films with double-digit ASLs in this period, as well: respectively: *Daffy Duck and the Dinosaur* (1939), 17.92 seconds; *Believe It or Else* (1939), 18.54 seconds; and *He Was Her Man* (1937), 10.45 seconds. The Tashlin cartoon with the longest ASL, and the only one with an ASL over ten seconds, is *Porky's Spring Planting*, at 10.15 seconds—a figure almost identical to the *average* ASL of the sample films (10.07 seconds). Tashlin's cartoons were just as likely to have relatively long ASLs as they were to have relatively short ones. Other Warner Bros. directors could and did cut just as quickly, or slowly, as did Tashlin during the same time period, to say nothing of editing practice at other animation studios. Deeper analysis may reveal these directors' differing strategies in using editing for comedy, and would likely yield finer-grained comparisons.

Maltin makes another strong claim—similar to that of Greg Ford—about Tashlin's cartoons. He holds that, since Tashlin used such devices as rapid editing, montage sequences, and unusual camera placement, his cartoons were more *filmlike* than those of his contemporaries. But Maltin overlooks an essential fact that one might think would weigh heavily on the minds of animation historians, whose field of inquiry has been rather severely marginalized within film studies. Animation *is* film. It is no more or less "cinematic" than live-action. No matter whether a moving image is shot in a studio or painted onto cels (or transferred physically onto the emulsion, as in Man Ray's 1923 film *La Retour à raison*), it is still a work of cinema. A film that features unusual camera placement and rapid editing is no more "cinematic" than a film shot in a single take with a static, chest-high camera.

Tashlin assuredly did use rapid editing in several cartoons: the scene from *Porky's Romance* is just one example. But if we study the *functions* of his techniques, a closer examination reveals that Tashlin forged humor from long takes just as skillfully as he did from quick cutting.

An excellent example of Tashlin's use of long takes to generate humor occurs in *Porky the Fireman*. Eager to extinguish a blaze, Porky yells to a canine fireman who leans against a hydrant, "OK, t-t-t-turn her on! Hurry up! T-t-t-turn her on!" The dog then lopes languidly along the curving path of the hose from hydrant to Porky, a movement shown in a dawdling tracking shot. When he reaches Porky, the dog says, "What did you say?" If the slow walk is the gag, this line of dialogue is the "topper": the secondary gag that enhances, by punctuation, the initial one. Porky, enraged, screams, "I s-s-said, 'Turn on the water!'" "Oh," replies the dog. Still without employing a cut, Tashlin then tops the topper: the dog moseys back to the hydrant, once again following the course of the winding hose. When the dog finally turns on the hydrant, Tashlin *again* tracks his camera laterally along the hose's path, this time at a greater speed as we follow the bulge made by the rushing water. Finally, Tashlin tops the topper-topper: when the bulge of water reaches Porky's nozzle, the hose releases but a single droplet, which falls to the sidewalk, accompanied by the tiny *tink* of a triangle. This shot is notable not just for its forty-seven-second duration, but for the way it demonstrates Tashlin's skill with gag escalation.

Wholly Smoke provides another fine example of long-take comedy. To create different effects at various moments in the narrative, Tashlin makes considerable adjustments to the editing rate. The film naturally breaks down into four brief narrative "acts," each of which reveals a different approach to editing.

> Act One: The Set-up (58 seconds; ASL: 29 seconds): As the church bell tolls, Porky's mother summons him downstairs for Sunday school and gives him a nickel for the collection plate.
> Act Two: The Complication (120 seconds; ASL: 10.91 seconds): In an alley, Porky meets a tough, cigar-smoking bulldog, and bets him a nickel that he can smoke the cigar just as well as the dog can.

Act Three: The Musical Number (181 seconds; ASL: 5.48 seconds): Porky has a wild, musical nicotine hallucination, in which anthropomorphic cigarettes, cigars, and the like warn him of the dangers of tobacco.

Act Four: The Denouement (36 seconds; ASL: 4.5 seconds): Porky realizes how foolish smoking is, swiftly grabs the nickel back from the bulldog, and places it in the collection plate.

Tashlin takes a different approach to the relationship between editing and humor in each of these sections. Act One consists of only two shots, and both extensively substitute camera movement for editing. The film's first shot is of a priest ringing the churchbell as if it were a carnival attraction. The second shot is a masterpiece of simulated camera movement: Tashlin tracks backward through a window into a living room; pans/tracks right as Porky's mother calls for her son; tilts/cranes up the staircase to find Porky on the landing; tilts/cranes quickly back down again as he slides down the banister; pans left and (artificially) zooms in for a medium close-up on the mother; dollies backward through the *other* window and into the front yard; tracks right along the outside of the house as Porky walks, hidden from view, out the front door; and continues tracking right, smoothly and uninterruptedly, as Porky walks out the door and along the sidewalk. Only one of these camera moves (the rapid tilt/crane down the banister) is used for humorous ends: it emphasizes the rapidity of Porky's descent, a joke compounded by the fact that he is somehow able to stop on a dime just short of the newel post.

When, in the second act, the jokes occur more regularly and rapidly, the rate of editing increases. The bulldog challenges Porky to a "smoke-off": he performs tricks with his cigar (pulling a smoke rabbit out of his hat, bouncing the stogie off his heel), all of which Tashlin shows in a single twenty-second take. When Porky tries to replicate the tricks, he fails, comically: his smoky duck lays a real egg on his head, and so forth. Tashlin shows Porky's failed attempts in three separate shots, joined by fast dissolves. The contrast is important: when the smoke tricks are introduced, longer takes encourage us to admire the clever visual design. But when the tricks are repeated for laughs, Tashlin isolates each trick into its own joke-unit, and cuts more rapidly between them.

In the film's third section, the visual gags fly fast and furiously. The master of ceremonies is the smoky demon Nick O'Teen, who leads Porky, and us, through an all-singing, all-dancing cavalcade of the horrors of tobacco use. One-off sight gags abound: matches strike themselves on a matchbox so that their blackened heads resemble a minstrel chorus; the slinky Fatima of the cigarette label becomes the zaftig, beveiled "Fat-Emma"; and, in a possible reference to Oskar Fischinger's Muratti ads, cigarettes dance in line formation to spell out "NO SMOKING." These are blackout gags: quick zingers with little payoff beyond their mere existence.

Act Four is the most rapidly cut in the film. Here, the brevity of the shots and the rapid increase in editing tempo convey a sense of speed.[13] Porky races from the tobacco shop to the church, where he realizes he has ill-advisedly surrendered his nickel to the bulldog. He runs to the alley, grabs the nickel, smashes the dog's cigar into his face, and darts back to his pew just in time to tithe. Most of the shots in this section last for less than two seconds. In Act Four, rapid editing denotes, simply, speed. Humor and rapid editing do not have a one-to-one correspondence in this or other Tashlin films; the director's approach is richer and more varied.

In his 1930s Warners cartoons, Tashlin employs three different techniques for the integration of gags and narratives. In several films, he simply makes no attempt to blend jokes and story. Such cartoons as *Speaking of the Weather, Have You Got Any Castles?*, and *You're an Education* (1938) are little more than strings of disconnected gags.[14] The first five minutes and forty seconds of *Have You Got Any Castles?*, for instance, consist of a long series of brief, one-off gags. The thinnest possible story is tacked on in the film's last fifty-six seconds, and is little more than a chase scene.[15]

Several—but not all—of the 1930s Porky Pig films depend more heavily on story than does *Speaking of the Weather*: their humor is more thoroughly rooted in situation and character than in disconnected gags. Much of the comedy in *Porky's Double Trouble*, for instance, centers on Porky's coincidental resemblance to Killer, a notorious bank robber. In fact, until this plot contrivance is introduced, the film is relatively free of jokes.

Most complex is a third method of gag/narrative integration, which combines elements of the other two, and which is exemplified in the key film *Cracked Ice* (1938), released under the Merrie Melodies banner.

The film's first section is plotless, consisting of a series of disconnected blackout gags. At precisely the halfway mark, Tashlin introduces an elaborate gag that serves as the basis for the simple narrative that dominates the remainder of the film. In this complicated setup, an inebriate pig uses a magnetized dish of soup bones to trick a St. Bernard into surrendering some of the liquor in his neck-mounted barrel, but, when pig and dog collide, the magnet falls into the water of a frozen pond, where it attaches itself inextricably to a passing fish. The fish swims through the stream of seeping liquor, instantly becomes drunk, and begins darting about crazily under the ice. In short order, the magnet attracts the metal blades of the pig's skates, causing him to career wildly about on the ice. The topper to the whole scenario is that the pig's frantic movements win him first prize in an ice skating contest, but when he fills his victory chalice with liquor, the magnetized fish passes beneath it and the cup zips away. This two-part narrative structure (which Tashlin would use again) allows him to develop the rudiments of a story with a beginning, middle, and end. While less narratively rich than many of his later cartoons, *Cracked Ice* is more narratively complex than, for instance, *Have You Got Any Castles?*, which merely appends a cursory, arbitrary chase scene to the end of its scattershot structure. Though Tashlin did not employ the narrative structure of *Cracked Ice* in his features, a different kind of partial integration of gag and narrative would become important in several of Tashlin's Jerry Lewis films.

Several of the twenty-one cartoons that Tashlin made between 1936 and 1938 are representative of broader trends in his work; a brief consideration of a few of these films is instructive. *Wholly Smoke*, again, and *The Case of the Stuttering Pig* (1937) are our standard-bearers here.

Wholly Smoke, though it does not lack for straight-on compositions (Figure 1.4a), frequently employs camera placement and shot composition themselves for gags, or non-gags. The film's first two shots, discussed above, use audacious framings and movements that call attention to themselves. Later, a low-angle shot of Porky responding to the bulldog's challenge humorously emphasizes our hero's false confidence (Figure 1.4b). In the musical sequence, Tashlin uses a showy, deep, diagonal composition for the burnt-match chorus: the shot is "artful" in a way that humorously contrasts with its whimsical content (Figure 1.4c). A high-angle shot of dancing cigarettes (Figure 1.4d) makes humorous reference to the lavish musical numbers of Busby Berkeley.

Figure 1.4 *Wholly Smoke*
A. Straight-on composition
B. Low-angle composition
C. Deep diagonals
D. High-angle shot

On the level of sonic humor, *Wholly Smoke* features numerous gags (and non-gags) that involve dialect and intonation. At one point in the musical number, a meerschaum pipe with a Teutonic moustache sings in heavily accented English, "Little boys zhould not zmoking zigarettes!" The pipe's thick accent is funny in itself, and it also emphasizes the humorous qualities of its line of dialogue. Later, a white pipe-cleaner man dips his head into a well-used pipe, emerges with a soot-blackened visage, and emits a mock-Calloway wail: "Little booooooooys shouldn't smoke!" Tashlin seems particularly interested in designing jokes that specifically make use of the soundtrack, a tendency he would exploit more fully in his feature career. Best known for his visual skills, Tashlin's abilities with sonic humor merit some attention.

Though hardly a work of satire, *Wholly Smoke* points toward Tashlin's penchant, fully realized in several features, for using artifacts of popular culture as the basis for comedy. Tashlin uses the hallucination scene as an opportunity for pop-culturally savvy, borderline-racy gags of a punny nature. The film caricatures famous performers, and uses racial and sexual humor on several occasions. Largely for these reasons, Tashlin's film comes off as fairly "modern"—an acknowledged product and reflection of the culture industries that gave rise to it.

The plot of *The Case of the Stuttering Pig*, one of Tashlin's best 1930s films, is simple.[16] Solomon, the departed uncle of several young pigs, has left them his entire fortune; however, his will stipulates that, should anything happen to them, his friend Lawyer Goodwill will inherit his riches. Shortly after reading them the will, Lawyer Goodwill takes a potion that turns him into a monster, and proceeds to capture each of the pigs with the intent of killing them and claiming Solomon's inheritance. However, his nefarious scheme is foiled by, of all things, a spectator in the cinema that is ostensibly showing the film. The monstrous Lawyer Goodwill repeatedly insults the "big creampuff" sitting in the third row of the cinema, only to have the creampuff somehow alert the police to the villain's wrongdoing, and thus ensure his capture. Humor of this type would become increasingly important to Tashlin.

The film includes another gag that suggests Tashlin's interest in exploring the relationship between gag and narrative. In a cellar, Lawyer Goodwill mixes up a batch of "Jekyll & Hyde juice" by pouring it back and forth between two glasses. Quaffing it rapidly, he looks into the camera and waits for the potion's effects to take hold, but the expected transformation fails to transpire. Then he has a bright idea. Pouring another glass of elixir, he walks to a countertop, where sits a very convenient milkshake mixer. The device effectively aerates the potion, and Lawyer Goodwill promptly turns into a giant, malicious goon. Tashlin takes a key narrative event and turns it into a gag not only by delaying it, but by acknowledging the constructed nature of the delay—and, by extension, of the story itself.

Tashlin's Porky

Though he later expressed a hatred of the character, Tashlin clearly learned a great deal about comic performance through his repeated use of Porky Pig.[17] Porky appeared in more Tashlin films than even Jerry Lewis. Since so much of the humor in Tashlin's films is dependent on the personae and performance styles of his comic actors, it is important to take account of the ways in which Tashlin employed Porky in his 1930s Warner Bros. cartoons.

A Warner Bros. cartoon character of the 1930s was more subject to changes in appearance than those of other studios. Though model sheets ("blueprints" of cartoon characters shown from different angles, used by animators to keep character design consistent) had existed for some time by the late 1930s, Warners animators were, according to Michael Barrier, not required or even encouraged to follow their guidelines until as late as 1939. In fact, the skilled animator and designer Robert McKimson was promoted to head animator in August 1939, precisely to keep his colleagues "on model."

> Until 1939, there wasn't much reason to worry about consistency in how the characters looked because there were so few continuing characters, and most of them were used by only one director apiece. . . . But when characters like Elmer Fudd and the early Bugs Bunny began to appear in different directors' films, the case was made for a head animator who would . . . smooth away the imperfections in others' more creative work. McKimson was ideally suited for such a job.[18]

McKimson assumed this important role shortly after Tashlin left Warner Brothers for the second time, meaning that Tashlin's 1930s Porky Pig cartoons were made without official design strictures. Like his colleagues, Tashlin could and did make changes to Porky. Maltin credits him with important alterations to the character's appearance: he "made his design even more grotesque, giving him apple cheeks and a compressed body."[19]

In Porky's first film, Friz Freleng's *I Haven't Got a Hat* (1936), the pig's appearance is significantly different from that of his familiar modern incarnation. In the first definitive model sheet for the character, Porky is quite fat and round, with squat legs, bulbous cheeks, and a snout whose height is about a third of that of his head. On this 1936 model sheet, the height of Porky's head comprises just less than one-third of his total height. The Porky of *I Haven't Got a Hat* is nearly spherical, so heavily did Freleng emphasize the pig's porkiness. The only hints of sharp or straight lines anywhere on Porky's body are the nearly unnoticcable ones that delineate his hoof and a notch in his eyeball; every other line is round and soft, imbuing the character with cuteness, friendliness, and jollity.

A model sheet from Tashlin's 1937 film *Porky's Romance* shows that, if anything, Tashlin made the character rounder still. In Tashlin's model sheet, Porky's cheeks are not small and kidney-shaped but so round as to be nearly spherical. Similarly, the pig's legs in the 1936 model sheet were already fat and round, but his thighs, knees, and calves are all nevertheless distinguishable. In Tashlin's model sheet, Porky's legs are little more than small circles attached to the larger circle of his body. Tashlin even rounds out such details as Porky's eyeballs—on Freleng's sheet, the pupils are notched; on Tashlin's, they are solid, rounded dots. As well, Tashlin made Porky's mouth less wide, and his ears smaller and rounder. The result is a character that is even more bulbous and spherical than he was under the pen of Freleng. More to the point, in rendering the character so globoid, Tashlin communicated Porky's amiability, innocence, and eagerness, as well as the naïveté that would become the character's most prominent trait. These traits, and their visual-comic framework, were apparent to the viewer at a glance; it is a fine example of what Henry Jenkins has called the "economy of gags," a hallmark of the vaudeville aesthetic that so strongly influenced Hollywood comedy.

By the time of *Wholly Smoke*, Porky bears relatively little resemblance to the pig of these two model sheets. In Figure 1.4a, Porky is a wide-eyed schoolboy who has apparently been dieting; with the weight loss came renewed definition of Porky's limbs.[20]

Every one of Tashlin's modifications to the character is in the service of rendering Porky more adorable (for want of a better word) and humanlike. The Porky of *Wholly Smoke* and *Porky's Spring Planting* is much closer in appearance to the pig's modern incarnation in that his proportions are less extreme. The naïveté suggested by Porky's appearance makes the character's sputtering fits of exasperation all the funnier: his rounded boyishness is a comical counterpoint to his frantic spasms of frustration.

Phenotype in animation is one thing, but performance is another, and far more complicated, for the simple reason that cartoon characters are not actually actors. However, they *do* have important commonalities with their three-dimensional counterparts. Human beings like Jerry Lewis and animated figures like Daffy Duck are narrative agents whose actions determine the courses of their stories. The difference is that Jerry Lewis *plays* a character, but Daffy Duck *is* a character. But to allow that Daffy is a character is not the same thing as saying that he is a performer. Is there a performative element to an animated character, and, if it exists, how can we speak about it? Donald Crafton provides a framework for thinking about this subject. Not only *can* cartoon characters perform, he argues, but they never stop performing. "Unlike in real life, where it is possible to film people unawares, in animation, everything is a performance. Everything we see on the screen has been constructed to be a performance. There is no cartoon candid camera."[21]

Moreover, Crafton argues, cartoon characters, like their human analogues, can and do act.

> This is what . . . Eisenstein would have called typage; they act out their personality traits. Daffy blows his top; Mister Magoo bumbles. But toon characters also act in roles, for instance when they do routines for the audience: Donald Duck and Porky Pig recite nursery rhymes (in separate films), Popeye and Bluto try to outdo each other with feats of derring-do, Porky behaves like a temperamental movie star and he tears up his contract. But again, the difference between performing in and out of roles is simulated. The private lives of the characters at home in Toon Town are just as constructed as their workaday lives as cartoon stars.[22]

Animated performance is of a different type, but it is still performance. When an animated character raises its eyebrows or delivers a line of dialogue, it can have the same effects as when performed by a human actor. Acting instructor Ed Hooks has written an entire book on this very subject.[23] Animator Richard Williams considers acting one of the skills that a good animator must master. Williams believes that acting in live-action and acting in animation are closely related—he even draws examples for would-be animators from the advice of such performers as Michael Caine and Ned Beatty. "The thing is," he writes, "to be aware of [acting] and use it to express things—to develop the ability to project it through our drawings or invented images by getting into the character we're depicting, in the situation they're in, knowing what it is they want—and *why* they want it—that's acting."²⁴

By studying production practices at Warners' Schlesinger Unit, we can assess Tashlin's role in establishing the persona and performance style of Porky Pig, the studio's first cartoon star. Between July 1935 and December 1938 (a period that represents the first stages of Porky's evolution, as well as Tashlin's major tenure with the character), nearly every one of Warners' principal animators made multiple films with Porky. Tashlin and Clampett tie for the most Porky films, with thirteen apiece; Avery made ten; Jack King, six; and five other directors made one, two, or three Porky Pig films each.²⁵

Certain of Porky's character traits—most notably his famous stutter and a certain wide-eyed naïveté—have been facets of his personality since the character's inception, and these lend his character some continuity. Generally, though, the first few years of Porky's existence show the Warners animators experimenting with personalities to discover which was best suited for their new star. This process is entirely analogous to the practice of casting a new human actor in roles of varying kinds in an effort to find the persona that registers with the filmgoing public.²⁶

Steve Schneider argues that Porky did not achieve a "coherent identity" until Robert Clampett directed him in 1937. Clampett, Schneider writes, "made Porky snappy and cute, downplayed his stammer, and cast him as an eager, if naïve, delver into the world's wonders. . . . [Porky became] an innocent observer."²⁷ During this time, Porky also developed into a straight man for the zanier Looney Tunes characters, notably Daffy Duck. Schneider aptly observes that Porky, in his straight-man role, was "unprepared for personalities who flaunt convention and rationality alike."²⁸ Schneider's observations are astute, but he omits entirely Tashlin's contributions to the character. Barrier, too, downplays Tashlin's contributions.²⁹

In the Schlesinger Unit, characters were allowed to develop organically. Writers and animators collaborated freely, and would often change their colleagues' ideas.³⁰ Because of the collaborative nature of the Warners animation unit, it is difficult to say with certainty which of Porky's character traits were given him by Tashlin, and which were borrowed or adapted from his colleagues' films. Additionally, there is relatively little variation in Porky's persona: he has always been a meek, unassuming, naïve young pig. Porky is unfailingly kind and gullible, and more than a little cowardly, silly, and clueless. But Porky is not just an inveterate simpleton: he has heroic qualities, as well. In *Little Beau Porky*, he does not hesitate to take on Ali Mode's army singlehandedly, if timorously. Porky is also resourceful: in *Porky's Poultry Plant*, while piloting a plane in pursuit of a hawk, his propeller is destroyed. He manages to maneuver the plane into a windmill so that its blades become his new propeller; thus, he resumes his chase. As Clampett puts it, "Porky was very laughable, but even more important, he had a touch of Chaplinesque pathos about him. The audience laughed at and felt sympathy for Porky Pig. He was our first full-fledged star."[31]

Warner Bros. made only ten Porky Pig films before Tashlin directed the character. By comparing some of these early Porky films to Tashlin's, we can see some of the ways in which Tashlin put his pig to work as a performer.

In Jack King's *Boom, Boom* (1936), Porky is a soldier on the front lines of World War I. He must brave anthropomorphic bullets and sneering Huns to rescue his general, who is imprisoned in a remote, bombed-out windmill. Porky exhibits both cowardice and bravery in turn, and King uses both emotions for comedy.

About halfway through the film, Porky, terrified of setting foot on the battlefield, cowers beneath a table while his bunkmates tauntingly sing "You're in the Army Now." Porky's brow furrows, his lips quiver, and tears of nervousness fall from his right eye (Figure 1.5a). As the song ends, he lets out a sustained "Ooo-ooo-ooo" whimper that drops in tone as it goes on. Porky's head drops, too, and he moves it quickly from side to side: a visual analogue to the drop in pitch. The scene is made humorous by Porky's over-the-top cowering, which King conveys through the pig's facial contortions and posture. In a way, this small moment gets at the core of Porky's character, in that it shows a character whose cowardly actions are meant to be humorous.

For a soldier on a dangerous mission in the middle of a bomb-scarred battlefield, Porky moves, in a later scene, with unusual sprightliness. He smilingly hops from one hoof to the other toward a windmill's window, so that he may peer inside (Figure 1.5b). It's a bizarre, inappropriate wartime action, but it highlights another key facet of Porky's persona: even his bravery is often played for comedy.

When Tashlin worked with the character, he refined and altered some

Figure 1.5 Porky Pig cowering and hopping gaily about the battlefield in *Boom, Boom*

of his performance techniques. *Porky's Romance* demonstrates several of the important changes that Tashlin made. Released in April 1937, *Porky's Romance* appeared nearly two years after the release of Porky's first film, and more than a year after the release of *Boom, Boom*, giving the animators some time to refine their star's performance style. In this film, Porky brings flowers, candy, and jewelry to his girlfriend Petunia to entice her to accept his marriage proposal. At the beginning of the film, when Porky visits a series of stores to acquire Petunia's gifts, he is a very happy pig: when he emerges from the florist's shop, he walks so jauntily that his hat bounces gaily and rhythmically atop his head. When he arrives at Petunia's house, Porky bounds up her front steps, slides down the banister, and then bounces back up to the landing. All the while, his eyes are huge and his smile is broad. When Petunia opens the peephole in her door, we see Porky with a nattily cocked straw hat and a look of immense self-confidence on his face (Figure 1.6a).

Moments later, after Petunia has spurned him, Porky plods away from the door in a state of all-consuming sorrow. His steps are now slow and heavy; his eyes are no longer wide, but half-closed and heavy-lidded; his mouth hangs in a deep frown; and his ears droop desultorily as he deliberately descends the stairs (Figure 1.6b). Tashlin uses nearly every facet of Porky's face, body, and movement to reflect his emotional change. This is good cartoon acting.

Tashlin adds significant nuance to Porky's performance. Immediately after Petunia whisks Porky into her living room, she sets about gobbling up the chocolates. As she stuffs her maw, Porky makes several attempts

Figure 1.6 *Porky's Romance*: A dapper Porky and a downtrodden Porky

Figure 1.7 *Porky's Romance*: Porky's first, second, and third attempts to placate Fluffnums

to pluck just one of the bonbons for himself, only to be thwarted by the growls of Petunia's insufferable dog, Fluffnums. The first time the dog snarls, Porky widens his eyes, raises his eyebrows, and pats Fluffnums gently on the head six times (each pat accompanied by a clinking piano note), as if to say, "Nice doggie. Relax while I take just one teensy candy" (Figure 1.7a). When Fluffnums's growl stops his second attempt to snag a sweet, Porky responds more angrily: he angles his eyebrows sharply downward and a slightly malicious smile crosses his lips (Figure 1.7b). This time, Porky pats the dog only three times, and the notes that accompany the gesture are pitched much lower. When his goal is blocked a third time, Porky's brows, now drawn with thicker lines, bend sharply downward and stay there for several seconds. The smile is gone, replaced by an out-and-out sneer, and Porky gives up any attempt to placate the dog with mock affection (Figure 1.7c). When he finally manages to grab a bonbon, he sticks out his tongue at the irritating creature, only to have the dog snatch the candy from his hand.

In this brief scene alone, Porky displays a far greater range of emotions than he does in the entirety of *Boom, Boom*. Moreover, his emotions here are of a significantly subtler variety than those in the earlier film, in which he is either fearful or uncomfortably brave. Porky's nuanced performance in this scene demonstrates that, in Tashlin's hands, he was capable of much more than cowering and stuttering. Tashlin showed, in *Porky's Romance* and other films (notably *Porky at the Crocadero*), that Porky could be a very expressive figure. This skill with comic performers would serve Tashlin well later in his career, when he directed such talented figures as Bob Hope and Jerry Lewis.

Screen Gems, 1941–1942

Though Tashlin's Columbia cartoons are overlooked today (largely for being almost entirely out of circulation), animation historians generally write favorably about them, just as, at the time of their release, Tashlin's contemporaries held them in high regard. Leonard Maltin quotes the influential animator John Hubley, who was an animator at Columbia: "Under Tashlin, we tried some very experimental things; none of them quite got off the ground, but there was a lot of ground broken. We were doing crazy things that were anti the classic Disney approach."[32] As Production Supervisor at Screen Gems, Columbia's animation unit, Tashlin oversaw a dramatic rise in the studio's animated output.[33] "Although his specific credit varies," Prouty writes, "[Tashlin] was certainly responsible for the creative atmosphere in which [Columbia's 1941–1942 cartoons]—the company's best in years—were produced."[34]

Since he appears to have had, at Screen Gems, significant creative freedom, it is tempting to read Tashlin's Columbia cartoons as unfettered expressions of his artistic temperament. For the first time in his career, Tashlin was in almost complete command of his own films. Given this freedom, he continued to explore many of the subjects and techniques he employed in his Warners work.

Certain stylistic fillips and methods of joke-telling carry over from Warner Bros. to Columbia. Many jokes—like the goofy wartime humor of the "B-19½" airplane in *Cinderella Goes to a Party* (1942), and grimace-inducing puns like the human "autograph hound" scratching at his fleas in *A Hollywood Detour* (1942)—echo the manic, punning, Looney Tunes

Figure 1.8 Showy animation in *A Battle for a Bottle*

sense of humor. Some homages are even more direct. In *A Battle for a Bottle* (1942), a tomcat waltzes with a stolen bottle of milk, warbling "Drink to Me Only With Thine Eyes," a song that, since at least Tex Avery's 1936 film *I Love to Singa*, was an all-purpose Warner Bros. signifier for schmaltz.[35]

Concerto in B-flat Minor (1942) employs an elaborate non-gag of the type Tashlin used at Warners. A Scottish terrier enters a concert hall in mid-symphony; carefully locates his seat on stage; meticulously removes his coat, scarf, and gloves; dons his glasses; plays a solitary note on the triangle . . . and leaves in just as elaborate a fashion as he arrived. The situation is not really humorous, but is made so by the fact that its duration barely justifies its minimal payoff: it is almost an anti-gag, very similar to the hose joke in *Porky the Fireman*. Another clever visual non-gag occurs in one of the first shots of *A Battle for a Bottle*, a showy composition of a cat's reflection distended by a milk bottle's convex topography (Figure 1.8). This is the same impulse behind the shadows in *Little Beau Porky*: technically accomplished animation that is not put specifically in the service of comedy.

Figure 1.9 The wicked stepsisters in *Cinderella Goes to a Party* prepare for the ball

One of Tashlin's finest visual gags of any kind appears in the first shot of *Cinderella Goes to a Party*. We see, in silhouette, Cinderella's wicked stepsisters, dressing for the ball on either side of an ornate vanity (Figure 1.9a). As they gossip, the fat one cinches up her torso inside a girdle and the skinny one stuffs a pillow inside her slip (Figure 1.9b). Then the women simultaneously yank identical dresses over their heads, their movements perfectly synchronous and symmetrical (Figure 1.9c). The result: they look identically slender and lovely—in silhouette, at least. This gag is a terrific synthesis of beautifully timed movement, excellent character design, sharp use of silhouette to strengthen the joke (and reduce visual clutter), and social/sexual satire.

Tashlin also further explored diegetic rupture in his Columbia cartoons. At the end of *Under the Shedding Chestnut Tree* (1942), the film's main character hangs from the glyph "THE END" that sits high in a tree; at the beginning of *Wolf Chases Pigs* (1942), characters run past trees on which are affixed signs that bear the names of the film's creators. As Hubley suggests, such techniques were entirely opposed to the Disney approach to storytelling in animation.

The strongest ties to Tashlin's earlier Warner Bros. work may be structural. Several of Tashlin's Columbia films, like many Warners cartoons of the 1930s, possess a vaudeville-like blackout gag formula. The influential film *The Fox and the Grapes* (1941) is the quintessential example: in an effort to steal the grapes of the devious Crow, Fox tries all manner of elaborate devices (levers, slingshots, etc.), failing every time. (When he finally *does* get the grapes, the ultimate topper is that they're sour.) Variations on the blackout gag structure also occur in the Columbia cartoons *The Great Cheese Mystery* (1941), *A Hollywood Detour*, *Under the Shedding Chestnut Tree*, *A Battle for a Bottle*, and *Woodsman, Spare That*

Tree (all 1942). The frequent occurrence of this structuring device in Tashlin's Columbia films points to his—and, more generally, classical Hollywood animation's—kinship with vaudeville humorists.

Warner Bros., 1942–1944

When Tashlin returned to Warners in 1942, he was employed by a far different studio than the one he had left four years earlier, even if most of the personnel remained. (One of the most significant changes was the departure of Tex Avery for MGM.) Warner Bros. animation had developed a stronger identity and greater professionalism; this was evidenced by firmer character design; a wider stable of reliable recurring characters, most notably Bugs Bunny, as well as Elmer Fudd, Daffy Duck, and a sort of proto-Tweety; a willingness to experiment with film for the sake of experimentation, not just for purposes of product differentiation; and a concretizing of their trademark robust, rowdy, wacky, self-reflexive, and, above all, intelligent sense of humor. In many ways, Tashlin's 1930s Warner Bros. work anticipated these changes: his Porky Pig films were vital to the studio's roster of stars; his interest in experimenting with film form antedates Jones's. These tendencies were intensified in his third and final tenure at Warners.

The Warner Bros. style of animation began to jell right around Tashlin's 1938 departure, and was largely in place by his 1942 return. This evolution was the result of two major events: the development of the character of Bugs Bunny, and the promotion of Chuck Jones to the position of unit supervisor.

Bugs debuted in Ben "Bugs" Hardaway's April 1938 film *Porky's Hare Hunt*. His familiar persona was not honed until 1940, when Jones cast him in the "important transitional cartoon"[36] *Elmer's Candid Camera*, and Avery made a series of films with Elmer and Bugs as hunter and hunted.[37] With regard to both character design and personality, Avery's *A Wild Hare* (July 1940) is, according to Barrier, probably the film in which Bugs comes into his own.[38]

Precious little information exists regarding the box-office of the Warner Bros. cartoons, but the development of Bugs Bunny was clearly a turning point in the popularity of the studio's animation. Mickey Mouse may have still ruled the roost, but Bugs was gaining: though it was not until 1945 that Bugs Bunny cartoons were selected by American and Canadian exhibitors as the number-one short subjects, the films would receive that honor for the next sixteen years.[39] With Bugs's success came what would these days be termed "brand identity": audiences now associated the Warners name with reliably enjoyable cartoons. Given this cushion of popularity, Warners animators could and did embark on artistic explorations that, in turn, resulted in the early 1940s flourishing of the Warner Bros. house style.

After Tashlin's 1938 departure, Chuck Jones took over his unit.[40] It was Jones who was largely responsible for the look of Looney Tunes starting in the early 1940s. Jones took his animation perhaps a bit more seriously than other unit supervisors, holding night classes for his unit's animators and instilling in them a spirit of artistic discipline.[41] Jones was interested in experimenting with film form, playing with match cuts and dissolves in two 1942 cartoons, *Conrad the Sailor* and *Hold the Lion, Please*. Michael Barrier writes of this experimental spirit, "From all appearances, Jones introduced matched cuts and dissolves not because they would solve a problem or add some strength to a particular cartoon, but as an intellectual exercise. What was really new about *Conrad*, at least for the Schlesinger cartoons, was the attitude embodied in it: that each cartoon could be a small laboratory where any idea could be tried for its own sake."[42]

Jones would assume the role of lead experimenter in the Warners stable. As Barrier suggests, this attitude toward filmmaking was healthy for the studio, and played a major part in enhancing the studio's reputation for professionalism, design, and comedy.

Situation Normal: All F***ed Up

In his final stint at the Schlesinger Unit, Tashlin directed four cartoons that were part of the "Private Snafu" series.[43] The Warner Bros. style of humor, which already occasionally pushed at the limits of propriety, was further unleashed in the Snafu films, whose intended audience was the men of the armed services. The cartoons never venture into out-and-out vulgarity, but they come closer than anything the Production Code Administration would have approved for general release. Tashlin was not the only Snafu director who seized this opportunity to ramp up the films' risqué humor: the first film in the series, *Coming! SNAFU!* (Jones, June 1943), features a realistically drawn woman who disrobes to Snafu's rendition of "The Strip Polka."

Tashlin took it further. In *The Home Front* (November 1943), the narrator says, "It's so cold it would freeze the nuts off a Jeep." Though this joke is literalized by two hexagonal pieces of metal falling from an icy military vehicle, the double entendre could not be clearer. Unsurprisingly, this gag was controversial, but, according to Greg Ford, the Warner Bros. cartoonists "rallied behind Tashlin in support of the gag. The incident may have helped to nudge Warner Bros. cartoons toward more adult-level comedy."[44]

Seconds after the "Jeep" joke, Tashlin engages in further ribaldry: he cuts to the interior of Snafu's Quonset hut, the walls of which are covered with pin-up girls in various states of undress. A short while later, we see Snafu's grandfather, back home, take in a burlesque show that goes on far longer and with far more jiggling than is required to complete the gag. Later, a horse gaily distributes its own manure across a field; after massive crops spring instantaneously from the soil, the horse says to the camera, "This stuff sure makes things grow, don't it?"

The Home Front is unusual because Tashlin's inclusion of these and other off-color jokes nearly steers the film away from its intended purpose. The SNAFU films have a standard structure: in the first part, Snafu complains about or shirks his duties; in the second, the dire repercussions of this shirking unfold—usually death for Snafu or defeat for Allied forces; in the third (if he survives), Snafu realizes the error of his ways.

Since these films were designed as behavioral instruction for soldiers, the third section is vital: without it, Snafu might come across as merely humorous, rather than dangerously foolish. But the Snafu films were also saddled with a strict time limit: they almost never exceed five minutes (the standard duration for a Hollywood cartoon was seven minutes), a restriction presumably brought about by both the need for conciseness and the fact that shorter films weigh less than longer ones, and were thus cheaper to transport overseas. *The Home Front* is so packed with gratuitous, off-color jokes that the third act is actually absent. In the first section, Snafu complains that he is cold and miserable, and that everyone back home surely has it easy. To counter his assumptions, "Technical Fairy, First Class," a military fairy godfather character who recurs in the series, shows him that his friends and family are actually building tanks, planting victory gardens, and the like. By the time the second act is complete, the film is at the 4:20 mark, and quickly draws to a close, forsaking any scene in which Snafu explicitly learns his lesson. In other films, he is transformed into a horse's hindquarters, or even killed; here, he merely marvels at how wrong he was. *The Home Front*'s lack of a "moral" section undermines its effectiveness. Moreover, it hints at Tashlin's abiding and arguably foolhardy interest in subverting official strictures for the inclusion of prurient humor—a tendency that would become especially relevant during his live-action career.

Warner Bros. Studio Cartoons, 1942–1946

Between 1942 and 1946, Frank Tashlin directed thirteen cartoons for Warners, only about a third as many as his talented colleagues Chuck Jones, Friz Freleng (thirty-seven films each), and Robert Clampett (thirty-three).[45]

Like Clampett and Tex Avery, Tashlin maintains a tone of fast-paced anarchy in his 1940s cartoons. But Tashlin is more catholic than these directors in his gag dispersal, relying not only on character and design, but on composition, camera movement, and editing. A sequence in *Porky Pig's Feat* (1943) highlights Tashlin's use of camera movement as a carrier of comedy. In an attempt to avoid payment of their hotel bill, Daffy and Porky pull various tricks on the hotel manager, one of which sends him tumbling down a huge spiral staircase. As the manager bounces down the steps, Tashlin cranes and tilts down to humorously show the staircase's enormity (Figure 1.10a). The next shot is a long, low-angle view of Porky and Daffy leaning over the banister, watching their nemesis plummet. The subsequent shot is an extreme close-up of Porky's eyes, in the pupils of which is reflected the hotel manager. He first appears in Porky's right eye, then bounces toward frame right, to be reflected in his left eye (Figure 1.10b). Then, Tashlin pans right to show Daffy's eyes in close-up: in reflection, the bouncing figure gets noticeably smaller, an indication of the significant and painful downward distance he has traversed in just a few seconds (Figure 1.10c).

First, the crane and the tilt emphasize the great height of the fall; in this case, the greater the height, the funnier the joke. Second, the cut from the long low-angle shot of the characters at the banister to an extreme close-up of their eyeballs is a fairly bold choice, and is mildly funny in and of itself, if only for its suddenness. Finally, Tashlin redoubles the effect of the eyeball-reflection gag with the pan from Porky's eyes to Daffy's. Both the pan itself and the reflection's diminution emphasize

TISH-TASH IN CARTOONLAND : 45

Figure 1.10 Humorous use of a high-angle shot, and comical eyeball reflections in *Porky Pig's Feat*

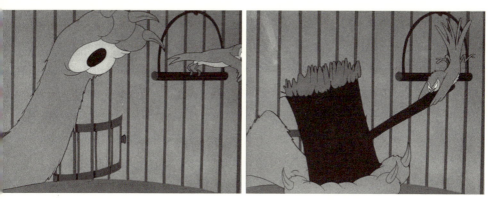

Figure 1.11 Offscreen-space humor in *Puss 'n' Booty*

the distance that the hotel manager falls. With these devices, Tashlin milks this simple joke for all it has.

This same gag relies, in part, on the space beyond the frame edges, a recurring comic device for Tashlin. We see the beginning of the hotel manager's fall as well as the eyeball reflections, but Tashlin stretches the gag by having the fall continue offscreen. In *Puss 'n' Booty*, one of his best 1940s Warners cartoons, Tashlin frames a shot inside a birdcage so that a small portion of the cage lies beyond the right frame edge. It is from this sliver of invisible space that Tashlin derives his gag, in which a tiny canary reaches offscreen to grab a gigantic mallet, with which he clobbers the paw of a marauding cat (Figure 1.11).

Visual humor of the types described above was a hallmark of the Looney Tunes of this era; humor rooted in character design and move-

Figure 1.12 An extended gag about impossible chicken movements in *Swooner Crooner*

ment was another. This is one of Robert Clampett's particular strengths and claims to fame, the evidence for which may be found in almost any of his mid-1940s films. But Tashlin was at least Clampett's equal in comic figure design and movement. In fact, Tashlin pushed his characters' designs and movements a bit further than did his colleagues: when a character's body stretches, melts, or quivers in a Tashlin cartoon, it does so with unusual vigor and expressivity. In *Swooner Crooner* (1944), Tashlin takes great care with the design and movements of his bobby-soxer chickens, one of whom melts into what Donald Crafton calls "a creamy puddle" in the presence of her favorite singing roosters.[46] Another chicken shoots straight up into the air on a jet of pure euphoria, pauses, then rockets to the ground to land beak-first in the earth (Figure 1.12). All the while, her body stays rigid with joy, and its weight quickly causes her to topple over, bringing a clod of dirt with her. It is a fine example of Tashlin's use of eccentric movement for humor.

Perhaps Tashlin's greatest achievement in the areas of character- and performance-based humor is *Nasty Quacks* (1945), his penultimate Warner Bros. cartoon. Daffy's frenetic energy is the comic center of the film: he zips around the house, enters the frame from all sides, and giddily tells unamusing shaggy-dog stories. Tashlin conveys this energy partly through the use of long takes. A scene at the breakfast table, in which Daffy enrages his owner's father with an irritatingly unfunny story, takes place over five shots and eighty-nine seconds (including shots of seventeen, twenty-three, and thirty-nine seconds) for an in-scene ASL of almost eighteen seconds. These long takes serve several purposes. First, and most plainly, the scene delivers a minimally interrupted performance from Daffy, encouraging us to focus on his behavior and dialogue. (I believe this to be one of Daffy's funniest performances.) Second, the long takes engender in the viewer, even if subsconsciously, a palpable sense of the passage of time, thereby allowing us to share in the father's agony of having to listen to this type of story for the umpteenth time. Finally, these long takes encourage us to focus on the visual contrasts between Daffy and his nemesis. Daffy is small, slender, ecstatically manic, and he moves with expressive speed; the father is stoic, stone-faced, and absolutely motionless.

The differences between Daffy's and the father's movements are a continual source of comedy, but each character's movements are humorous in and of themselves. Daffy is a ball of energy in this film, rarely slowing down and never stopping. Tashlin also imbues him with some bizarrely funny specialized movements that add to the film's frenzied tone. The most notable of these is when Daffy, aware that Agnes's father has attempted to slip him a mickey, walks across a table to switch his water glass with the father's. Daffy ambles across the table with a weird, bent-knee shuffle: his legs are bent at right angles, and they move alternately at the hip joint.[47] The principal gag here—the switching of the glasses—would be no less funny had Daffy moved in a less eccentric manner. But Tashlin understands that Daffy's manic energy is an important comic element in the film, and turns to it at this moment.

Daffy is hilarious in this film, but it is Agnes's father whose movements Tashlin mines most thoroughly for comedy. The character design here is superb: the father is a huge, ovoid man who conveys an overall impression of roundness. But the parts of his body that Tashlin uses most often for comedic purposes are those few parts drawn with straight, sharp lines: his feet and legs. This graphic incongruity is especially visible during a butter-knife duel with Daffy, but the father's movements are funniest in a scene in which he thinks he has finally rid himself of his anatine nemesis. As he sings happily, the father prances about the house on what can only be called twinkletoes: his legs and feet flick rapidly back and forth, propelling his large body around the room with humorous, unexpectedly smooth swiftness. This character neatly embodies humorous contrasts between fat and thin, round and sharp, large and graceful.

Warner Bros. cartoons often employ reflexive gags: jokes that call attention to their film's status as a manufactured work of art. This form of humor is one of the many devices that links American animation to such comic traditions as vaudeville. Tashlin is one of the reasons that this style of comedy is so strongly identified with Warner Bros. animation. In Tashlin's *Porky Pig's Feat*, Porky, referring to Bugs Bunny, says, "I saw him in a Leon Schlesinger cartoon once." In *Booby Hatched* (1944), Robespierre, a half-born duckling (only his legs jut out of an eggshell), tramps through a forest in a blinding snowstorm crying, "Help! Help!" All of a sudden, the snow stops in mid-drift, and Robespierre turns to the camera to say, "This is the saddest part of the picture, folks." At the beginning of *Nasty Quacks*, Daffy grows from duckling to duck as calendar pages fly past. He grows so fast, in fact, that he bumps his head against the upper frame line, whereupon he mincingly scolds the animator: "You're goin' too fast, you crazy!"

Tashlin continued to favor gags that shatter narrative unity. *Plane Daffy* (1944) is an excellent example. Daffy, pursued by *oiseau fatale* Hatta Mari, hides inside a refrigerator. Before she can shoot him, Daffy quickly sticks out his head to say, in a weird, high-pitched voice, "Well, whaddya know? The little light—it stays on!" He then zips out of the fridge and escapes. The greater part of the pleasure in this gag arises from the fact that it stops the story dead in its tracks with a patently absurd observation.

Another gag in the same film has Daffy racing across the room, a blur of orange and black (Figure 1.13a). Then, unaccountably, he happens upon a platform with a staircase at each end. When he reaches the first step, the blurring instantly ceases, and Daffy walks daintily up the steps (Figure 1.13b). Reaching the plateau of the platform, Daffy zips along, once again a blur (Figure 1.13c); upon reaching the top of the other staircase, he daintily tiptoes down the steps (Figure 1.13d), then resumes running (Figure 1.13e). Just as the refrigerator appears solely as an opportunity for Daffy's offhand joke, the stairs appear solely to interrupt Daffy's pace; in both cases, Tashlin temporarily delays the progression of the narrative to make a joke. A notable gag in *Swooner Crooner* has absolutely nothing to do with the story. In this film, Porky Pig plays a poultry farmer who notices that all of his chickens have gone missing. He frantically searches his entire farm, at one point uprooting a water pump, only to discover that inside of it is a water cooler.

It is somewhat surprising that Tashlin's 1940s Warners cartoons, like those of his colleagues, were, despite their topicality, only infrequently satirical. This situation changed somewhat in the studio's vaunted war-

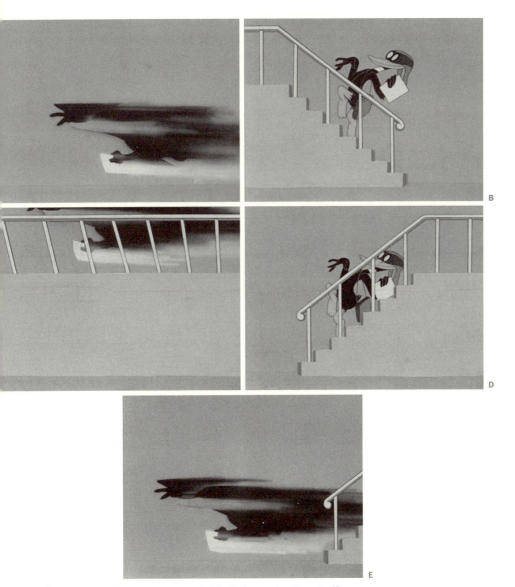

Figure 1.13 The humorous contrast of Daffy's pace in *Plane Daffy*

time films, which regularly and gleefully parody such figures as Hitler and Mussolini. (To this vein of comedy Tashlin contributed *Scrap Happy Daffy*, *Brother Brat*, and *Plane Daffy*.) It was not until he directed live-action films that Tashlin hit his stride as a satirist.

Frankie Goes to . . . Church?

In 1947, after he had left Warners for the last time but before his feature career commenced, Tashlin made a peculiar animated film that differs in many significant ways from all of his other film work. *The Way of Peace* is entirely lacking not only in satire, but in visual humor, sexual humor, character-based humor, and every other major facet of Tashlin's style examined in this volume. It is, in fact, unrecognizable *as* a Tashlin film—the only one of his pictures that may be so described. An analysis of *The Way of Peace*'s differences and shortcomings reveals how thoroughly Tashlin's style depended on various methods of comedy.

The Way of Peace is, by some margin, the most unusual film of Tashlin's unusual career.[48] Funded by the American Lutheran Church, it preaches an eschatological gospel of nuclear annihilation. The film is extremely heavy-handed and humorless: not a single gag of any kind appears in this film, making it the only Tashlin film that is definitively *not* a comedy. But it is a fascinating film: it combines traditional, clay, and puppet animation with a few live-action shots, and the very fact that it was a one-off film financed by a church sets it at odds with the rest of Tashlin's work.[49]

Deprived of comedy by churchly strictures, Tashlin made a film that is not just humorless, but poorly paced and oppressively didactic. Unsubtle visual metaphors abound (brick walls of misunderstanding, shadows of evil acts); the live-action shots are clumsily integrated, as if Tashlin resorted to them because animation had become too time-consuming. A lengthy scene of Jesus's birth slows down the film significantly, and stands in near-humorous contrast to the cursory treatment of the rest of his life: one brief scene of preaching, and then the crucifixion. The film's climax, in which nuclear missiles destroy the entire earth in spite of Christ's message of peace, drags: even the most doomsaying Christian would surely tire of its repeated images of global carnage.

The Way of Peace is Tashlin's least funny film and his worst film. Without his comic mainstays, the film falls apart, proving just how dependent his style was on such techniques.[50] *The Way of Peace* highlights, by their absence, the key facets of Tashlin's animation style: particular methods of staging, pacing, visual humor, character-based humor, non-gags, self-reflexivity, sexual humor, and satire. Denied the use of these techniques, Tashlin's style collapses. Unable to put his talent in the service of comedy, Tashlin delivers a film that bears little or no resemblance to the rest of his work. Though not a comedy itself, *The Way of Peace* illustrates how crucial the comic mode is to Tashlin's style.

2 TASHLIN, COMEDY, AND THE "LIVE-ACTION CARTOON"

Precisely what is cartoonlike in Tashlin's gags?
There is no adequate answer to this question in the critical literature.
—Brian Henderson, "Cartoon and Narrative in the Films of
   Frank Tashlin and Preston Sturges"[1]

A persistent argument about Frank Tashlin is that his cartoons anticipate his live-action features, and that his live-action features resemble cartoons. I wish to propose an alternative to this long-standing argument, which I believe mischaracterizes Tashlin's work.

Tashlin was a comic artist. His print cartoons; his animated cartoons; the gags and scripts that he wrote for such artists as the Marx Bros., Red Skelton, and Laurel and Hardy; the live-action features that he wrote, directed, or produced—all of these certainly belong to the comedy genre. We must now ask *how* Tashlin's films are funny, and if they are funny in ways that are particular to either live-action or animation. That Tashlin happened to move from animation to live action explains relatively little about him. Rather, the most important thing about Frank Tashlin is that he provides the most extensive, compelling case study for the deep generic connections between Hollywood animation and the American comic tradition.

Tashlin provides an excellent opportunity to ask questions about the generic identity of Hollywood animation. Animation is by no means restricted to a single genre, and yet the great majority of American animation, including all but one of Tashlin's animated films, does indeed fall within the genre of comedy. Other national animation traditions are not so generically restrictive. Japan's large *anime* industry—which for decades has produced not just comedies, but works of science-fiction, horror, and melodrama, to list only some of the best-represented genres—is probably the clearest counterexample, but Canada's, France's, and China's animation industries, to name a few, are also relevant here. Why, then, are most American cartoons comedic, and can a study of Tashlin's cartoons help us understand anything about this correspondence?

Ontologically, animated and live-action films diverge from one another but also overlap. Without initiating the book-length study that this topic merits (and which is long overdue), suffice it to say that the key difference between animation and live-action is that the former is made one frame at a time. This difference, though seemingly small, generates far-reaching ontological disparities, all of which are rooted in the same thing: that animation affords a far greater degree of *control* over the filmed image than does live-action filmmaking.

To be strict—and pedantic—about it, it is true that even live-action film is made one frame at a time, in that each frame of film does indeed spend a stationary split-second behind the taking lens so that a blur-free image may be exposed. However, in real-world terms, no live-action film is made by counting, monitoring, or adjusting each individual frame as it pauses instantaneously for exposure. In animated films, movement is simulated, one frame at a time, by animators; in live-action films, the movement is still simulated, but this simulation is provided by the rapid, motorized movement of the film through the camera.

Another matter that separates animation from live-action is that, in the former, even such tools as cinematography and editing become subsumed within the domain of *mise-en-scène*: the arrangement of elements in the frame. All camera movements are simulated by changes within the *mise-en-scène*, not by the manipulation of an actual camera. As well, depending on one's perspective, there are either zero cuts in an animated film, or a cut every twenty-fourth of a second, both of which cases render trivial the very notion of *editing*. While the *effects* of both cinematography and editing are identical in animation to the effects of these tools in live-action filmmaking, these devices in and of themselves are, in animation, folded into the dominion of *mise-en-scène*.

What this means is that, on a visual level, animation is a near-totalizing *mise-en-scène* experience, and, moreover, that those animators who are skilled *mise-en-scène* artists have the potential to command great expressive power from this realm of filmmaking. Frank Tashlin is one such artist. The principal skill that Tashlin carried over from animation to live action was a fine-grained control over all elements of *mise-en-scène*. Moreover, since the American animation industry, during Tashlin's animation career, made far more comedies than films of any other genre, Tashlin had ample opportunity to employ his *mise-en-scène* skills in the service of comedy.

Of necessity, Tashlin, as an animator, crafted all of his gags by deploying his *mise-en-scène* talents on a frame-by-frame basis. Such prolonged experience with the minute mechanics of visual comedy gave Tashlin an advantage when he moved into live-action film, but it does not mean that Tashlin simply transferred his animation technique to his live-action films, nor that his live-action films are in some way "cartoonlike." The principal comic influences on Warner Bros. and Columbia animation (and on nearly all other American animation studios) are the same sources that influenced the great majority of American comedian-centric comedies: vaudeville performers and the slapstick tradition. That we can detect some continuities between Tashlin's cartoons and his live-action features should not come as a surprise: they derive from the same traditions, and their creator spent the early part of his film career observing, replicating, and modifying—on a precise, frame-by-frame level—a form of visual comedy that explicitly draws on these traditions. This is decidedly *not* the same thing as saying that Tashlin's features are cartoonlike, or vice versa.

"Cartooniness" in Context

The impulse to understand Tashlin's features as "live-action cartoons" was first advanced by the cineastes/cinephiles of the French New Wave, specifically Jean-Luc Godard at *Cahiers du Cinéma* and Roger Tailleur at *Positif*. In the half-century since New Wave critics wrote with excitement about Tashlin, few advances have been made in the field of Tashlin studies. Almost without fail, more recent authors observe that his cartoons look forward to his features, and that his features resemble cartoons. The pervasiveness of this assumption cannot be overstated: virtually everything ever written about Tashlin—from scholarly journal articles to the "trivia" section at imdb.com—makes reference to the apparent connection between his cartoons and his features.[2] It is summed up succinctly in the opening sentences of animation historian Dewey McGuire's piece on Tashlin's cartoons: "There are two things everyone knows about Frank Tashlin. One, he made animated cartoons using the language of live-action features. Two, he made live-action features using the language of animated cartoons."[3]

To say that Tashlin's features contain gags similar or identical to gags in his cartoons is merely to acknowledge that animation is a fine forum for the development of gag-craft, especially the crafting of gags that depend for their humor on visual devices. It is thus rather surprising that so few American animators made the leap to the realm of live action, which may well have benefited from the work of skilled visual-comic stylists.

The American studio cartoon is one of the great cinematic repositories of disconnected, modular, near-narrativeless structure. Several of Tashlin's films, especially those from the 1930s, exhibit this structurelessness; in many of them, he simply makes no attempt to present anything resembling a coherent story; examples include *Speaking of the Weather, Have You Got Any Castles?*, and *You're an Education*. Even in his cartoons with more fully developed narratives, such as *Porky's Double Trouble, Little Pancho Vanilla*, and *Cracked Ice*, gags provide a kind of alternative structure that runs parallel to that offered by the story. As discussed in the previous chapter, Tashlin's 1940s cartoons such as *Plane Daffy* and *Swooner Crooner* are replete with absurdist, one-off gags that challenge the primacy of narration.

Such live-action films as *Cinderfella* demonstrate precisely the same kind of modularity and uneven narration (see Chapter Six for more development of this element of Tashlin's style). Indeed, such an approach to narrative is one of the marks of anarchic Hollywood *live-action* comedy, as well as one of the strongest indicators that American animation and American live-action comedy derive from the same tradition. We find examples in nearly every one of Tashlin's live-action features: *Son of Paleface, Marry Me Again, Artists and Models, Will Success Spoil Rock Hunter?, The Man from the Diners' Club, The Private Navy of Sergeant O'Farrell*, and many others. These films provide ample evidence of the director's penchant for an episodic, gag-centric structure that either diminishes or is at odds with any degree of narrative unity.

Jokes that interrupt, challenge, or complicate a cinematic narrative are the exclusive provenance of *neither* animated nor live-action comedy. The fact that we find many such gags in Tashlin's feature comedies indicates not that Tashlin was making "live-action cartoons," but that he learned that both comic animation and comic live-action features were venues in which it was appropriate to display an irreverent, comic disregard for cohesive narrative.

Tashlin is by no means the only director of live-action comedies to include moments of diegetic rupture or interruption; such moments are in fact even *more* common in the films of such workmanlike directors as Norman Taurog, Hal Walker, and Norman Z. McLeod (discussed in greater detail in Chapter Seven) — and yet these directors' films, inasmuch as they are considered at all, are not said to evoke animation. In fact, the presence of such anarchic, fourth-wall-rupturing comedy is largely dependent on the presence of such vaudeville or Borscht Belt veterans as Bob Hope, Danny Kaye, Jerry Lewis, and others who fit into Steve Seidman's "comedian comedy" tradition. Such performers' personae are permanently associated with this form of narrative breakage. We find this deliberate rupturing of narrative cohesion in many Tashlin features, but we also find it in non-Tashlin comedian comedies, such as Walker's *At War with the Army* (1950) and *Road to Bali* (1952), McLeod's *Road to Rio* (1947) and *Casanova's Big Night* (1954), and Taurog's *The Stooge* (1953) and *Pardners* (1956), to name a scant few.

With regard to vaudeville's reliance on gags that played out quickly and clearly, the standard seven-minute duration of the Tashlin-era Hollywood cartoon links it to the comic traditions of the vaudeville stage. Films with durations as short as those of the "Golden Age" cartoon could hardly afford to devote significant screen time to complex characterization. To this end, cartoon characters were nearly always designed so that their phenotypes strongly suggested character and comic traits. Important characters such as Porky Pig were designed so that their personae and comic abilities and potentials were understandable at a glance. Taking this technique even further are the great many Warner Bros. cartoons from the 1930s and 1940s that depend so heavily on caricatures of pop-culture icons: singers, movie stars, radio personalities.[4] Tashlin and other Warners animators included such characters often, thus avoiding the issue of characterization altogether. In Tashlin's *oeuvre*, examples may be found in *Have You Got Any Castles?*, *The Woods Are Full of Cuckoos*, *A Hollywood Detour*, and several others.

Gags involving the breaking of the fourth wall — a vaudeville bulwark — are common to every phase of Tashlin's career, from his earliest print cartoons through his last features. But, again, diegetic rupture is by no means peculiar to animation, and in fact has long been an integral part of both Hollywood cartoons and live-action Hollywood comedies — a strong sign of their shared heritage. Tashlin was not unique in including such gags, though he did have a particular facility with them, even in his most tightly unified films.

A more generalized set of similarities between Tashlin's cartoons and features can be seen in their composition. Certain compositional and framing strategies link the films of these two realms; more pertinently, they connect the films of both realms to traditions of vaudeville comedy. Tashlin's 1930s cartoons are characterized, in large part, by frontality: actions unfold as if under a proscenium arch, on a plane parallel to that of the lens. These cartoons occasionally make use of unusual camera angles, but the overwhelming majority of their shots are frontally composed, a technique that borrows from vaudeville's emphasis on the visibility and centrality of the comic performer.[5]

To take but two examples, the actions in seventy of the ninety-nine shots (71 percent) in *Porky in the North Woods*, and thirty-four of the forty-one shots (83 percent) in *Porky's Spring Planting*, unfold perpendicular to the lens axis, and are taken from neither particularly high nor low angles. Tashlin's 1940s cartoons more frequently make fuller use of unconventional angles, especially for comic purposes: recall the scene of the hotel manager falling down the stairs in *Porky Pig's Feat*. But these films, too, depend heavily on frontal staging. Of the seventy-two shots in *Puss 'n' Booty*, fifty-two (72 percent) are frontally composed; even fifty-two of the seventy-six shots (70 percent) in *Porky Pig's Feat* itself are frontal—and these films contain more canted-, low-, and high-angle shots than any other Tashlin film of any kind.

Like the cartoons, most of Tashlin's live-action features are frontally composed; many are shot in so staid a fashion as to appear stage-bound: *Susan Slept Here* (based on a play) and *The Geisha Boy* are just two prominent examples. This frontality is partly a function of Tashlin's reliance on performative comedy, a tendency that in itself evokes vaudeville-style comedy. Tashlin admitted to letting Lewis's performance determine the placement of his camera. "Jerry never rehearses . . . Just one take and that's it. . . . So you can't really do anything interesting with the camera—his habits dictate your style."[6] That he allowed Lewis (and, possibly, other performers) to play a part in dictating his camera placement reveals two important things about Tashlin's style. First, it confirms that he is a director for whom comic performance is of great importance. Second, it shows that the general frontality of Tashlin's features is an adaptation to the fact that a highly controlled *mise-en-scène* is far less easily achieved in live-action film than in animation. Frontal camera placement is, for Tashlin, the best way to allow performative comedy to unfold.[7]

Sonic comedy also connects the films of the two realms. Tashlin appears to have learned a great deal from Carl Stalling, the brilliant musical director of the Schlesinger cartoons, and Tregoweth Brown, who was responsible for Warners' cartoons' sound effects. Stalling, who scored no fewer than thirty-nine Tashlin cartoons, was known for, among other things, his facility with comic quotations of recognizable pieces of music.[8] Brown built up a large library of comical sound effects from which all the Warners directors could and did draw. The Schlesinger cartoons get great comic mileage out of sonic incongruities and exaggerations, as well as devices that "naturally" lend themselves to comedy, such as gongs, kettledrums, whistles, and horns. Tashlin uses a kettledrum, for instance, to accentuate the hotel manager's weighty stride in *Porky Pig's Feat*, and a *boing* to underscore the action of a dog jumping on a scale in *Dog Meets Dog* (a Columbia cartoon, demonstrating that Tashlin brought this technique with him on his studio travels). Ultimately, this sort of sonic humor derives from vaudeville and its antecedents. Vaudeville historian Joseph Laurie writes of accompanists who achieved renown by "ad-libbing on the keys."[9] He also lists common vaudeville instruments and noisemakers with especially comical qualities: cowbells, ratchets, horns, banjos, "gobletphones," balloons, saws, washboards, accordions.[10]

That such uses of sound carried over from vaudeville to cartoons and from cartoons to Tashlin's features is one of the strongest pieces of evidence for identifying Tashlin's comic lineage, and for linking his cartoons and features along historical-stylistic lines. The little-discussed *Marry Me Again* contains several pertinent examples. Less than a minute into the film, Bill Anderson (Robert Cummings) is handed a draft notice, an act accompanied by musical quotation of "You're in the Army Now." Later, a scene of Bill and his friend drunkenly rampaging around a room is accompanied by "Drink to Me Only With Thine Eyes"; when a vehicle drives through a haystack, we hear "Turkey in the Straw." These are particularly Stalling-like touches, in that the musical excerpts are sonic riffs on a single visual element: they are just like Stalling's instrumental quotation of the first two lines of "Oh! You Beautiful Doll" in a shot from

Porky's Romance of a great big Petunia gorging herself on bonbons. In another scene from *Marry Me Again*, a scrawny, odd-looking young man is administered a physical exam. When the army doctor taps him on his back and shoulders, we hear a hollow knocking sound. ("Splendid officer material!" the doctor exclaims.) This is the kind of sound-effects gag at which Brown was expert. Even in his later features, Tashlin does not abandon this type of comedy: Chapter Six discusses similar sound gags in *The Man from the Diners' Club*, *The Alphabet Murders*, and *The Glass Bottom Boat*.

Many of the arguments for the alleged cartooniness of Tashlin's features refer to "impossible comedy," the idea being that Tashlin, in breaking the laws of physics, turns his films into "live-action cartoons." The problem with such an argument is that this type of humor is one of the most stalwart mainstays of American comedian comedy. The "swaying" and "trumpet" gags from McLeod's *Road to Rio*, mentioned in Chapter Three, are perfect examples, as is a gag in Jerry Lewis's *The Bellboy* that has Lewis's character arranging hundreds of chairs into neat, even rows within the space of a couple of seconds of diegetic time.

The fact that we can find this form of comedy in many, many films *not* directed by Frank Tashlin should be sufficient grounds for dismissing the "live-action cartoons" argument. This kind of impossible comedy is utterly commonplace in mid-century American comedian comedies, and it ultimately derives from and is an intensification of old slapstick routines. It is quickly and easily grasped, and so ludicrous as to nearly guarantee a belly-laugh response; such humor plainly derives from vaudeville tradition.

Similar arguments have been made for Tashlin's use of Jayne Mansfield—specifically, her unusual physical proportions—in her two films for Tashlin. Greg Ford, for instance, pushes the cartoon/live-action connection in commenting on the apparent influence of Hatta Mari, the curvaceous spy in Tashlin's cartoon *Plane Daffy*, on the physical appearance of Mansfield in her Tashlin films—as if Tashlin could physically mold a living human to conform to a phenotypic ideal; as if Tashlin could somehow have predicted the existence and appearance, six years before her public début, of Jayne Mansfield; as if Mansfield wasn't already plenty curvaceous before she ever met Tashlin.[11]

What Tashlin *did* do—and what her other directors generally failed to do—was to depict Mansfield in such a way as to draw humorous visual attention to her voluptuousness, a quality Tashlin found inherently funny. He clad her in absurdly form-fitting clothing, going so far as to affix a tassel to each of her buttocks in *The Girl Can't Help It*; he had her sprawl her curvy body across a massage table that occupies the great majority of a CinemaScope frame in *Will Success Spoil Rock Hunter?* For Tashlin, Jayne Mansfield was but another potentially humorous facet of *mise-en-scéne*.

Many have argued for the essential likeness of Tashlin's cartoons and his features by referencing his use of color. The director's association with print and animated cartoons has caused critics such as Jonathan Rosenbaum and J. Hoberman to view him as a vivid colorist.[12] However, neither Tashlin's print cartoons nor his animated cartoons are exclusively black and white or full color: he drew many cartoons of both kinds for various humor magazines in the 1930s. (Indeed, Rosenbaum and Hoberman both display a common but baseless assumption: that cartoons, whether printed or animated, have a strong association with color. In truth, there is no such association: historically, cartoons are equally likely to be either black and white *or* color.) Tashlin also directed monochromatic and polychromatic cartoons and features. Of Tashlin's fifty-nine animated cartoons, twenty-seven, or about 46 percent, are in color; of his twenty-three features, seventeen, or 74 percent, are in color. But the decision to shoot a film with or without color was not completely his: it was not until April 1943—by which time Tashlin had made some thirty-six cartoons—that Leon Schlesinger declared that all Looney Tunes would thereafter be made in color.[13]

There are three important points here. First, it was not always Tashlin's decision to shoot his films in color or black and white. This was, crucially, a budgetary matter, as the costs of color film stock and processing may have been, depending on the particular year that a film was a released and on the studio that released it, greater than those of black and white.[14] Nor is it the case that Tashlin "evolved" from black and white to color: *Son of Paleface*, his second full feature, is a Technicolor film, while *The Alphabet Murders*, his fourth-to-last film, is in black and white. Most important, the mere fact that many of Tashlin's cartoons and features were shot in color is not a sufficient basis from which to argue for their essential similarity. In fact, by framing the question within the context of comedy, we find major differences between the cartoons and the features.

Tashlin's print cartoons provide useful context. For the cover of the May 1933 issue of the humor magazine *Hooey*, Tashlin drew a racy gag that depends entirely on color. The title of the cartoon is "The Traffic Cop's Daughter," and it depicts a man and a woman embracing on a couch. The man's huge eyes indicate his delight in what he sees: a sly look in the woman's eyes, and her lips colored green. Green, that is, for "go"—she is the traffic cop's daughter, and she's giving him the "all-clear" sign to proceed. This is a color-specific gag: if her lips were red or pink (or if the cartoon were uncaptioned), the cartoon wouldn't make any sense.

That Tashlin made color-based jokes as early as 1933 makes it all the more surprising that *none* of his animated films employ color for comic purposes. The nearest miss occurs in *Booby Hatched*, in which several duck eggs, resting in a nest in a wintry barn, turn blue with the chill. But this is barely a gag: blue is merely cartoon shorthand for "cold"; if anything, the gag here is Carl Stalling's quotation of "Am I Blue?" on the soundtrack. Of Tashlin's twenty-seven color cartoons, not one of them contains a gag like the one in "The Traffic Cop's Daughter," in which the punchline is conveyed by hue.

The mere fact that a device exists in a number of films is not proof that the films are similar; more important are the ways in which the device is used. It is true that Tashlin's cartoons often make excellent use of color, but he is not necessarily more skilled with this device than Robert Clampett or Chuck Jones. (In fact, it is surely Jones whose use of color is the richest and most complex.) Many of Tashlin's features, too, are filled with rich, vivid hues—there is no disputing that he had an excellent eye for color. It is only very rarely that Tashlin uses color for comic purposes in his features, however. The paint-cans gag from *Artists and Models* (discussed in Chapter Four) and the joke about the DeLuxe color process in *The Girl Can't Help It* (discussed in Chapter Five) are two of the few examples. Ironically, it is the very *absence* of color-based comedy that connects Tashlin's cartoons and features.

Tashlin did once remark on the connections between Warner Bros. animation and the vaudeville tradition. In a 1971 interview with Michael Barrier, he says,

A lot of our humor came from Jack Benny, and I'll tell you how. Jack Benny was on [TV] Sunday nights, when Jack was very, very big. We'd come in Monday morning, all of us were talking about Jack. Jack had running jokes—there'd be a knock on the door, Mr. Kitzel [a character on the show] would stick his head in the door and say one line. That rabbit [Bugs Bunny] started doing that—"What's up, doc?" Bing, door closes, out. We'd get all of this from Jack Benny. We really stole from all over, and perhaps, as it came out from the assembly line, put some originality into it.[15]

Jack Benny enjoyed great success in radio, television, and film, but his career began in vaudeville. Other Warner Bros. animators have made related claims. Chuck Jones, in discussing his art, makes reference to his admiration for Buster Keaton and Charlie Chaplin, and likens Bugs Bunny to "a cross between Harpo and Groucho."[16] Tex Avery, though specifically discussing his later MGM work, could just as well be speaking of his Warner Bros. films when he says, "The real problem [in directing humorous cartoons] was to build up to a laugh finish. . . . If you build up to a point and then the last gag is nothing, you've hurt your whole show, audience-wise. So in all of them we attempted to be sure that we had a topper."[17] Avery uncannily echoes Jenkins's characterization of vaudeville structure, which holds that shows were designed to have "socko" endings.

Instead of arguing for the cartooniness of his features or for the "cinematic" nature of his cartoons, we may more usefully consider Frank Tashlin as a vaudeville-influenced comic artist who found success in multiple realms of artistic expression. In this way, he is not dissimilar to such undisputed comic mainstays as Groucho Marx, Jack Benny, Red Skelton, Ed Wynn, Bob Hope, Danny Kaye, and many others who found comic success in multiple media: stage, radio, film, television. (Indeed, Tashlin himself dabbled in all of these media, in some more successfully than in others.)

For some reason, however, the general trend among those scholars and historians who have considered Tashlin is to insist on a *de facto* disconnect between animated and live-action film. As discussed above, animation and live action are two distinct but overlapping modes or realms of filmic expression. Perhaps the most important of the many areas of that overlap is that of genre. Most of the claims for Tashlin's uniqueness, which have been made almost entirely on the basis of this perceived cartoon/live action connection—have been overstated, but this is not to say that Tashlin did not possess his own particular directorial style. On the contrary: a Tashlin film reveals itself as such fairly readily to even a minimally trained eye; his cinematic style may be traced by careful study of its recurring elements and the ways in which he varies and permutes them. Tashlin is an unusual case because his work provides an uncommonly perspicuous demonstration of the *continuities* between animated and live-action American films. The fact that a film is animated does *not* prohibit it from being influenced by certain forms of live-action film. Which is to say, again, that any resemblances we may find between Tashlin's animated and live-action work should come as no surprise, for they evolved from the same set of comic, performative, and historical circumstances.

This shared comic lineage does not explain everything about Tashlin's style; surely, nothing can: the relevant influences are many and complex. The films made in one realm are not simply identical to those of the other. Certain fundamental differences between live action and animation all but guarantee that films of the one type will not perfectly resemble films of the other. Indeed, these two modes of filmmaking offered Tashlin different ways in which he could deploy and permute the elements of his style. By posing the question historically, we find that the similarities and differences between the films of the two realms are more nuanced.

Neither sexual humor nor sexuality in general, for instance, play major roles in Tashlin's cartoons, though it is a mainstay of his features. Sexual humor *is* present in such Tashlin cartoons as *Porky's Double Trouble, Cinderella Goes to a Party, The Stupid Cupid*, and few others, but it is nowhere near as prevalent as in his features, a fact due at least in part to the weakening of PCA guidelines.

Somewhat surprisingly, neither do Tashlin's cartoons make much use of satirical humor, save for the mild celebrity caricatures present in several of them. It is only in his wartime cartoons that Tashlin employs satire of any kind: *Plane Daffy* and *Scrap Happy Daffy* gleefully poke fun at the leaders and philosophies of the Axis powers.[18] With the important exception of the "Private Snafu" films, which were made under relaxed censorship rules and for a specialized audience, none of Tashlin's other cartoons makes satirical gestures of any kind. Tashlin's live-action features are much more strongly satirical, aiming barbs at consumerism, popular culture, advertising, and many other subjects.

A more obvious but perhaps more important difference between the cartoons and the features is that of running time. The longer running times of the features provided Tashlin with, simply, a greater number of opportunities to develop, combine, and permute the elements of his style. With running times roughly a dozen times those of his cartoons, the features permitted him to include a greater number of jokes; to work with more complicated narratives (and their attendant gags); and to develop jokes and experiment with patterns of comic repetition.

The differences in running times led to another important difference: the features' far greater raw durations permit more flexibility with gag staging and timing. Not only did Tashlin have more time to develop his gags, but, in many cases, he had a great deal more space: a dozen of Tashlin's features were shot with one or another widescreen process.[19] As David Bordwell has shown, most early widescreen films had longer ASLs than did flat films. Bordwell finds that "the ASL of early widescreen films is four to seven seconds longer than the eleven-second non-widescreen norm." By 1959, however, the ASLs of CinemaScope films dwindled to approach those of non-widescreen films.[20] Several of Tashlin's key CinemaScope films, including *The Lieutenant Wore Skirts*, *The Girl Can't Help It*, and *Will Success Spoil Rock Hunter?*, were made in this brief window of acclimation to the new widescreen process.

However, given greater time and, often, more space, Tashlin does *not*, generally, increase the durations of his gags. Most Tashlin gags are sight gags, which means they can be read nearly instantaneously: it does not take more than a second for a viewer to grasp *The First Time*'s jokes about bananas, *The Girl Can't Help It*'s joke about Jerri "hiding" behind a shrub, or the joke about the rapidly swelling ankle in *The Disorderly Orderly*. Again, this kind of visual clarity may be traced, at least in part, to vaudeville technique.

In Tashlin's features, there are few equivalents of the long-take comedy that he uses fairly regularly in his cartoons — the archetypal example here is the firehose gag in *Porky the Fireman*. Many of the long takes in his features are showcases for extended comic performance by his actors. A scene from *Cinderfella* in which Fella (Lewis) grovels theatrically contains shots of fifteen, nineteen, twenty-six, and forty-three seconds, all of which serve the intended goal of highlighting Lewis's performance. In every case, however, the very longest takes in Tashlin's live-action films are not used for comedy. Rather, Tashlin uses multiple-minute-long takes in his features for exposition. In many cases, such scenes have a perfunctory ring: it is as if Tashlin wishes to cover as much story material as possible within a single take so that he may focus his talent and attention on the moments of comedy. An early scene in *The Girl Can't Help It*, for instance, lays out the entirety of the film's plot within a single take of 136 seconds. An expository scene from *Rock-a-Bye Baby* is even more cursory in its treatment of story matter. A single 129-second shot spells out the central plot complication of the film. As if to signal the end of the exposition, Tashlin cuts from the expository shot to a shot that contains a mild visual non-gag: Marilyn Maxwell posing in front of a lifesized photograph of herself in a near-identical pose. Thus, the exposition out of the way, the comic portion of the film begins. For Tashlin, a longer shot duration does not often lead to a longer gag duration. Rather, it affords him an opportunity to experiment further with the relationship between gag and narrative.

Tashlin's use of long takes points to the fact that he needs to be considered a director of *mise-en-scène*, rather than a director of editing. Simply put, editing is not particularly important to Tashlin's style, nor is it one of his major strengths as a director. Tashlin's style is not one that depends especially heavily on visual contrast, a careful adjustment of pacing, or the breaking down of a space into its component parts. It is a style of sight gags, performative comedy, and careful composition for comic effect—all of which are functions of *mise-en-scène*. It is Tashlin's major strength as an artist, and it is the underlying reason for the relative ease with which he moved from animation to live action.

The Exception that Proves the Rule: *Say One for Me*

A film that reveals a great deal about Tashlin's comic style happens to be one of his least funny, least "cartoonlike," and least Tashlinesque. *Say One for Me* was released in 1959, less than two years after the release of *Will Success Spoil Rock Hunter?*, though the two films have so little in common that they do not even appear to have been made by the same intelligence.

Say One for Me is unusual for many reasons, the first of which is its religious subject matter: its narrative revolves around one Father Conroy (Bing Crosby), a New York priest. The tone of the film is gentle and pious, terms that simply do not describe any other of Tashlin's works. This piety, borne of the Production Code Administration's skittishness regarding the depiction of religion, manifests itself in *Say One for Me* in several ways. The film avoids satire entirely, for instance, and nearly eschews comedy altogether. Though it is set within the milieu of the New York City entertainment industry, a frequent subject of Tashlin's slings and arrows, the best he can muster here is a mild joke about audience fickleness, which occurs in a tiny subplot. Needless to say, the film lobs not even the most lightweight of brickbats at organized religion. Unsurprisingly, the film is also completely devoid of sexual comedy. As discussed below, the PCA expressly mandated that not even the slightest hint of sexuality—especially if presented irreverently—could encroach upon the overtly religious subject matter of *Say One for Me*.

The film is almost entirely humorless, and what little comedy it possesses is not of the kind normally associated with Tashlin. He does not draw upon his performers' comic skills, for one. Crosby, a fine and underrated comedian, is given no comic scenes; at most, he avuncularly delivers a gentle one-liner to a parishioner. The comic duties of the film fall almost entirely to supporting player Ray Walston, who, as an alcoholic pianist, is the pivot of numerous gags about jittery hands and hidden bourbon. Such humor was permitted in a religious-themed film because the Walston character is not a member of the church, but of the nightclub subculture, and is in fact redeemed by Father Conroy's efforts.

Neither are there any sonic or sight gags in the film, unless the mere presence of a horn-playing seal that takes the stage during a talent contest can be said to count. Nor, on any occasion, does Tashlin break the world of the diegesis, perhaps because such a move would have been considered too impertinent for the film's subject matter. The matter of the integration of gag and narrative is not an issue, due to the utter dearth of gags. What few there are—Walston hiding his highballs, for the most part—are fully integrated into the world of the story. *Say One for Me* cannot rightly be considered a comedy. It is a romantic melodrama with musical numbers and a few light moments; its tone is not, in the main, comic.

Tashlin may have been a shrewd censorship warrior, but he lost the battle for *Say One for Me*. The PCA is primarily responsible for the film's utter earnestness, as it was extremely strict on the subject of religion. Between the early 1930s and the late 1960s, writes film historian Gregory D. Black, "Catholic prelates and priests played a dominant role in determining what was seen on the screen. A Catholic priest, Father Daniel Lord, wrote the Production Code that defined what was acceptable movie content for Hollywood. From 1934 until the early 1950s a staunch lay Catholic, Joseph I. Breen, rigorously enforced Lord's code at the Production Code Administration (PCA), often over the protests of studio executives, producers, directors, and screenwriters."[21]

A warning from PCA director Geoffrey Shurlock to 20th Century-Fox executive Frank McCarthy to take special care with *Say One for Me*, due to the "delicate and tasteful nature of this story as a whole," sums up the tenor of the negotiations.[22] Shurlock wrote, "There are several references to scanty costumes in this script. Because of the nature of this story, it would seem to be only prudent and in good taste to exercise the greatest of care not to offend on this score."[23] And McCarthy wrote Tashlin of the importance of obtaining the Legion of Decency's approval.

> Of course there is no objection, Frank, to your creating a cheap nightclub atmosphere, but we cannot go overboard in scantiness of costume or in suggestiveness of dancing. We must get an A-1 rating on this picture from the Legion of Decency in order to realize our greatest audience potential, and the Legion is much stricter on costumes and dancing in pictures designed for the family trade than it is in those designed for more adult audiences.[24]

In addition to stripping the film of even the slightest bit of raciness, Shurlock, McCarthy, and John Trevelyan of the British Board of Film Censors made extremely detailed corrections to the script's treatment of churchly matters. Trevelyan gave Fox executive J. Pattinson very specific instructions not to show the "specially sacred" portions of the Catholic wedding and Mass ceremonies, and urged that extreme care be taken to "hold the balance between Father Conroy's rather free and easy sermons and jokes in the pulpit and the seriousness of the message that he is putting over."[25]

The extreme caution of these censorship agencies prevented Tashlin from engaging in any risqué humor. The PCA files contain no letters from Tashlin, but the film itself speaks his reply: every single one of the censors' suggestions has been followed. Tashlin's acquiescence is quite unlike his combative attitude to the censorship of *Artists and Models* and

Will Success Spoil Rock Hunter?, as discussed in Chapter Five. We may speculate, from his defeated tone in a 1962 interview, that the experience was not a little demoralizing.

> I liked the original script [by Robert O'Brien]—the idea of a show business priest. We had a monsigneur in [as an advisor] and he loved it. One day he brought his guy in, Martin Quigley [publisher of *Motion Picture Herald*, a Catholic layman, and a powerful voice for movie industry "self-regulation" since the late 1920s], and he raised hell. He hated it. The monsigneur ran for cover. And so there were deletions and changes. And it was generally ruined by the cuts.[26]

Say One for Me is not only one of Tashlin's least funny films—only *The Way of Peace* is more dire—but one of his least good films. It is far longer than its thin plot requires: at 119 minutes, it is Tashlin's longest. The performers, especially Crosby, are misused: none of their talents receive appropriate attention. The film's pious tone is, at times, uncomfortably shrill. Visually, it is staid and thoroughly conventional; few if any compositions are clever or unusual. Tashlin was probably not the best choice to direct it.

Despite the fact that *Say One for Me* is so thoroughly unlike the rest of Tashlin's films, it reveals a great deal about his style. Stripped of his principal aesthetic strategies, Tashlin turned in one of the worst films of his career. Working outside of the genre of comedy severely and necessarily compromised Tashlin's directorial method. Film style, for Tashlin, *was* comic style. Unable to deploy his style in the way in which he was accustomed, Tashlin made a non-comic film that provides no evidence of his talent or authorship. The success of Tashlin's films required a comic framework.

3 "HURRY UP! THIS IS IMPOSSIBLE!"
TASHLIN'S EARLY FEATURE FILMS

Frank Tashlin's transition to live-action filmmaking was eased by his five years as a screenwriter. His screenwriting experience, coupled with the directorial skills he had honed as an animator, helped to ease this transition. Nonetheless, I have not conducted any detailed analyses of the films that Tashlin wrote but did not direct, since I do not think it wise (or even possible) to demarcate the authorial line between writer and director. Moreover, there is no good reason that Tashlin should be granted special authorial dominion over the films that he wrote or cowrote but did not direct. It seems more sensible simply to acknowledge that he probably learned a great deal about comedy screenwriting during these five years, and to leave it at that.

The Lemon Drop Kid, the film that gave Tashlin his first experience in live-action direction, is a problematic example, as he directed only about a third of it. Even though Tashlin archivist Howard Prouty offers a minute-by-minute tally of the scenes directed by Tashlin and those by original director Sidney Lanfield, it seems foolhardy to detail any microscopic differences between the scenes directed by these two men.[1] I do not wish to make too much of what is only a partial Tashlin film, especially one on which he presumably aimed to make his new scenes mesh fairly well with those of Lanfield's that remain. However, Tashlin's next two pictures, *The First Time* and *Son of Paleface*, offer insight into the development of the director's live-action style.

In *The First Time*, Tashlin takes a standard domestic romantic comedy and makes it recognizably his own by, for instance, including of a great deal of sexual and visual humor. It is also an excellent example of Tashlin's ability to employ performance-based humor when his performers did not have especially strong personae. In this way, it looks forward to his films with Jayne Mansfield.

Son of Paleface might be called the first "mature" Tashlin film, in that it combines nearly all of the facets of his style: sexual humor, satire, visual gags, non-gags, diegetic rupture. The film also provides an opportunity to study the ways in which Tashlin designed gags around Bob Hope's firmly established persona and performance skills — a subject relevant to the discussion of the director's eight films with Jerry Lewis.

The First Time: *The First Time*

The First Time reveals a great deal about Tashlin's style, as well as his career. When Tashlin's contributions to *The Lemon Drop Kid* satisfied both Hope and his producer, Robert Welch, they approached him to direct the upcoming *Son of Paleface*, the sequel to Hope's very successful 1948 comedy *The Paleface*, which Tashlin cowrote. Howard Prouty writes, "Reluctant to tie himself down to a single studio, Tashlin drag[ged] out the negotiations, and in the meantime sign[ed] to direct [*The First Time*] at Columbia for producer Harold Hecht."[2] When Tashlin did sign with Paramount to direct *Son of Paleface*, it was on a non-exclusive contract.[3] As an animator, Tashlin moved from studio to studio with great frequency: his two two-and-a-half-year stints at Warners were his longest periods of residence at any studio. Even as a neophyte feature director, Tashlin was apparently hesitant to make any long-term commitments.

The First Time is a fairly typical domestic comedy about the difficulties that arise as a young couple, Betsey and Joe, conceive and raise their first child. The child-rearing story is mapped atop a narrative arc about Joe's frustrations with his job, and another about the deterioration of the couple's marriage. Tashlin moves from one baby-, job-, or relationship-related situation to another, in an echo of the way some of his cartoons shuttle from one gag setup to the next. He crafts gags around, for instance, the baby's bottle, an argument at the dinner table, and Joe's feigned obsequiousness around his boss. The narrative arcs are resolved unsurprisingly: Joe quits his awful job as a washing-machine salesman, and Betsey and Joe resolve their differences and have a second child.

Bill Krohn overstates the case when he writes about the film, "Tashlin leaves no doubt that he could have made a name for himself without ever violating the rules of screen realism."[4] It is true that, in *The First Time*, Tashlin employs few gags that rupture the diegesis or are not fully integrated in the film's narrative, but this does not mean that such techniques were not important tools for him. *The First Time*, with its generally mild tone and conventional narrative, is not particularly suited for such types of comedy; *Son of Paleface*, a parody, violates screen realism in numerous ways, a subject addressed below. Still, *The First Time* does violate "screen realism" on a few isolated occasions: a baby plays maracas rather well and, in another scene, manages to bend a spoon; a gag involving candles, discussed in detail below, seriously strains plausibility.

The First Time does not lack for gags (or non-gags) that depend on clever visual design. One example is a simple non-gag that relies on skillful blocking. Joe and Betsey are both awakened by their hungry baby, but neither knows that the other is awake. So they both prepare bottles and, sleepily unaware of each other's presence, just miss each other—by a matter of seconds—when their paths nearly cross in the hallway. We can see their near-meeting, but the characters cannot: this is the extent of this non-gag, which is constructed purely out of careful *mise-en-scéne*. Another minor sight gag is one of the fairly small number in Tashlin's body of work to rely on editing, in this case for the purpose of a clever contrast: a dissolve humorously juxtaposes Betsey's fashionable, well-dressed mother with Joe's frumpy, housedress-clad mother.

The First Time also contains one of Tashlin's best visual gags. At the dinner table, Joe and Betsey have a heated argument about Betsey's skills as a housewife.[5] Between them are two lit candles. When Joe speaks, the flame of the candle nearer him flickers and extends in Betsey's direction, and vice versa. (Figure 3.1a) When the discussion becomes more heated, the flames extend farther. (Figure 3.1b) The joke is, at first, quite subtle: the flickering of the flames is plausibly coincidental or unintentional. But as the gag develops, the distortion of the flames precisely corresponds to the amount of rancor in the actors' voices. This joke is in many ways a summary of Tashlin's comic style. It is more clever than funny; it depends on visual humor; and it cleverly emblematizes sexual tension in an unusual and memorable sight gag.

One very funny scene in *The First Time* uses silence, demonstrating Tashlin's skill with this important element of sonic expressivity. In a mocking response to her husband's persistent, boorish claims about her failings as a wife, Betsey plays her wifely role to the hilt. She dresses seductively, prepares Joe's meal, pours him a beer, and generally behaves like a dream wife—all in order to mock Joe's caveman attitude. Part of the joke is that, while Betsey coos constantly, Joe does not utter

Figure 3.1 The candle-flame gag from *The First Time*

a word: he merely smiles and gazes in wide-eyed glee at his wife. Tashlin pointedly uses an absence of dialogue to highlight the differences in their behaviors and personalities, a fact essential to the film's narrative.

The First Time bursts with sexual humor. (The film's cheeky title is a giveaway here.) A key motif is that of bananas: when Betsey finds herself eating unusually large numbers of bananas, she correctly interprets it as a sign that she is pregnant. The raciest of several banana jokes is depicted in Figure 3.2: Betsey hungrily eyes a banana that Joe eats. This scene hints that Betsey is pregnant for a second time, but Tashlin suggests a lewder alternate reading. Betsey's focused ogling of the banana, that most phallic of foods, indicates that she is eager to have sex. Given the feral look on Barbara Hale's face, this reading is all but unavoidable. The strength of the joke is in its ambiguity: the "real" meaning of the gag is probably the sexual one. But the gag can also be read within the film's motivic structure: bananas are simply visual shorthand for "a baby is on the way." The beauty of the gag is that its narrative significance is unchanged, no matter which reading is applied: in either case, Betsey's appetite for bananas indicates that she is ready to procreate.

Such humor did not go unnoticed by the officers of the Production Code Administration. In a letter to Columbia Pictures chief Harry Cohn, PCA head Joseph Breen writes, "While it appears some of the emphasis on the bananas has been reduced [as per earlier letters], we still feel, in the interests of good taste and avoiding embarrassment on the part of mixed audiences, that you still go a little too far in emphasizing the fact

Figure 3.2 Barbara Hale hungrily eyes Robert Cummings's banana in *The First Time*

of Betsey's pregnancy. We recommend most earnestly that this emphasis be, wherever possible, further reduced."[6] Despite Breen's bid for a banana ban, the motif survives in the final cut of the film, and is in fact one of its bawdier gags.

Breen also warns against what is surely the film's bluest scene. Under the mistaken impression that she is a babysitter, Joe picks up a young woman named Fawn (Tashlin regular Jean Willes) on a street corner. The scene's dialogue is, in part, as follows:

Joe: Well, it's certainly a blessing I found you, after the other two I picked up tonight.
Fawn: Two?
Joe: The first one was about fourteen.
Fawn: Fourteen.
Joe: Yes.
Fawn: What type *do* you like?

Joe: Oh, it, um, it doesn't particularly matter to me. The other one I picked up was about seventy.
Fawn: Where you been—at sea for a year?
Joe: At sea?
Fawn: You must be really desperate.
Joe: Well, I always say a fella should get out of the house sometime. Thank heaven I found someone who won't mind looking at TV.
Fawn: Oh, no, that's fine with me. I prefer making my own amusement.
Joe: Well, that's the way it should . . . *(a glimmer of realization flashes across his face as Fawn seductively blows cigarette smoke in his direction)* Uh, you're a sitter, aren't you?
Fawn: Just between you and me—two Scotches and I'll sit anywhere.
Joe: Well, I don't think my wife would stand for any drinking.
Fawn: Your wife? What's she got to do with us?
Joe: Well, it was her idea, you see, that I pick you up tonight. So we could have the night out.
Fawn: Stop the car.

The scene is humorous if and only if the audience understands Joe's and Fawn's mistaken assumptions: he thinks she's the babysitter; she thinks he's interested in having sex with her, and, for a few moments, the prospect appeals to her. "We are . . . of the opinion that this girl, both through appearance and dialogue, is unmistakably a tart," writes Breen, no fool. "There should be no inference whatever that she is a loose woman."[7] But such an inference—indeed, far more than an inference—assuredly remains.

It is unclear how Cohn and Tashlin were permitted to retain these two bits of blue humor. Perhaps Cohn felt that the risk of including some blue material was worth taking: *The First Time* was an inexpensive production that stood a fair chance of turning a profit whether or not the racy scenes remained. It is difficult to resist the temptation to assign some of the credit to Tashlin himself: he would ignore the PCA's recommendations many more times in his career. The Tashlin that emerges from later letters to and from the PCA is a shrewd negotiator who appears to take some delight in upsetting the authorities, and it does not seem a stretch to say that he played a key role in circumventing the censorship of his films.

The First Time lampoons not only sexual mores but consumer culture, a frequent Tashlin target. Here, an emblem of domestic convenience — a Whirl-o-Mat washing machine — serves as shorthand for advertisers' broken promises. In order to support his family, Joe is forced to follow in his father's footsteps as a Whirl-o-Mat salesman. He hates the job, largely because he is now responsible for extolling the virtues of machines that routinely destroy the clothes they are supposed to clean. Joe finally vents his frustration about the job in a scene in which his overbearing boss has arranged a demonstration of the company's products for several members of the Better Business League. Joe seizes the opportunity to expose the Whirl-o-Mat's many flaws: it shakes violently and sputters suds all over the stage, his boss, and the Better Business Leaguers. It is a tellingly Tashlinian touch that he caps off a mockery of consumer culture with a messy, noisy sight gag.

Tashlin uses the leads of *The First Time*, Barbara Hale and Robert Cummings, to great comic effect, despite the fact that neither of them had particularly strong screen personalities. (Cummings, indeed, is one of the 1950s' quintessential Everyman figures.) *The Disorderly Orderly* is a Jerry Lewis Movie, and *Son of Paleface* is a Bob Hope Movie, but *The First Time* is a fairly typical romantic comedy that is not predicated on the talents of particular performers. Much of the performative humor in the film is of a kind that is not crucially linked with the stars' personae or abilities. For the same reason that Tashlin does not include more than a handful of impossible gags, Hale's and Cummings's very normalness is an important part of the film, whose subject matter is rooted in the everyday.

This ordinariness distinguishes the stars of *The First Time* from the star of *Son of Paleface*. Bob Hope — who had conquered vaudeville, radio, and film by the time *Son of Paleface* went into production in August 1951 — had a persona and performance style that would have been quite familiar to movie audiences. In signing to direct *Son of Paleface*, Tashlin was faced with the challenge of crafting personality comedy around an actor with a strong, established persona. This skill would turn out to be one of Tashlin's strengths.

Son of Vaudeville: Tashlin and Bob Hope

In the hierarchy of 1950s Paramount, Bob Hope was far more important than Frank Tashlin. In fact, Tashlin might not have been promoted from writer to director had it not been for the intervention of Hope and producer Robert Welch. Welch, who also produced *The Lemon Drop Kid*, suggested that screenwriter Tashlin take over the reins from director Sidney Lanfield, who was unseated after poor previews. Hope writes that, after a preview of *The Lemon Drop Kid* pleased Paramount president Barney Balaban, he suggested to Balaban that the picture "could profit from some additions."[8] Balaban agreed and, according to Hope, budgeted $200,000 for retakes. (That Balaban agreed to this additional financial outlay is itself indicative of Hope's value to the studio.) Hope continues,

> Frank Tashlin, whose wacky humor I admired, was assigned to do a rewrite. He ran the picture, together with a recording of laughs from the preview. Then he put blank film in the picture where he planned additions. Frank showed me *The Lemon Drop Kid* that way, explaining what would be added to the blank scenes.
> "Sounds good," I said. Bob Welch agreed.
> "I'll do the rewrite," Frank said, "if you let me direct it."
> We agreed, and that's how Frank Tashlin became a director.[9]

Satisfied with Tashlin's work, Hope and Welch asked Tashlin to direct *Son of Paleface*. They had the power to boost Tashlin's career, not the other way around.

It is important to detail the development of Hope's persona and performance style to get a sense of how Tashlin made use of the presence and talents of his star. How and when did Hope's persona coalesce? How well established was this persona when Hope first worked with Tashlin? Which elements of Hope's persona did Tashlin build on, which did he alter, and which did he reject?

Bob Hope honed his skills on the vaudeville stage, so a general understanding of the performance techniques of that medium is relevant. Henry Jenkins argues that vaudeville had an "actor-centered mode of production."[10] "Performers," he writes, "were never subservient to the script; rather, narrative, where it existed at all, facilitated their familiar tricks."[11] Vaudevillian Eddie Cantor confirms Jenkins's claims, writing that, furthermore, vaudeville comedy was "mostly extemporaneous and required quick and often inspired thinking.... Every Monday, with the changing bill, our comedy changed to suit."[12] Besides improvisation, another essential vaudeville skill was the ability to develop a rapport with the audience. One of the most important hallmarks of vaudeville is that its performers addressed the audience directly—a tactic that was anathema on the legitimate stage.

Vaudeville's structure was modular: a typical show consisted of dozens of brief bits strung together with nothing more than the lowering of a curtain between them—if that.[13] This modular format inevitably had an impact on performers' styles. Brief gags were preferred over long ones, a fact that affects comic timing; a joke or skit had to end with a bang, thus providing important lessons about emphasis; a short performance time encouraged broad, accessible gags, and this made the belly-laugh the coin of the realm. Finally, according to vaudeville historian Joseph Laurie, vaudeville comedians had to be well-versed in, among other types of comedy, ethnic humor, double entendres and parody, cross-dressing, and blue humor.[14] This précis of vaudeville performance techniques describes, albeit insufficiently, the comic milieu from which Bob Hope emerged. More important is an understanding of the specifics of Hope's comic persona itself.

John Lahr enumerates several important components of this persona: Hope's average Americanness; his topical-but-safe jokes; his "slightly skewed good looks"; his breezy, casual, naturalistic manner; and his quick-wittedness and ability to ad-lib.[15] A definition of Hope's screen persona might be something like: a cowardly, cheap, "regular guy" with a quick wit and a sharp tongue who is, at the same time, wolfish, sexually immature, and somewhat effeminate and/or homosexual.[16] Hope's characters' normalness, tight-fistedness, and cowardice are all readily identifiable by viewing any two or three of his films, but his persona's complex array of sexual meanings merits a closer look, as it bears on his relationship with Tashlin.

Hope's radio shows made frequent use of bawdy humor, and such jokes did not disappear when he made the move to film. In *Give Me a Sailor* (1938), Hope's third feature, sailor Jim Brewster (Hope) likens women, for reasons arcane, to forts, and remarks to his brother, "You haven't seen as many forts as I have." A weak joke, for sure, but it hints at a potentially taboo subject: Jim's philandering. A short while later, Jim and his brother are playfully wrestling on a ship's bunk when a third sailor opens the door and sees them. The audience is encouraged to view the scene through the sailor's eyes: two homosexual men frolicking on a bed.[17] These two gags address two of the important and apparently contradictory sexual elements of Hope's persona: his oft-professed ability to seduce women, and his implicit homosexuality. Many are the jokes that suggest Hope's effeminacy.[18] In *The Ghost Breakers* (1940), Hope's character, upon coming across a large feather, makes a joke that he used to dance for Sally Rand; later, he quips that his "slip is showing." In *Monsieur Beaucaire* (1946), he even declares, "I'm a man! Well, sort of."[19]

Still, Hope's comedy never veered into the truly offensive. Lahr writes,

> Hope, who never worked dirty, had no qualms about working racy. [For example:]
> Dorothy Lamour: Don't take me seriously, Bob. I was pulling your leg.
> Hope: Listen, Dottie—You can pull my right leg and you can pull my left leg. But don't mess with Mr. In-Between.[20]

In Lahr's example, the humorous reference to Hope's anatomy is deflected by the clever quotation of the popular Johnny Mercer/Harold Arlen song "Ac-Cent-Tchu-Ate the Positive." But the cleverest part of the joke is that it pokes fun at Hope's frequent costar and friendly rival Bing Crosby, for whom the song was a massive hit in 1945.

The Hope persona that carried many a Paramount moneymaker took some time to develop—it had fallen into place around 1940, two years after his feature debut.[21] The key film in the fixing of his screen personality was *The Cat and the Canary* (1939). Joe Morella, Edward Z. Epstein, and Eleanor Clark posit that, in this film,

> Hope was finally [after six features] cast in a role tailored to his talent.... In Wally Hampton [*sic*: Hope's character's name is Wally *Campbell*] Hope had found the skeleton of the screen character around which he would mold his future screen image.... [The character's] reluctant heroism ... and his penchant for quips when confronted by perilous situations eventually became Hope's film trademarks.[22]

Hope himself called the film the "turning point in my career": it was, in his opinion, the first "A" picture specifically tailored to his talents.[23]

In his previous films, the comic features mentioned above are much less evident in Hope's characters. In *The Big Broadcast of 1938* (Hope's first feature), for instance, his character, Buzz Fielding, is a ladies' man who is quick with a quip, but this does little to distinguish him from other light comic actors of the day. None of the Hope trademarks—boastfulness, cowardice, sexual confusion—are present. By the time Tashlin first wrote for him, in cowriting the script for *Variety Girl* (1947), Hope's screen persona had been more or less fixed for about seven years.[24]

For Paramount, Hope's studio for decades, Hope was a valuable commodity. His rankings in the annual International Motion Picture Almanac list of "money-making stars" are impressive: not once is Hope absent from the list of top ten moneymakers between 1941 and 1953.[25] This kind of popularity could conceivably have allowed Paramount to take some chances with Hope, off-casting him or marketing him in a different manner. But the studio rarely exercised this option: Hope's success was not something that studio executives wanted to spoil. Paramount offcast him only once, in the musical biopic *The Seven Little Foys* (1955). Barring this one exception from relatively late in his career, Hope's studio placed its star in films very like those he had already made for them: light, character-centered comedies with zany humor, whimsical songs, flimsy stories, and plenty of opportunities for Hope to crack wise. Sometimes they were period films and sometimes they would send up a particular genre, but they remained, above all, Bob Hope pictures. In his two-and-a-third films with Hope, Tashlin did not tamper in any major way with Hope's established screen personality. In *The Lemon Drop Kid*, Hope is, as ever, a lovable rogue full of get-rich-quick schemes; in *Son of Paleface*, he is full of bluster, greed, lust, and cowardice—all Hope trademarks.

In order to consider how the nature of Hope's performance style might have been changed for his Tashlin films, it is useful to compare his Tashlin work to some of his earlier films.[26] Both *Caught in the Draft* (David Butler, 1941) and *Son of Paleface* contain comic scenes in which Hope attempts to seduce a woman. By comparing these two narratively similar scenes, we may discern whether Tashlin encouraged significant changes in Hope's performance style, and, moreover, whether Tashlin learned anything from his leading man.[27]

About fourteen minutes into *Caught in the Draft*, the Hope character, movie star Don Bolton, tries to woo the Dorothy Lamour charac-

Figure 3.3 Bob Hope feigning agony and gesturing broadly in *Caught in the Draft*

ter, Tony (short for Antoinette). Bolton, smitten with Tony, has sent his assistants to trick her into paying him a visit, using the thin ruse that he has injured his back and would feel better if he could see her. She politely consents; their meeting takes place at Bolton's Hollywood estate.

As Tony arrives, Don is sitting in a wheelchair in the yard, a blanket on his lap and a rigid plaster girdle under his sweater. His face is the picture of steely reserve, and his left hand rests on his chest in a gesture that says, "Alas, I am in a great deal of pain, but I shall suffer unflinchingly through it" (Figure 3.3a). Hope leans forward as Lamour approaches. When he sees that Tony has taken the bait, his eyes widen and he smiles, but then catches himself and readjusts his body to convey fortitude in the face of pain. Lamour approaches and stands beside his wheelchair. Hope gazes fixedly into her eyes, glancing away only once, for an instant. His delivery conveys false bravery: when he says, "Oh, it's nothing serious. Just a broken back," his voice trails off slightly to show that he has grimly but bravely resigned himself to his fate.

Tony compliments him on his lovely swimming pool, to which he responds, "Oh, it's adequate." Then he prissily shines his fingernails on his sweater and admires them—a clichéd gesture to signify the boredom of the idle rich. But Hope also uses it to show its inherent phoniness. No one *really* uses this gesture genuinely; it is only used to mockingly indicate boredom. Hope accesses both levels of its significance.

When Tony comments on Bolton's *other* swimming pool, Hope responds, "Oh. Last year's," and emits a soft chuckle: "A-ha-ha-hah." His dialogue reinforces the fact that the lazy Bolton has done little to merit his wealth, but the chuckle is actually of greater interest. The "post-joke laugh" is a common Hope technique, and he uses it here, as he often does, to convey the fact that his line is a lame ploy to impress a woman. But the laugh also indicates that Bolton is fully aware of the ineffectuality of the joke; he uses it as a means to change the subject. He chuckles again moments later, when, after Tony asks to see the X-rays that he has just received, he says, "Oh, I'm just skin and bones."

Tony recognizes the X-rays as those of a woman, calls Bolton's bluff, and angrily stomps away. Faced with the exposure of his scheme, Bolton grabs his chair's armrests, elbows bent outwards. His face contorts into a grimace of shame: lowered eyebrows and a slightly open, frowning mouth. Hope then pulls a classic "somebody help me out here" gesture: he looks quickly off to his right — where there is no one — before looking back at Lamour (Figure 3.3b). Bits of broad music-hall performance such as this one find their way into Hope's films with some frequency.

When Bolton realizes his cover is blown, he leaps out of the chair and rushes after Tony, pleading with her one last time. Against her better judgment, Tony agrees to go out with him. As soon as she consents, Hope delightedly reaches under his sweater, unzips his corset, and blissfully runs his fingernails all over his itchy midsection. "Oh-ho-ho! Freedom!" he exclaims. As Lamour giggles (seemingly authentically), Hope broadly rolls his eyes heavenward in a gesture of pleasure and gratitude.

Since Tashlin cowrote the scripts for two Hope films before he ever directed him (*Variety Girl* and *The Paleface* [1948]), he clearly had some knowledge of Hope's comic style. Regarding Hope's persona, Tashlin said,

> All comedy is derivative; it draws from what has gone before. Bob's walk derived from that enormously inventive comic, Ted Healy, as did Jack Benny's and Ken Murray's. Bob drew his character from the timid fellows of Harold Lloyd, Buster Keaton, and Harry Langdon. But he added a new dimension: braggadocio.
>
> Bob uses his brashness to cover fear. The formula is simple: 1. the villain threatens Bob; 2. Bob responds with a challenge; 3. the villain pulls a gun; 4. Bob dissolves. There is a startling similarity between Bob and Donald Duck. Both became immensely popular during World War II. Both were braggers [sic] who backed down in a pinch but somehow prevailed.[28]

Tashlin astutely observes that one of the keys to Hope's comic persona was the gap between his characters' boastfulness and their abilities. This, and other performative talents of Hope's, are relevant to a study of *Son of Paleface*.

A scene of attempted wooing occurs at about the fifty-minute mark in *Son of Paleface*. Mike (Jane Russell)[29] has told Junior (Hope) to meet her in her room, and he readily agrees: he thinks he will finally get to be alone with her. Mike has other plans, however: she will slip him a mickey, commit a robbery while he's unconscious, then return to wake him up. Since she knows Junior is naïve enough to believe that they have spent a romantic evening together, he will thus provide her with an alibi.

In an effort to impress her with his machismo, Junior grossly overestimates the attire of a cowboy: he arrives clad in furry white chaps, an oversized gunbelt, a black and white cowhide vest, and a badly dented hat whose capacity surely exceeds ten gallons. He strides with exaggerated bowleggedness, as if he hasn't dismounted from his horse in years. As he struts into the room, Hope rests his thumbs inside his gunbelt, a gesture that clearly tells us that he is trying, and failing, to make it all look natural (Figure 3.4). To communicate this much through a simple, barely noticeable gesture is no small task, and it indicates Hope's great skill in physical comedy.

Junior offers a cowpoke apology: "I didn't aim to be late, but I was busy. I was sashaying m' mavericks and brandin' m' stray buckboards 'til I was plum hornswoggled. By the time I got to m' car, some plum had done swoggled m' horn." Hope speaks in a deep, gruff voice flecked with a broad western accent. Mike ignores him. Though Hope's delivery is such that these lines sound like they could be improvised, his words appear verbatim in the final draft of the film's screenplay.[30]

Once inside, Hope says, without prompting, "OK, gal, get lucky," grabs Russell roughly, and attempts to force a kiss on her lips. His broad gestures are now used for clumsy wooing: he swings his arms in a sweeping embrace around Russell, clamping his hands firmly on her back and shoulders. Hope leans his whole body forward, pressing it into Russell's with some force. She resists, and a second stab at soliciting smooches is similarly spurned.

When Mike steps into another room to start up the phonograph, Junior yammers on in his faux-western drawl, trying to dupe Mike

Figure 3.4 Buckaroo Bob in *Son of Paleface*

(and himself) with the cowboy act. "Ah, music. Music and a big, yella moon, moseyin' atwixt the clouds. There's nothin' lahk music and a big yaaaallla moon to keep a critter hankerin' for the bunkhouse dew on the sagebrush. Ooh-la-la!" Junior has a great deal of difficulty with even simple tasks, like rolling a cigarette; when he cheats by extracting a pre-rolled one from his tobacco pouch, he does so with chest-swelling pride.

The final phase of the sequence occurs after Junior has quaffed a drink laced with knockout drops. He and Mike dance, and Junior all but abandons his cowboy swagger as he cuts a rug like the East Coast dandy he actually is. Hope commences a strange hopping jig while staring directly into Russell's eyes. He quickly bounces on his heels while slowly rotating in place with Russell, whose movements are far more reserved. A solo dance by Hope leads to a couple of near-falls and a jostled phonograph. At one point, as Russell confusedly looks on, Hope extends his left arm toward the camera and undulates his shoulder as he bites his lip in an expression of determination—a strange and hilarious gesture (Figure 3.5a). Though he takes his eyes off of Russell's for a moment at this point, for the rest of dance he stares fixedly at her with a mildly

Figure 3.5 Peculiar dance moves and the effects of knockout drops in *Son of Paleface*

wolfish grin on his face. When the drug kicks in, Hope's movements stutter and his lips quiver; he looks baffled, but soldiers on in a vain attempt to play it cool (Figure 3.5b). His high-pitched titters do not help his cause: instead of aiding him in brushing off the moment, they make him seem childish and silly. After a few more hilariously determined but hopelessly uncoördinated dance steps, the mickey hits him, and he passes out. Mike hangs Junior on a coathook, where he will spend the evening in blissful ignorance.

There are several salient differences between these two narratively similar scenes from *Caught in the Draft* and *Son of Paleface*. One of the most important has to do with physical comedy. The situation in *Caught in the Draft* requires Hope to play all but the last twenty-five seconds of the scene from a wheelchair, a fact that obviously limits his physical performance. If in the wooing scene in *Son of Paleface* he were deprived of his ability to walk bowlegged or to dance humorously, it too would be less funny. The latter scene involves far more physical humor, and Hope's gestures are, appropriately, grander.

The *Son of Paleface* scene also makes heavier use of sonic humor, in that Hope's affectation of an accent is extremely pronounced. As a parody, *Son of Paleface* affords Hope the opportunity to push his performance in ways that *Caught in the Draft* does not permit. Tashlin was cognizant that parody permitted him greater freedom. In a letter to his friend Fred Niemann, Tashlin (who seems to have conflated the definitions of "parody" and "satire") wrote, "*Son of Paleface* . . . [is] a broader type of comedy—kidding the chaps off all the Westerns you've ever seen. Satire, at best, is difficult to do on the screen, but I'm trying to pull it off."[31] Hope's goofy bowleggedness and thick, fake accent in *Son of Paleface* are techniques appropriate to a film that lampoons the conventions of the western. Such techniques would probably be out of place in the more middle-of-the-road comedy of *Caught in the Draft*.

These are not insignificant differences, but they are outweighed by the similarities in Hope's performances across the two films. In both scenes, Hope fixes his gaze directly on the eyes of his leading lady and rarely looks away. Surely, this is good advice for any actor who wishes to convey sincerity (or false sincerity), but Hope stares with particular determination at both Lamour and Russell. With these gazes, Hope conveys a dogged eagerness to impress, a move that backfires on him in both cases. In these attempts to appear sincere, Hope instead appears naïve and foolish, as though he were following the advice of an ill-intentioned older brother. The gap between bragging and acting, as Tashlin notes, is a source of the humor in these scenes, and this facet of Hope's persona remained in place across the ten-year span between the films.

There is a similar gap in Hope's employment of certain small hand gestures: the nail-shining in *Caught in the Draft* and the hooking of the fingers into the gunbelt in *Son of Paleface*. In both cases, Hope uses a stock gesture to communicate an attitude, as well as to comment on the gesture's very ridiculousness. Bored rich people do not *really* shine their nails on their vests; cowboys do not *really* hook their thumbs in their gunbelts. The humor of these gestures derives from the fact that the characters do not understand the difference between sincerity and affectation. Again, these small and skillful bits of physical comedy indicate a consistency in Hope's performance style.

In both films, Hope occasionally titters oddly at his own jokes. This post-joke laugh serves the same purpose in the two films: demonstrating that Hope's characters are nervous, childish, and in over their heads in situations for which they did not adequately plan. More important, these little laughs alert the audience that Hope is in on the joke, even if his characters are not. They are ways for Hope to show that, even though *he* knows the gags are corny, his characters think they're pretty good. Such appeals to audience empathy, made from within the confines of rather silly, over-the-top characters, are surely among the truest measures of Hope's enduring popularity; these gestures also demonstrate his genuine mastery of the comic mode.

Hope's style of comedy was too well established—and too valuable to Paramount—to be significantly altered. The differences in Hope's performances in these two scenes are differences of degree, not kind. Tashlin neither added to nor subtracted from Hope's repertoire of performance techniques; instead, he amplified and adapted techniques already present. These amplifications and adaptations, discussed in further detail below, give some indication not only of Tashlin's method with performative comedy, but with his other comic interests as well.

Tashlin exploited another important dimension of Hope's star persona: the impossible humor that was, to some extent, built into it. Primarily through his seven "Road" films with Bing Crosby, Hope was associated with jokes that depend on the shattering of the laws of physics.[32] *Road to Rio* (Norman Z. McLeod, 1947) provides two brief examples. On a cruise ship, Hope and Crosby, in an effort to pilfer a nearby diner's food, attempt to nauseate him. As they noisily discuss repulsive foodstuffs, they move their bodies in such a way as to induce seasickness. But their movements are beyond the capacities of any human being: they sway as if their feet are nailed to the deck, and their entire bodies dip and rotate at impossible angles. Aided by unseen harnesses and wires, Hope and Crosby defy gravity (Figure 3.6). Later in the same film, a cleaning woman accidentally knocks Hope's trumpet into a tub of sudsy water. When he performs on the ship's stage moments later, he brings down the house when bubbles issue forth from the bell of his instrument.

In *Son of Paleface*, Tashlin takes advantage of this dimension of Hope's persona, using him in numerous impossible gags. At one point, Junior finds himself on the wrong side of a door as it is busted off its hinges. He falls on his back, the door atop him, as a horde of angry people—and one horse—trample over the door, squashing him. When he extricates himself, we see that Hope's famous ski-jump nose is now a broad, flat smear (Figure 3.7a). Earlier in the film, after rapidly downing an enormous, incredibly strong drink, Junior undergoes all manner of physical transformations: his head spins in place, steam shoots out from his collar and ears, the Harvard "H" on his sweater curls up, and his entire head shrinks (Figure 3.7b).

Figure 3.6 Crosby and Hope undulate impossibly in *Road to Rio*

Figure 3.7 Impossible humor in *Son of Paleface*

Because of his earlier career in animation (a field in which anything goes, so long as it can be drawn), it is tempting to say that Tashlin was the first to use Hope in impossible comedy. However, the impossible dimension of Hope's persona dates at least as far back as 1940; Tashlin may have emphasized it, but he did not invent it. Again, this is a matter of degree, not kind: Tashlin selected from Hope's rich and complex persona, emphasizing those elements that best meshed with his own style.

The impossible humor inherent in the Hope persona spills over into *Son of Paleface* as a whole. That is to say: Hope's persona allows Tashlin to employ physics-defying jokes that do not explicitly involve Hope's person, but are consistent with the film's comic tone. Late in the film, when shooting wildly at rampaging Indians, Junior hits a painting of a waterfall, which promptly springs a leak. In perhaps the most famous gag in the film, a wheel of Junior's car is detached in a shootout. Roy (Roy Rogers) lassos the hub and hands the lariat to Junior, who, from the passenger seat of his rapidly moving jalopy, pulls mightily on the rope to prevent the car from toppling over. "Hurry up," Junior says to Roy, "this is impossible!" (Figure 3.8a).

Impossible humor is not the only kind of visual humor Tashlin employs in *Son of Paleface*. Early in the film, Junior is framed between the legs of a bronze statue of his father, juxtaposing his head and the statue's behind. The gag's topper, revealed by a dolly back, is simply the incongruous patch on the seat of the statue's pants. In an early scene, Junior shows up in the Old West town of Sawbuck Pass driving his noisy, smoke-belching jalopy. The car's tires kick up mud on two men who stand against a wall. Once thoroughly splattered, they move away, leaving mud-free outlines on the wall (Figure 3.8b). The mud joke is a quintessential bit of Tashlinian humor: a non-gag that depends on clever visual design.

In setups reminiscent of the gag from *Porky Pig's Feat* about the hotel manager falling down the stairs (Figure 1.10), Tashlin demonstrates his continued interest in using offscreen space for comedy in *Son of Paleface*. Here, Junior tries out a pair of spurs for the first time and falls down an offscreen flight of stairs. Instead of showing us the actual fall, Tashlin lingers on the reaction of Junior's sidekick, Ebenezer, and we hear the crash from beyond the frame edge. Later, Junior takes a drink of well water, then drops the bucket down the well. This moment is not actually a gag until a full thirty-four seconds later, when we hear a distant

Figure 3.8 An impossible gag and a non-gag in *Son of Paleface*

splash. Hope glances at the well and remarks, "No wonder that water was warm."

Son of Paleface is, in fact, particularly rich in sonic humor. In one gag, we hear a *boi-oi-oing* sound when Junior opens an unexpectedly empty chest. Later, when descending from a saloon bar, Mike lands on Junior's hand, and we hear a horrific crunch; when Junior stands up, we hear the sound of a creaking door. One of the film's best sound jokes occurs when Jane Russell sings "Wing Ding." Dancing in a revealing outfit, her every hip-shake is accompanied by the low *bwoooomp* of a kettledrum.

The kettledrum gag, as well as several others mentioned above, are but a few examples of the sexual humor that pervades *Son of Paleface*. Much of this type of humor is connected to Hope's complicated sexual identity. When he first sets eyes on Mike, Junior is so excited that the lid of his pipe flutters up and down—a sight gag with overt sexual overtones. A similarly impossible sexual sight gag occurs later in the film, when Mike's kiss literally lifts Junior off his feet; the topper is that his spurs begin to spin. In the same scene as the one with the pipe gag, Junior interjects a verse of sexual confusion into Roy's and Mike's rendition of "Buttons and Bows": "When I was twelve / Oh, what a joy / Mom told me / I was a boy!" An extended gag with Hope and Trigger the Wonder Horse sharing a bed even carries the unmistakable whiff of suggested bestiality, indicating, perhaps, that, though Tashlin was hardly the only director to make use of the confused, infantile sexuality of Hope's persona, he may have been willing to push it a bit further.

For the most part, PCA recommendations for *Son of Paleface* were not followed. Curiously, though the PCA letters regarding the film warn against the inclusion of another gag with bestiality undertones (Roy's avowal that he prefers horses to women—a line that survived the censorship process), they make no mention of the scene in which Junior snuggles up with Trigger. As well, the PCA cautions against many double entendres that nevertheless survive in the film's final cut. Joseph Breen deems unacceptable a series of gags about Junior peeping through a keyhole as Mike takes a bath, but these jokes, too, make the cut.[33] In fact, Breen's letter of August 9, 1951, not only restates nearly all of the cuts suggested in his letter of July 26, but actually *adds* a number of concerns. Recall that many of the recommended cuts in *The First Time* were not made, either; this points to Tashlin's personal involvement in flouting PCA guidelines: no other key production personnel worked on both films. Perhaps unintentionally, Tashlin had begun to build a reputation with the PCA as a troublemaker.

Tashlin chooses a time-tested method of handling the integration of gags and narrative in *Son of Paleface*. The film has two heroes: Hope as Junior, the bumbling Easterner who comes west to claim his father's inheritance, and Roy Rogers as Roy, the government agent assigned to capture "The Torch," a bandit whose presumed next target is the town of Sawbuck Pass, where the film's action takes place. These two narrative arcs intersect in the character of Mike, a showgirl and saloon owner who moonlights as The Torch: she is the object of both Junior's affections and Roy's pursuit. Tashlin's strategy is simple: he assigns most of the responsibility for advancing the story to Roy, and most of the humor to Junior.[34] This is not to say that Junior is not at all involved in the advancement of the narrative. In fact, he is crucially involved: he unwittingly draws Mike into Roy's plans for her capture. That Junior advances the narrative unintentionally is emblematic of the fact that he is little more than another tool with which Roy can advance the story. Junior's own narrative arc—locating his father's gold—is less complex than the film's main story. Every scene that focuses on Junior's quest for his inheritance is an excuse for comedy; every scene that focuses on Roy's quest to capture The Torch is crucial to the advancement of the narrative. When Junior *does* contribute to the furthering of the story, Tashlin has him do so in humorous ways. A key example occurs when Junior— again unwittingly—assists in the capture of several of The Torch's henchmen. In an abandoned mineshaft, Junior falls into a wheeled coal cart, causing it to go around and around on a circular section of track. Tashlin uses fast-motion to show the cart crashing into one henchman after another, thus highlighting the gag's narrative function. Junior is a comic agent who, through pure accident, brings the film's principal narrative arc to a close.

This narrative strategy, which is rooted in the film's two-hero structure, is a reflection and an updating of the strategy Tashlin uses in several of his cartoons: gags in the first half, limited narrative in the second. Instead of splitting the film into a gag-heavy section and a narrative-heavy section, Tashlin splits the narrative responsibilities between two characters. Scenes of narrative advancement and scenes of comedy alternate fairly regularly in *Son of Paleface*.

Tashlin breaks the diegesis of *Son of Paleface* on several occasions. The film's brief opening scene, in which Junior's fiancée, Penelope (Jean Willes again), urges him to head west to seize his destiny, contains two interrelated examples. The film's first image is a freeze-frame shot of Junior and Penelope accompanied by a voiceover from Hope. After she speaks a few lines, Junior leans in to kiss Penelope, and the image freezes again; Hope says, in voiceover, "Very few people recognize me from this angle. Rather classic head, haven't I? You should see it when they take the cork out. But enough chit-chat—on with the story!" Seconds later, Hope's voiceover interrupts again: "I'm about to turn toward you lucky people. Fasten your safety belts, don't be impatient, and, please, no applause. You might miss the plot." Hope speaks his voiceover lines from a time and space outside the diegesis; he speaks as Hope, not as Junior. Moreover, the lines themselves, with their references to story and plot, break with diegetic unity.

At one point, this interrupting voiceover is itself interrupted by an "unexpected" insert of Bing Crosby behind the wheel of a car. Pretending to be slightly flustered, Hope resumes his voiceover: "This is an old character actor on the Paramount lot we try to keep working. . . . But I guarantee you this fellow will *not* be in the picture tonight!" Other gags that break story unity include Junior's referring to a pair of talking vultures as "Martin and Lewis," and a scene in which Cecil B. DeMille plays himself—jokes that refer to people who are definitively *not* a part of the Old West.

Tashlin seizes the opportunity presented to him by *Son of Paleface* to lampoon the conventions of an entire genre. To address just two of the most important genre conventions: the western hero, it is often said, embodies the tension between east and west.[35] In *Son of Paleface*, Tashlin mocks this convention via the character of Junior, who is an effete East Coast dandy as well as the west's worst excuse for a cowboy. The climactic gunfight, which Thomas Schatz calls "the most fundamental of all western plot conventions," is reduced to the absurd: Junior picks off invading Indians by pure chance by firing wildly from a spinning barber's chair.[36]

With the denouement of *Son of Paleface*, Tashlin moves beyond parodying the western to lampoon a trope of Hollywood narration. Mike and Junior have married, but Mike has had to serve time in prison for her crimes. Junior and Roy meet at the jail on the day of her release. Roy says, "You sure been a faithful husband, waitin' all these years," to which Junior responds, "Aw, it wasn't so bad. After all, I saw Mike on visiting days. But, you know, it wasn't any fun talkin' to the woman you love through a wire screen." Just then, Mike emerges from the jail, but she is not alone: at her heels run four small children, each dressed in a miniature version of Junior's Harvard driving coat. Roy, confused, points to the kids, and asks Junior, "Yours?" Junior turns to the camera and says, "Let's see 'em top this on television."

The movie does end with the expected heterosexual romantic union, but the circumstances of the union are comically impossible. Junior does indeed get the girl at the end of *Son of Paleface*; so thoroughly does he get her, in fact, that he manages to sire four children while she is behind bars. Junior's implied sexual prowess is not true virility, but a mockery thereof; the very fact of his fatherhood is unbelievable. This type of ending was not uncommon in American comedies of the time (a subject addressed in Chapter Seven), and Tashlin employs it frequently; this is the earliest example in his work. As is the case with much of his sexual comedy, Tashlin's skewering of the Hollywood ending is deliberately ambiguous. The scene is both a happy ending and a lampooning thereof.

Hope's line about television's censorship strictures is important. In addition to poking fun at both the film and television industries, the joke ruptures the diegesis in several ways: by Hope's direct address to the camera, which shatters the fourth wall; by mentioning television in a movie that takes place in the Old West; and by its implied reference to Hollywood censorship.

Finally, the last laugh in the film is an impossible sight gag: Junior's jalopy rears up on its hind wheels like a bucking horse, and he and his family drive off into the sunset. The closing scene of *Son of Paleface* neatly encapsulates nearly every one of Tashlin's major stylistic concerns, and offers ample evidence that, by his second feature, his style was maturing rapidly.

4 THE ARTIST AND HIS MODEL
TASHLIN AND JERRY LEWIS IN THE 1950S

It would probably be going too far to say that, in Jerry Lewis, Tashlin discovered his muse. However, over the course of their eight films together, the two men clearly found in each other what we might call compelling congruencies. When Lewis became a director himself, he acknowledged Tashlin as his mentor. Asked to name his biggest directorial influence, Lewis told Peter Bogdanovich, "Mr. Tishman, spelled T-A-S-H-L-I-N. He's my teacher."[1]

Their close association and the similarities between their directorial styles has led some scholars to speculate about where Jerry Lewis ends and where Frank Tashlin begins. That the two artists exerted influence on one another is undeniable, but the specifics of that shared influence are not fully clear. By close analysis of their first two collaborations, *Artists and Models* and *Hollywood or Bust*, we may observe how Tashlin afforded Lewis the opportunity to refine his performance style, and how Lewis afforded Tashlin the chance to explore his aesthetic interests.

Mr. Lewis and Mr. Tishman

Fairly early in his career, Lewis developed a persona and a performative style that struck a comic nerve with a large audience. Identifying the essence of these qualities is of no small importance in understanding Tashlin's work, as Lewis appeared in more than one-third of Tashlin's features.

A fascinating 1952 article by Robert Kass runs through Lewis's on-screen personality traits. Though the author has other intentions, he arrives at some astute conclusions about the nature of Lewis's persona.

> Despite unpredictable behavior, tantrums, and fits of weeping, he is rather nice—because he is harmless. Men can look down with comfortable superiority upon his athletic and sexual failures; women feel a tender protectiveness as toward a retarded child; the young like him because his unorthodox

reactions to authority express the rebellion of which they themselves dream. And to everyone Lewis represents the sole unconcerned, unworried individual in today's terrifying world.[2]

Kass provides a good start, but Lewis's screen persona is more complicated than this.

Dean Martin and Jerry Lewis started shooting their first film, *My Friend Irma*, the film version of Marie Wilson's popular radio show, for Paramount producer Hal Wallis in February 1949.[3] Shawn Levy recounts Wallis's reasoning for casting the duo in supporting roles: "*My Friend Irma* was effectively presold, and surely the same people who went for Wilson's dumb blonde act would go for Jerry; if the picture flopped, on the other hand, it would do little damage to Martin and Lewis's future, since it wouldn't really have been their film."[4] When assigned to play Martin's childish sidekick Seymour, Lewis became incensed; he wanted a more "actorly" role. Wallis, an expert negotiator, managed to get Lewis to accept his role as the duo's nuttier half. Writes Levy, "[Lewis] was, after all, to play Seymour, or roles like it, throughout the flush of his career. Yet he began that era refusing to make a film in exactly the guise that had already brought him fame. He would never again shun the character so fully, though he would spend years trying to find nuances in it — primarily a level of pathos he aspired to after studying Chaplin and Stan Laurel."[5]

Given the evidence in the films, Levy's argument is convincing. Lewis's first feature role was instrumental in determining the types of roles he would play throughout his career. The desire to enrich his persona with pathos is of great importance to any study of Lewis, and is addressed in detail in Chapter Six.

Martin's and Lewis's respective personae were established early on in their nightclub years, and were firmly in place by the very end of the 1940s, when they made their first film. Dean was the suave, easygoing Lothario who got the girl, and Jerry was his manic, apelike sidekick who caused the problems that Dean had to solve. These character types would not change for the duration of their partnership, primarily because Wallis was unwilling to unnecessarily alter a successful formula. When *Scared Stiff* screenwriters submitted drafts in which they had given Martin more comic bits, Wallis chided them. "A Martin and Lewis picture costs a half-million, and it's guaranteed to make three million with a simple formula: Jerry's an idiot, Dean is a straight leading man who sings a couple of songs and gets the girl. That's it, don't fuck with it, go back to the typewriter."[6] In their two films as a duo for Tashlin, Martin and Lewis do not deviate in any significant way from these personae.

Another important dimension of Lewis's screen persona is his sexuality, which, like Hope's, is complex. Lewis's sexual persona differs from that of Hope's in that, whereas Hope is wolfish but homosexual and/or effeminate, Lewis is girl-crazy and immature. Lewis is not so much emasculated as he is underdeveloped: he is reduced to blabbering and extreme uncoördination by the mere presence of attractive women. Plentiful examples of this behavior may be found in *Scared Stiff* (George Marshall, 1953), and *Jumping Jacks* (Norman Taurog, 1952), among others.

As for his performance style, much of it can be attributed to traditions of Borscht Belt comedy. Lewis honed his performance skills in the Borscht Belt circuit, a school of comedy that owes a great deal to vaudeville. The two forms are distinct, but the one is surely the little brother of the other. Joey Adams writes, "[Around World War II], vaudeville took to the hills—Old Man Vaudeville that was supposed to be dead and buried was now alive and kicking.... The weekend shows and musical comedies were replaced by three-act bills. The Borscht Belt became the Borscht Circuit for professional acts and big-time show business. Jugglers, dog acts, magicians, hypnotists, acrobats and the rest of the vaudeville fraternity dusted off their music, brought out their yellowed scrapbooks and headed for the Hills."[7]

Stefan Kanfer writes that, in the Catskills, the humor was far bluer than that allowed in vaudeville. While vaudevillians on the Keith circuit were subject to many restrictions, "none of these rules prevailed in the mountains. There, audiences could be addressed frontally and insulted constantly. Rabbis and diets, money and sex became the staple subjects of comedy; double entendre was the order of the day, and when energy vied with taste there was never a question of which would win."[8]

Borscht Belt comedians did much more than merely address patrons. They teased them, harangued them, and spilled soup on them: direct address gave way to physical engagement. Borscht Belt comedy amplified certain tendencies of the vaudeville humor that had spawned it.

Comedians who worked the Borscht circuit had to be, like vaudevillians, well-versed not only in joke-telling, but in singing, dancing, mimicry, even juggling and calisthenics. Even more heavily than vaudevillians, Borscht Belt comedians relied on spontaneity and extemporaneousness. The Catskills is where Lewis obtained his impressive improvisatory skills.

Early in his career, Lewis mastered both verbal and physical comedy, a rare perfecta that puts him in the company of W.C. Fields, Mae West, the Marx Brothers, Bob Hope, and other exalted company. A 1965 piece by John Russell Taylor accurately addresses Lewis's verbal comedy. "[He has] an entirely personal way of mangling English, with nouns turning into verbs, verbs into adjectives, notions duplicating themselves, twisting, turning, dividing and re-forming in a babble which stays always tantalisingly on the edge of comprehension, just this side of total disintegration into gibberish."[9] Lewis's uncommon gift for verbal comedy was not lost on Tashlin.

Murray Pomerance usefully broadens our understanding of Lewis's performance style:

> He is strident, brash, dysfunctional, uncoordinated, immature, inarticulate, imposing, hyperactive, . . . irritating (even debilitating), rude, untutored, uncivilized, inconsiderate, and often ugly . . . — all this, and to an extreme degree. Further, when he whines and wheedles, screeches and drones, the amplitude of his vocalization, as recorded, exaggerates volume and pitch so that his expression is an acoustic weapon, what conventional listeners would call unmusical. When, in his walk or posture, he configures himself asymmetrically . . . he seems without grace, therefore unblessed, even morally twisted. The syntax of his speech is likely to be warped, his social response apparently miscalculated, his needs uncivilized. Jerry doesn't know how to behave.[10]

More than any other director—even Lewis himself—Tashlin understood Lewis's mastery of these (and other) dimensions of performance.

You're Never Too Young for *Artists and Models*

To get a sense of how different directors can shape Lewis's performance, let us consider two scenes: one from *You're Never Too Young* (Norman Taurog, 1955) and one from *Artists and Models*. As with the scenes from *Caught in the Draft* and *Son of Paleface* discussed in Chapter Three, these scenes have been chosen not only because they were made within months of each other, but because they are narratively similar.[11] In both scenes, Lewis's character confounds and humiliates Martin's character. Most important, both scenes demonstrate the full range of Lewis's performative talents. The first has Wilbur Hoolick (Lewis) masquerading as a French master barber. Bob Miles (Martin) requests a haircut and inevitably winds up on the wrong end of Jerry's overenthusiastic incompetence.

Lewis wears a wig, a false goatee and thin, upswept moustache, and he affects an over-the-top French accent. As he says, "I zink we shall start wiz ze scalp treatment," he walks toward the camera with a huge grin and bugged-out eyes (Figure 4.1a). His arms bend upwards at the elbow, and he spreads and stiffens his fingers like talons.

Bob refuses "ze scalp treatment" and settles into the chair, which is controlled by an armrest-mounted switchbox. Lewis hits a switch, the back of the chair flops down, and Martin tumbles to the floor. Lewis then manages to get into the chair himself, contorting his body to mount the chair backwards, then turns around and plays customer himself. "Could you please just take ze beard?" he says to Martin, stroking his goatee.

As Lewis attaches an apron around Martin's neck, he sings "Alouette" in mock French. This is a fine example of Lewis's gift with nonsense words; these have the added humor value of sounding faintly French. The physical equivalents of these nonsense words are the hand gestures that Lewis employs. Trying overly hard to act the part of the skilled professional, Wilbur runs his fingers over Bob's cheeks, chin, and forehead in a vain attempt to relax him. But the gestures do not resemble true tonsorial technique: individual fingers randomly stroke Martin's eyebrows, hairline, and the area below his lower lip. These gestures, combined with the nonsensical faux-French, confuse and frustrate Bob — not least because, every few seconds, Lewis grabs Bob's head and thrusts it back against the headrest, a gag augmented by a coconut-bonking sound effect.

Wilbur decides to do just what the barber next door is doing: fancifully tossing an egg in the air and catching it.[12] Jerry handles the egg-tossing with great aplomb, bouncing it off of his bicep and juggling it with a skill that surprises us, since we expect an instant mess. All the while, Lewis sings in his mangled French. Inevitably, the egg winds up all over Martin's face. Lewis registers embarrassment, but the hint of a

Figure 4.1 Barbershop antics in *You're Never Too Young*

smile creeps across his lips. He just barely catches himself before bursting into laughter at this ancient gag.

Moments later, Lewis presses a button that makes the chair vibrate crazily, subjecting Martin to heavy jostling. As if in sympathy, Lewis shakes his body in time with the chair: his head, upper body, and arms vibrate until the chair stops moving. Lewis exclaims, "Ees good! Eet make you relax!" We see a subtler sympathetic gesture a few seconds later, just after the wings of the automatic headrest clamp down on Martin's skull. In medium close-up, Lewis rapidly crosses his bulging eyes in a remarkable distillation of the outward-to-inward motion of the headrest (Figure 4.1b).

The final gag in the sequence also involves the chair, which raises itself on a telescoping post up to the ceiling, taking both men with it. Just after Lewis presses a button to make the chair stop climbing, he delivers a line in an unusual way. "*Voilà!* We stop good, *oui?*" Lewis's voice betrays its New Jersey origins here, his "Hey, laaaady!" rattle poking through the veneer of fake French: Paris by way of Newark. It's a small, almost unnoticeable occurrence, but an important one, as it demonstrates Lewis's vocal control. The brief but genuine Joisey intonation offers humorous contrast to the extended run of phony French, which Lewis resumes after uttering this line.

His 1956 split with Martin indirectly led to major changes in Lewis's persona and performance style. In both of Tashlin's films with the duo, however, Lewis's mature, pre-breakup persona is on full display. *Artists and Models* is the single best example of the meshing of Tashlin's directorial style and Lewis's early performance style. A scene from *Artists and Models* contains a similar situation: Eugene (Lewis) subjects Rick

(Martin) to physical humiliation, this time with the unwitting assistance of several masseuses. The situation is that Rick brings Eugene to a massage clinic after the latter has injured his sacroiliac by posing as a model for a cartoon character. (A Tashlinian situation if ever there was one.)

The scene begins with Rick, carrying an immobile, crooked Eugene under his arm, entering a massage parlor and depositing his friend on a table (Figure 4.2a). A masseuse climbs atop the table, and then atop Eugene, in an attempt to straighten him out. As she yanks his ankles and pushes on his lower back, we hear a series of sharp cracking noises; at the same time, Lewis begins grunting and moaning comically. The nurse sits on Lewis's rump, slowly forcing his chest against the table; she then pushes her feet against his, shoving them down with another series of cracks. Just before his legs hit the table, Lewis emits a series of loud grunts and briefly looks directly into the lens. Finally fully extended, Eugene pants and wheezes with exasperation.

Moments later, the masseuse bends Lewis's left leg beyond the capacity of even the most generous hip joint (Figure 4.2b), and Lewis reacts with a loud, wailing, moan/grunt: "oh-ohh-Ohh-OHHH-AAAH-AAAAH-AAAAAH," each syllable of which is pitched slightly higher than the previous. The result is a strange, singsong wail that is both painful and funny. Lewis repeats this wail, more or less verbatim, as the masseuse lifts his leg again; this time, he sticks his tongue out of his mouth and jerks his head slightly with each syllable. The topper for this phase of the scene occurs when the masseuse lifts Eugene's right leg well beyond the point of impossibility, an act aided by prop legs and the partial concealment of Lewis's body. Lewis matter-of-factly mutters, "Oh, pain. Oh, plenty of pain," just before emitting his loudest yelp yet; the cracking sound effects also reach their highest volume at this moment. When his right foot winds up over his left shoulder, Eugene pauses to grab his shoe and remark, "Oh, I gotta get new soles." The masseuse then takes one ankle in each hand and braids Eugene's legs together, prompting another barrage of crunching and cracking as well as a long series of howling "OO-OO-OO"s. Again, Lewis pauses to crack wise: "Anyone for taffy?"

The final phase of this extended gag begins with the masseuse again flattening Lewis's body against the table. In so doing, for some reason she places her right leg on the table beneath Lewis's thighs, and then

Figure 4.2 Jerry Lewis, both right-angled and elastic, in *Artists and Models*

shoves him down onto the table with a crunch. The two of them become entangled, and Eugene summons Rick to help them. Eugene, acting the part of an expert masseur, directs Rick to insert himself between the two bodies on the table, a tactic that only complicates matters. Eugene calls for another masseuse. This woman, at Eugene's instruction, climbs on the table, lifts his foot, and stands astride the mass of bodies, in the process shoving her backside right into the face of the first masseuse. Rick, realizing that Eugene has gotten him into another fine mess, resigns himself to being stuck for a while. Eugene rearranges body parts into various unhelpful positions, which is the essence of the gag: the more Eugene tries to extricate himself and Rick, the worse the entanglement becomes. Nonetheless undaunted, he asks, "Is there another lady?" and yet a third masseuse appears. She, too, joins the enmeshed bodies. Eugene continues to give instructions to the masseuses, somehow managing to extricate himself from the other four people. As he positions and repositions their arms and legs, Eugene realizes that he is now cured of his injury and free from the pile of bodies. Sheepishly, he says to the entangled Rick, "I'll tell you what: I'll see you at the apartment later." Rick responds, "I don't think so. I may have lunch here." "Oh, what a mess," says Eugene as he leaves the room and the scene fades to black.

The massage table scene from *Artists and Models* is similar in certain respects to the barbershop scene from *You're Never Too Young*. Both are fine examples of Lewis's skill with vocal humor. In Taurog's film, Lewis uses phony French (and authentic Jerseyspeak); in Tashlin's, he uses all manner of comic nonverbal moans and grunts, as well as his trademark peculiar dialogue: "Oh, pain. Oh, plenty of pain." As well, both scenes give Lewis a chance to flaunt his skills as a physical comedian. Of a piece are Wilbur's use of ridiculous hand gestures to demonstrate his tonsorial skill and Eugene's contorting of the masseuses' bodies in an effort to untangle himself. In both cases, Lewis uses physical gestures to suggest clueless dilettantism.

However, at the level of physical humor, the scenes differ in many ways. For much of the massage table scene, Lewis is the manipulatee, not the manipulator. The masseuse contorts Eugene, whereas in the earlier scene Wilbur contorts Bob. Nevertheless, Wilbur remains the focus of the physical comedy. In the barbershop scene, Lewis's performance is physically unrestricted, whereas he plays most of the massage table scene prostrate. His legs replaced by the phony pair, Lewis contorts his head, face, and tongue, and flaps his arms in a show of comic pain: even when restricted, Lewis uses all available body parts for comic gesture. These limitations cut down on Lewis's wilder gesticulations, encouraging a subtler performance based on vocalization and restrained gestures. "Subtler" is a problematic descriptor of any Jerry Lewis performance; nevertheless, Tashlin is able to coax a more compelling performance from his star by saddling him with physical restraints. Lewis's command over his movements and postures in this scene is superb.

The two scenes are tellingly different in other ways, as well. Both directors employ Lewis's vocalized comedy, but Tashlin does the more creative work with comic sound effects. In *You're Never Too Young*, the only sound-effects gag is the *bonk* we hear when Wilbur knocks Bob's head against the headrest. In *Artists and Models*, Tashlin uses repeated cracking and crunching sounds to *structure* the scene: as the scene goes on, these noises get louder, which makes them both funnier and more wrenching. The more severely Eugene's body is bent, the louder the sound effect. As well, Tashlin uses music to let us know that the gag has reached its apex. Before we notice that Eugene has extracted himself from the mass of masseuses, we hear a whimsical oboe theme that tells us "something silly has just happened." Tashlin uses this musical cue to prepare the audience for the joke.

The scene from *You're Never Too Young* lacks two essential features of the *Artists and Models* scene: sexual humor and impossible humor. While many a Martin and Lewis routine (especially in their television work) alludes to or contains apparently homosexual content, the barbershop scene is not representative of this particular subtext. The massage table scene, however, is rich in sexual comedy, though not of the same-sex variety. As it ends, Rick is pinned to a table by no fewer than three women, two of whom are young, blonde, and voluptuous. As soon as he extricates himself, Eugene leaves the room, ostensibly embarrassed at having caused such a foul-up. But the scene encourages an alternate reading: the virginal Eugene leaving the sexually accomplished Rick, already established as a womanizer, to his orgiastic pleasures.

The impossible humor of the massage table scene is rooted in the humorous bending, stretching, and twisting of Eugene's body. No such comedy exists in the barbershop scene, though it is true that the hyperactive barber's chair pushes at the limits of plausibility. It is a fine but important distinction: Taurog stretches the rules of physical reality, but Tashlin breaks them.

At no moment in the barbershop scene is the diegetic world compromised, but Lewis's brief but noticeable glance into the lens in *Artists and Models* acknowledges that there is a world beyond the camera. Tashlin uses Lewis's penchant for disruption to engage one of his own preferred comic modes: diegetic rupture.

Both of these "showcase" scenes have the Lewis character feigning expertise with tasks he cannot perform, and, in the process, embarrassing the Martin character. Beyond this, however, the scenes' relative importance to their films' narratives differs somewhat. Eugene's scene is better integrated into its film's narrative than Wilbur's. The barbershop setup is isolated from the rest of the story, which never again refers to matters tonsorial. In fact, it is little more than a highly vaudevillian "barbershop" skit dropped into the film as a pretext for the characters' meeting—a bit of unintegrated performance inserted wholesale into the narrative. The situation that sets up the massage table scene derives from Eugene's character: obsessed with comics, he injures his back by posing as a comic-book character. In this way, the scene from *Artists and Models* emerges more organically from the film's narrative than does the scene from *You're Never Too Young*.

Hollywood or Bust or Bust

Of Tashlin's two Martin and Lewis films, *Artists and Models* seems to be the more representative of his style, but *Hollywood or Bust* also offers a window onto his stylistic development. The production of *Hollywood or Bust* (Tashlin's final film with the duo, and the duo's final film) was troubled by the fractious relationship between its two stars.[13] Memoranda exchanged between the film's producers indicate a production plagued by, among other things, Lewis's fear of being upstaged by a dog[14] and his requiring hospitalization for "palpitations."[15] In reading the studio discourse, one gets the sense that Tashlin was fed up with his troublesome star; associate producer Paul Nathan, in a memo to producer Hal Wallis, writes, "Frank told me he is going to stay out of the middle of this project—come what may. He is going to shoot the script exactly as it is, without any temperament from anybody."[16] Nathan refers in another memo to the "millions of problems" that beset the production, and writes to Wallis that "[Tashlin] insists it has not been easy or fun for him, and at the end of the day is so beat that he can't stand it."[17] Whether this meant that Tashlin had resigned himself to a lesser film is uncertain: the film, though perhaps not as good as *Artists and Models*, is nevertheless at least partially representative of his mid-1950s feature style. Though it was made and released later, I will discuss *Hollywood or Bust* before returning to a fuller analysis of *Artists and Models*.[18]

The plot of *Hollywood or Bust* can be sketched quickly: Steve Wiley (Martin) and Malcolm Smith (Lewis) acquire a new car in a raffle, and, along with Malcolm's Great Dane, Mr. Bascom, drive it from New York to Los Angeles, Steve to escape his creditors and Malcolm so he may meet the girl of his dreams, Anita Ekberg (who plays herself). Along the way, they pick up Terry (Pat Crowley), with whom Steve eventually falls in love, and pause in Las Vegas, where Malcolm displays his uncanny ability to win at games of chance. After various arguments and fallings-out, the pair finally arrive in Hollywood, meet Anita Ekberg, and secure a starring role for Mr. Bascom in Ekberg's new film.

The film offers few challenges to the "road movie" archetype, and contrasts narratively with *Artists and Models*, whose plot is far more convoluted. *Hollywood or Bust*'s thin plot makes it difficult to discuss Tashlin's strategy of gag/narrative integration in the film: any digressions, gag-related or otherwise, are built in to the film's story structure. Most of the comic moments that might be seen to interrupt the flow of the narrative do, eventually, wind up contributing to its advancement, albeit in elaborate ways. One such instance involves Steve and Malcolm pulling over to give a ride to a sweet old lady who happens, they soon learn, to be packing heat: she steals their car and leaves them on the roadside. But this is not entirely a "throwaway" gag, for it sets up a key development: Terry drives her jalopy past the stranded Steve and Malcolm, and is persuaded to give them a lift; she soon becomes the romantic foil for Steve. The gags in the film are reasonably well integrated into the narrative, but the narrative is so episodic and uncomplicated that the distinction between integration and non-integration is negligible. If one wanted to make an argument for Tashlin's "cartoonlike" live-action style, *Hollywood or Bust* would be a good case study—not for the "cartoony" nature of its gags, but for its loose approach to the relationship between gags and narrative.

Hollywood or Bust is notable for several gags that employ offscreen space. One of the best occurs in an early scene in which Malcolm, sitting in the balcony of a cinema, excitedly makes his way to the stage to present his winning ticket in the theater's new-car raffle. So excited is he that he burrows a path under the theater seats, and Tashlin allows us to chart his stageward progress by watching patron after patron leap up with surprise and shock. Several other offscreen gags use impossible humor. In one, the camera stays on Steve waiting in the car while Malcolm steps inside his apartment to pack for their road trip; twenty-three seconds later, he emerges with four suitcases fully packed. Two other jokes are variations on a similar idea. The first occurs when Malcolm and Mr. Bascom run off into the distance, and then rematerialize in the same shot from an entirely different direction. (The gag is pulled off with doubles.) The other has Malcolm drive the car speedily in one direction, only to reappear seconds later from the diametrically opposite compass point—a gag accomplished, this time, with editing.

The film contains many one-off sight gags, several of which involve Mr. Bascom: driving a car, carrying a gas can, drinking champagne, and the like. A few others seem as if they were plucked directly from a vaudeville routine, such as the few quick shots, in a scene on an Arizona reservation, of "Big Chief Running Water" sitting under his own personal raincloud. Later, at a craps table, Steve tells Malcolm to "throw the dice," and of course he tosses them into the air and into the champagne glass of an elderly, well-dressed woman.

These fairly mild, tried-and-true gags have their counterpart on the film's soundtrack. At one point, Mr. Bascom barks in time to the song that Malcolm sings; at another, the boys drive through a covered bridge, causing their singing to echo. (This, and the film's other two uses of echoes, are perfect examples of Tashlinian non-gags: sound really *does* echo in enclosed, empty spaces, yet Tashlin presents these moments as if they possess special comic value.) Shortly after the boys meet Terry, Malcolm makes a confident but clueless stab at fixing her jalopy. Its engine falls out (another offscreen gag), and as it sits, sputtering, on the road, it issues a series of humorous squeaks, whines, and honks—sonic elements that "sell" this small gag.

Other gags in the film are more plainly Tashlinian. The film's title sequence, in which Anita Ekberg poses, in outlandish and revealing costumes (Figure 4.3), in front of various Los Angeles landmarks, establishes a slightly suggestive tone for the film, alerting us that the incipient pun in the film's title will be hatched using both VistaVision and Technicolor. The title song, sung by Martin and Lewis over this sequence, also notifies us that Hollywood humor of a self-reflexive stripe will be important to the film. Lyrics include "Land of stardust, and land of glamour / VistaVision and Cinerama," and "All agree: In Paramount we trust." In this brief, introductory, quasi-diegetic scene, Tashlin combines a joke about his female star's anatomy, a self-referential joke about the film industry, and a signal that lets the viewer know that the diegesis (which has barely commenced) may be subject to further rupture.

And the film's diegesis *does* get ruptured later in the film. One funny instance also occurs in the lyrics of a song, when, driving past the Hoover (a.k.a. Boulder) Dam and unable to resist the pun, Martin, Lewis, and Crowley warble, "Although the movie censor won't let us utter 'damn,' / They can't stop us from saying, 'Boulder Dam!'" Moments later, when they pull into Las Vegas, the trio spy a billboard for the Sands casino, which just so happens to be promoting an upcoming Martin and Lewis show. Just as it begins on a moment of diegetic liminality, so ends *Hollywood or Bust*, the final Martin and Lewis picture. In the film's very last shot, both leads step out of character and walk directly into the camera lens, acknowledging its presence and effecting a "practical" fade to black with their widely grinning faces (Figure 4.4).

Hollywood or Bust lacks the satirical barbs that characterize both earlier and later Tashlin films. Any jabs at the Hollywood apparatus are decidedly tame—ironic, considering the film's title and subject matter. For the most part, such gags consist of mere references to Paramount Pictures and VistaVision. The film's last scene is not a parody of the pat Hollywood ending, but a pat Hollywood ending in itself, even if the closing song does jokingly refer to a "happy ending and grand finale."

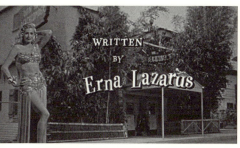 

Figure 4.3 Typically punny, Tashlinian objectification of the female form

Figure 4.4 Martin and Lewis storm the camera in the last shot of their last film.

The sexual comedy in the film, too, is fairly tame. Aside from Malcolm's somewhat surprising and lascivious mention of Anita's "undies," and a naughty joke in which Terry mistakes Mr. Bascom's wagging tail for one of Steve's appendages, the level of ribaldry in the film is fairly low.

There is one exception, though, to this general mildness: an extended musical number ("A Day in the Country") in which Malcolm and Steve sing about the pleasures of fresh air. But their bucolic surroundings offer a fringe benefit: the roads are lined with comely young women in alluring dress. Malcolm sings about and gestures offscreen toward an "old water mill," and Tashlin cuts to a panning shot, taken from behind, of three shapely young women who recline near said mill (Figure

4.5a). The "little red barn" Malcolm mentions does appear in the subsequent shot, but its quaintness is overshadowed by the scantily clad young ladies pitching hay in its yard. The gag continues in a similar vein for the duration of the song, eventually presenting a haycart laden with not just hay, but nine young beauties (Figure 4.5b); a tracking shot of scantily clad farmgirls sitting on a fence; and a shot of a tractor and cart, driven by and filled with even more curvaceous young women, some of whom are swinging carrots by the leaves (Figure 4.5c).

On one level, the women's mere presence is funny because of its incongruity. On another level, the gag is that the boys sing about the landscape's natural beauty, but this visual pleasure is supplanted by one more prurient. The gag is about an idealized sexual landscape in which every nook of the American countryside brims with fresh, young, eager women. Ultimately, this fine extended gag is a satirical jab at the overdeveloped, yet naïve, sexuality of the American male: in the America of *Hollywood or Bust*, the very countryside is a sexual playground, there for the plucking by "a couple of travelin' guys."

Despite all those nubile farm girls, the Production Code Administration had few objections to *Hollywood or Bust*, deeming the film acceptable under the Code.[19] Though the brief memo includes the standard warnings about the "proper and decent" attire required of all women in the film, Geoffrey Shurlock, writing on behalf of the PCA, grants the film his official seal of approval. (It is notable, though, that the Legion of Decency granted the film only a "B" rating, for reasons of "suggestive costuming and situations," a fact that suggests that the PCA and the LoD were not always in perfect accord.) As we shall see, the PCA negotiations surrounding *Artists and Models*, conducted a year earlier, were far more difficult.

Artists and Models Redux, or, How to Catch a Mouse by the Tail

The massage-table scene in *Artists and Models*, described above, is but one instance of the elements of Tashlin's style approaching a kind of maturation. A précis of the film's story, and an analysis of the ways Tashlin weaves gags into it, demonstrates some of the reasons that the film is one of Tashlin's key works.

The story of *Artists and Models* concerns two childhood friends who have moved to New York City so that Rick can make a living as a painter

Figure 4.5 The sexualized countryside of *Hollywood or Bust*

and Eugene can write children's books. Unable to find work in their desired fields, they bounce from job to unsatisfying job: the film opens with a scene of them employed as billboard painters—a job they lose partly through Eugene's obsession with comic books. So consumed with comics is Eugene that he dreams about the adventures of Vincent the Vulture and Zuba the Magnificent. Rick accuses Eugene of ruining any chances they have of making money, and threatens to move out of their apartment, but doesn't have the heart to leave his best friend behind.

New tenants move into Rick's and Eugene's boarding house: Abby (Dorothy Malone), a comic-book artist, and Bessie (Shirley MacLaine), a free-spirited model who poses for Abby's character The Bat Lady, with whom Eugene is particularly obsessed. Both women are employed by the publishing firm of Mr. Murdock (Eddie Mayehoff), who scolds Abby for not including enough blood and guts in her comics. In short order, Rick begins wooing Abby, and Bessie falls for Eugene. Rick uses his relationship with Abby to get in Murdock's good graces; he proposes a comic book based on Eugene's dream-character Vincent the Vulture. Murdock is intrigued, so long as Rick can pull it off with sufficient gore. The comic is published and becomes a big success.

By ridiculous coincidence, the name of the secret formula mentioned in *Vincent the Vulture*, "X-34 minus 5R1-6X36," is the same as that of the U.S. government's new "power formula" that will enable them to launch the first space station. Communist agents catch wind of this coincidence and determine that Rick, as the book's author, must be in cahoots with the U.S. military. The Communists send the sultry Sonia (Eva Gabor) to seduce Rick and extract the rest of the secret formula from him, but Sonia gets to Eugene first. On the evening of the Artists and Models Ball, Sonia brings Eugene to a suburban mansion and attempts, but fails, to seduce the formula out of him. Rick and Bessie go to the mansion and, with Eugene's help, defeat the Communist spies. They have just enough time to dash back to New York to join Abby in the ball's finale, where the two couples are "married" onstage just before the film ends.

The plot of *Artists and Models* has affinities with those of certain of Tashlin's cartoons, in that its final act introduces a self-contained narrative that has relatively little to do with the bulk of the story. The espionage portion of the story—which runs from about the film's seventy-seventh minute to its hundred and seventh—is pronouncedly disconnected from the rest of the story. The connection is deliberately thin: Tashlin emphasizes its unlikeliness in the elaborately silly name of the secret formula. Just as the latter half of *Cracked Ice* is connected to its first half merely by milieu, the espionage plot of *Artists and Models* is connected to the rest of its story by an intentionally thin plot device.

Until the espionage plot is introduced, *Artists and Models* is more thorough than *Son of Paleface* at blending scenes of comedy and scenes of narrative advancement. In the earlier film, Roy advances the plot while Junior is the focus of the comedy. In *Artists and Models*, Rick is more involved with comic scenes (in addition to the massage-table scene, Martin is very funny in a scene involving an elaborate game of pantomime) and Eugene, ostensibly the comic relief, is in fact the central figure of the espionage plot.

Though Tashlin exercises his satirical wit several times in the first two-thirds of *Artists and Models*, he ramps it up during the spy story. In the film's first scene, Tashlin lampoons the garishness of modern advertising by staging a series of gags around a gimmicky billboard. Two scenes—one of Murdock speaking effusively about blood and gore, and another of Eugene appearing on a televised panel discussion as a casualty of comic books—are typical of Tashlin's ambivalent approach to American popular culture. Both scenes satirize not only the increasingly graphic content of popular media, but the bluenoses who would ban them.[20] The satire of the movie's last third is quite different. On one level, it is a parody of spy movies: the Communist agents are bumbling fools; the hero is a man-child who defeats the villains by repeatedly stumbling into them. On another level, it satirizes, more generally, conventions of Hollywood narration: its tacked-on nature contradicts traditional notions of streamlined, integrated storytelling.[21] More broadly, the espionage plot satirizes the Cold War, American foreign policy, and the space race. *Artists and Models* represents the first large-scale cinematic flowering of Tashlin's sense of satire, a tendency concentrated in the film's final third.

Tashlin only breaks the diegesis twice in *Artists and Models*, but sight and sound gags are much more common. One occurs in the film's opening scene, which takes place on a billboard above the streets of Manhattan. Given a situation involving Jerry Lewis, a scaffold, and several cans of paint, it is no surprise that the scene climaxes in multicolored chaos on the sidewalk below (Figure 4.6). The vivid hues of the paints are made all the more vivid by Technicolor photography; the richness of

Figure 4.6 Color as comedy in the opening scene of *Artists and Models*

the colors emphasizes the drabness of the clothes of the men on whom the paint falls, and of the men themselves. Here, Tashlin uses color to bring into relief an additional level of humor: the gag *is*, on one level, the colors themselves. This is actually one of the very few Tashlin gags to explore the comic potential of color—a surprising fact, given Tashlin's (deserved) reputation for having a good eye for color.

A small, impossible non-gag occurs in a scene in which Eugene extols the virtues of pretending. Eugene touches a match to the wick of a candle, but it fails to ignite; instead, the candle next to it flashes alight. Moments later, Tashlin employs a traditional sight gag: Eugene removes a silver dome to reveal his feast: a single bean, which Eugene smothers with ketchup and eats with a fork and knife.[22] In a scene in Murdock's office, Tashlin uses a water cooler, one of his favorite comic props, as the pivot of several sight gags. The first occurs when Bessie kisses Eugene, who is leaning against the cooler, which begins to bubble and steam as Eugene becomes aroused. Less than two minutes later, Tashlin exploits the reflective properties of water and glass for two non-gags about Lewis's and Mayehoff's distorted faces (Figure 4.7). Finally, in an ex-

Figure 4.7 Tashlinian non-gags: Lewis and Mayehoff distorted by a water cooler in *Artists and Models*

tended, slapstick bit, Eugene winds up with the water bottle stuck inside his pants, and proceeds to make a watery mess of the office.

A small, funny gag demonstrates Tashlin's increasingly deft handling of offscreen space. Rick meets Murdock at the Stork Club for a business lunch, and Murdock brings along his mistress, a voracious eater. In a medium close-up of Rick, the mistress's hand snakes into the frame from the right to snatch food from his plate (Figure 4.8a). This activation of the offscreen space for humorous purposes is the comic highlight of this expository scene.

Artists and Models uses sound comedy often, including in the aforementioned "pretending" scene. As Rick looks on in disbelief, Eugene "plays" a drafting board, somehow making it sound like a piano. Other impossible sound-effects gags include an exaggerated *wobble* noise when a thrown letter opener vibrates after lodging in a door, and the *boing* produced by Eugene's uncooperative dickey. (At which Eugene exclaims, "I can't keep this dickey down, Ricky!") Tashlin also exploits Lewis's skill with vocalizing: some of the film's funniest moments are nothing more than the weird, sudden shrieks that Eugene emits in the middle of a dream about Vincent the Vulture.

Sexuality permeates the comedy of *Artists and Models*. An incomplete list includes the strange psychosexuality of the opening scene, in which a giant pair of female lips inhale Jerry Lewis; the suggestion of an orgy in the massage table scene; a scene in which Eugene climbs into the bathtub with Rick; a gag in which the tops of Eugene's shoes pop open when Bessie kisses him; and the framing of Lewis through Shirley Mac-

Figure 4.8 Comedy from beyond the frameline and between the legs in *Artists and Models*

Laine's legs in the "Inamorata" number (Figure 4.8b). And then there is the mousetail gag.

When Sonia whisks Eugene to the mansion to seduce his secrets from him, he is dressed as Freddie Fieldmouse, his costume for the Artists and Models Ball. Tashlin uses this ridiculous costume in several gags: its head spins around impossibly, it frightens a cat in a reversal of a familiar antagonism, Eugene gets so hot inside it that steam pours forth from the neckhole when he removes its head. But the funniest and most controversial use of the Freddie Fieldmouse costume involves its long tail. The joke is quick—only about five seconds long—and is shot in such a way that it is somewhat abstracted (Figure 4.9). But the thrust of this sight gag is clear: as Sonia leads Eugene to her boudoir, the mouse's tail, limp and dragging in the preceding shot, stiffens as a sign of Eugene's arousal.

The fact that this fairly explicit gag remains in the film tells us a great deal about Tashlin's comic style, as well as his strategy for dealing with censorship. Various gags in *The First Time* and *Son of Paleface* concern sexual arousal, but their raciness is always compromised in some way. The moment in *The First Time* in which Betsey stares greedily at Joe's banana certainly has sexual overtones, but it also carries the narrative weight of the film's motivic structure: bananas signify pregnancy. In *Son of Paleface*, the fluttering of Junior's pipe-lid when he first sees Mike is a sure sign of his arousal, but this is a kind of deflected distillation of the actual signs of human sexual excitement. The mousetail gag is the first occurrence in any of Tashlin's films of a sight gag that makes direct, specific reference to the physical facts of sexual arousal.

Figure 4.9 The mousetail gag

Tashlin wasn't fooling anybody with this joke, least of all the administrators of the PCA. PCA director Geoffrey Shurlock, in four successive letters over the course of about six weeks, urges *Artists and Models* producer Hal Wallis in no uncertain terms to cut the gag, and yet it survives. While it is impossible to discern from their correspondence the reasons that the gag made it into the final cut, an account of the negotiations is informative. Most of Shurlock's worries about *Artists and Models* have to do with what is known in PCA parlance as "sex suggestiveness." Of the forty-six items that Shurlock names in the earliest correspondence regarding the film, all but three have to do with sex suggestiveness or vulgarity.[23] Scenes that refer to birth control and drugs were cut; the remaining forty-three pieces of sex suggestiveness met with varied fates. The mousetail gag is not the only sex-suggestive gag to survive in spite of Shurlock's warnings. Such fragments of dialogue as "cleaving cleavage" and "bosom exposed" exist in the finished film, as do scenes involving showers and skimpy bathing suits, all of which Shurlock warns against. Most prominently, the mousetail joke survives.[24]

Many of the suggested changes that were *not* made to *Artists and Models* would have been very simple and inexpensive to make. The censorship negotiations occurred between January 20 and March 2, 1955; the film's shooting dates were February 28 through May 3, 1955. Principal photography and censorship talks overlapped by only three days, giving the filmmakers ample opportunity to make the suggested changes. But by the time the rough cut of the film was screened for the PCA (around May 17), it would have cost Paramount a great deal of time and effort to make the recommended changes, some of which would have involved cutting or replacing individual lines of dialogue within long takes.[25] For instance, Tashlin simply appears to have refused to cut the epithet "buttbrain" (said by Rick of Eugene), even though Shurlock explicitly warns against it in the memos of January 20 and 25. By the time of the rough-cut screening, replacing the word, which occurs in the middle of a carefully composed 40-second take, would conceivably have necessitated expensive reshoots. By shooting scenes in such a way as to make costly any changes to them, Tashlin guarded his vision of the film and ensured, as much as he could, that some of the bluer jokes remain. Some changes, however, *could* have easily been made even after the rough cut was complete—most notably the mousetail gag, which occurs in a single insert shot, and could easily have been excised without compromising continuity.[26] The presence of this gag argues not only for Tashlin's increasingly bawdy humor, but for his increasing unwillingness to accede to PCA demands.

Tashlin's creative interpretation and selective refusal of the PCA's recommendations may be evidence that, by the mid-1950s, the Production Code had lost some of its efficacy. Tashlin's films may themselves be chinks in the Code's armor, the very cases that contributed to the diminution of its authority. In all likelihood, both conditions obtained: Tashlin was responding to a perceived loosening of the Code, and seized the opportunity to loosen it further. As producer Paul Nathan wrote to Wallis, "Tashlin agrees with [any recommended change], then doesn't always write it."[27]

To put these negotiations in perspective, the Production Code weathered other challenges around this time. In fact, the early to mid-1950s were a period when auteurs mounted repeated and serious challenges to censorship: Otto Preminger with *The Moon Is Blue* (1953), Elia Kazan with *Baby Doll* (1956), Vincente Minnelli with *Tea and Sympathy* (1956).[28] Tashlin's challenges to the PCA's authority with *Artists and Models* were not made in isolation. The film's controversial moments were not even necessarily the least subtle of the era: *Baby Doll* is nothing if not overtly lurid. *Artists and Models* is both a turning point in the brashness of Tashlin's comedy and a representative example of the challenges and changes that the PCA underwent in the mid-1950s.

Gregory D. Black writes that, in the early 1950s, various forces both external and internal had begun to pose fairly serious challenges to the PCA, and that Shurlock, who became the director of the PCA in 1954, "was under intense industry pressure to modernize the code yet maintain the PCA."[29] Black writes of a committee convened in May 1956 to address this modernization; Shurlock, in addressing the committee, said that "almost anything can be treated as a story subject under the Code . . . provided it is done with taste."[30] The committee recommended that, when treated in good taste, heretofore taboo subjects such as abortion, prostitution, narcotics, and miscegenation were acceptable story material, but nudity and sexual perversion would remain banned.[31]

Black provides excellent case studies of how the PCA and the Catholic Legion of Decency responded censoriously to such mid-1950s films as *Tea and Sympathy* (problematic for the issues of homosexuality and adultery) and *Baby Doll* (problematic for its overt, leering sexuality). Though such films as *Artists and Models* and *Will Success Spoil Rock Hunter?* met with opposition from the administrators of the PCA, they were not, in the main, considered to be scandalous in the way that *Baby Doll* and *The Moon Is Blue* were. Why was it that Tashlin was able to get away with subject matter that was so problematic for other directors? The answer may have something to do with genre. Black's case studies are generally "serious" films: dramas, melodramas, "issue" pictures. Did the PCA have a different standard for comedies, and, if they did, what accounted for it?

Without extensive study of extant PCA files for early and mid-1950s comedies, it is difficult to come to a conclusive answer. However, we can speculate on the existence of two relevant dynamics. First, it may be the case that, because comedies were seen to be less "important"—they were, by their nature, not to be taken entirely seriously—PCA officials may have been somewhat more lax in their censorship of them. Unlike *The Man with the Golden Arm*, *The Moon Is Blue*, and *Tea and Sympathy*, all of which take place, more or less, "in the real world," comedies, including Tashlin's, often take place in worlds in which the impossible becomes possible. As such, comic films may have posed less of a threat for PCA censors.

If, as seems likely, the PCA was less hawkish about comedies, Shurlock and his associates may have unwittingly acted to diminish the Code's efficacy. Regardless of comedies' putative realism, a transgression of the Code was a transgression of the Code, and the very existence of a sexual joke like the mousetail gag set a precedent that directors of films of any genre may have used in disputing the findings of the Production Code Administration. As argued above, some of Tashlin's films may themselves have chipped away at the foundation of the code, and every time he was allowed to include a potentially problematic gag, the slippery slope of permissibility was further greased. While Tashlin may not have been a vocal advocate of the dissolution of the code, he certainly took no steps to ensure its continued and uncontested authority—indeed, he seemed to delight in challenging it.

If *Son of Paleface* is the first mature film of Tashlin's live-action career, *Artists and Models* represents an intensification of that mature style. Nearly all of Tashlin's major stylistic interests receive emphases in *Artists and Models* equal to those in his earlier features, and in many cases are intensified and enriched. Three of Tashlin's next four features—*The Lieutenant Wore Skirts*, *The Girl Can't Help It*, and *Will Success Spoil Rock Hunter?*—explore these concerns even more extensively. Chapter Five focuses on the last two and makes the case that they represent the peak of Tashlin's directorial talents.

5 THE DIRECTOR AND THE BOMBSHELL
TASHLIN AND JAYNE MANSFIELD

Critics, scholars, and Tashlin himself generally agree that *The Girl Can't Help It* and *Will Success Spoil Rock Hunter?* are the director's two best films.[1] It is a claim that this volume will not refute.

The starring performances by Jayne Mansfield in both of these films are crucial to their success. Mansfield was, in many ways, Tashlin's least skilled leading performer, and yet he uses her as the locus of some of his best performance-based comedy. Though more talented than her reputation suggests, Mansfield was nowhere near as gifted a performer as Bob Hope or Jerry Lewis, and her persona was not half as complex or well-formed. As this chapter argues, one of the reasons that Mansfield's comedy in these films is so successful is that Tashlin effectively uses her a channel for his other interests—satire, sexual humor, visual gags. Moreover, Tashlin employs Mansfield—and, crucially, her straight-man costars, Tom Ewell and Tony Randall—in ways that allow him to unify the many elements that comprise his style. In Mansfield, Tashlin's style had found its perfect vehicle.

The Girl Who Couldn't Help It

Like Porky Pig, Jayne Mansfield was something of a blank slate. While she certainly didn't lack a star persona, it was fairly uncomplicated, and, like Porky Pig's in the 1930s, it was malleable. When she first collaborated with Tashlin in *The Girl Can't Help It*, her persona was partially established, but her performance style was virtually non-existent. It was in the two films she made with Tashlin, in fact, that these elements were fixed. Mansfield gave for Tashlin not just her two finest performances, but her career-making performances.

Unlike Hope and Lewis, Mansfield was not a trained

comedian. It is an unfortunate reality of the studio system that, while Hope's and Lewis's first film roles came about as a result of their success in other realms of entertainment, Mansfield was first cast on the basis of her appearance. A former beauty queen, Mansfield moved to Hollywood in 1954, intent on becoming a star. After attracting attention with a stunt involving a swimming pool and an ill-secured bikini top, Mansfield was signed to a Warner Bros. contract.[2] She and her agent, Jim Byron, developed a promotional strategy built around not only her physical assets, but her willingness to mock them. Byron has said, "She was the satire of all dumb blondes. . . . One time Jayne arrived and I posed her by a sign on a crane which was there. The sign said, 'Excess Frontage Overhang.' It wasn't a problem coming up with individual stunts for her."[3]

This good-natured self-mockery is the very thing that distinguishes Mansfield from the more overtly glamorous bombshells of the time, most notably Marilyn Monroe. Tashlin did not invent this facet of her persona, but he did a great deal to develop it.

After taking supporting parts in three Warner Bros. productions of 1955—*Pete Kelly's Blues*, *Illegal*, and *Hell on Frisco Bay*—Mansfield was offered a lead role in the Broadway production of George Axelrod's play *Will Success Spoil Rock Hunter?* In the play, which resembles the film only titularly, Mansfield played a ditzy starlet, "more or less based on the studio-stupid image of Marilyn Monroe. Jayne opened the show clad barely in a towel, lying on a massage table."[4] The play was a success, and Twentieth Century-Fox bought the film rights and signed the star to a contract.

Mansfield's first picture as a Fox player was not *Will Success Spoil Rock Hunter?* but *The Girl Can't Help It*, in which the bombshell facet of her persona was cemented. Fox then took the cautious next step of off-casting Mansfield, starring her in an adaptation of John Steinbeck's novel *The Wayward Bus* (1957). However, the studio apparently found Mansfield's dimwitted bombshell persona to be the more bankable one: in *Will Success Spoil Rock Hunter?*, Mansfield's next film for Fox, the oversexed, clueless, lovable diva Rita Marlowe is the embodiment of the two principal components of Mansfield's screen persona: her overripe sexuality, and her ability to satirize same. Unfortunately, comprehensive box-office figures for the films are unavailable, and a scan of *Variety*'s reports for their respective first two weeks' box office is inconclusive.[5]

In any case, the Marlowe character precisely matched Mansfield's star image: this was typecasting of the highest order, and it represented a crystallization of Mansfield's screen persona.

For Tashlin, Mansfield represented a different kind of challenge than did Hope or Lewis. She came to him with an established but pliable image: curvaceousness and gentle self-mockery is a far less specific persona than that of Hope or Lewis. Mansfield was not necessarily an utterly blank slate on which Tashlin imposed his every whim, but he seems to have had a fair amount of freedom in his use of her. Tashlin emphasized certain elements of her thin persona to the point where they became, for the rest of her short career, her defining characteristics.

Tashlin played up Mansfield's tendency to satirize her bombshell image. She is used, in her Tashlin pictures, to much greater comic effect than in nearly all of her other extant films, and she appears to have been in on the game. Tony Randall, her costar in *Will Success Spoil Rock Hunter?*, once said of her,

> She was not an accomplished actress, but she was hard-working. She could be silly, but she knew it. She'd argue, and then make fun of herself for arguing. There was a scene [in *Will Success Spoil Rock Hunter?*] where she gets out of the plane wearing a chinchilla coat, and all of a sudden she's got a bikini on. Like a serious actress, she said to Frank, "Frank, would this girl do this?" Then she said, "Maybe she would. *I* would."[6]

A comparison of Mansfield's pre-Tashlin film performances and those in her two Tashlin films is illuminating. Despite the fact that her roles in *Female Jungle* (1954), *Pete Kelly's Blues*, *Illegal*, and *Hell on Frisco Bay* (all 1955) are small and non-comic, they do afford some understanding of her acting skills. A brief look at *Illegal*, a mildly glorified B picture, is worthwhile.

In *Illegal*, Mansfield plays Angel O'Hara, a nightclub singer and mob moll. She has but two significant scenes: one in which she receives a telephone call from a crooked attorney, and one in which she testifies at a criminal trial. The latter offers a small but revealing window onto Mansfield's performance style.

Called to the stand as a surprise witness, O'Hara enters the courtroom just in the nick of time. She wears a look of concern as she glances around the room: she does not know why she's been called here. Mansfield walks with hips a-swivel, as if she is on a fashion model's runway, not in a courtroom: she thrusts her chest forward and her backside backward. On the witness stand, Mansfield delivers all of her lines from exactly the same position: back straight, chin high, right hand awkwardly resting flat on the railing in front of her. She reads her lines flatly: no word receives more emphasis than any other. Her expression changes minimally; the only facial gesture she makes is a very broad, room-scanning eyeball roll just before she reveals the name of the crooked attorney to the stunned courtroom. She uses this stock gesture to denote the hesitation before a shocking revelation. It is not totally out of place in a shoddily made movie like *Illegal*, but it does little to convince us of Mansfield's acting talents.

To put it charitably, Mansfield's performance in *Illegal* is unpolished. She is given precious little to do, and doesn't do that much with it. Her performance in *Illegal* gives no hint of her comic talents, or of her capacity to mock her own image, though these elements of her persona had already been established. By studying a few of Mansfield's comic scenes in her Tashlin films, we get an idea of the adjustments he made to Mansfield's acting.

Jayne Mansfield as Comic Performer

In *The Girl Can't Help It*, Mansfield plays Jerri Jordan, the fiancée of the semi-reformed gangster Fats Murdock (Edmond O'Brien). Murdock hires Tom Miller (Tom Ewell) to turn his future bride into a star.

During a scene in which Miller rehearses with Jerri to get an idea of her vocal range, she emits sounds so horrible that they shatter a lightbulb. In the next scene, Miller and Jerri attempt to convince a disgruntled Fats that his protege is talentless. Jerri sits on a couch with her back straight, her shoulders back, and her jutting breasts squeezed into a very tight sweater. Miller insists that Jerri cannot sing; she adds, "I stink, Mr. Murdock!" Mansfield delivers the line matter-of-factly, pronouncing each syllable with exaggerated properness, as if correct elocution will bolster her argument. When Fats responds, "You don't stink!," Jerri retorts, "I do so stink! I'm telling you, I stink, stink, stink!" To deliver this line, Mansfield coils her body slightly, hunching her back and drawing her shoulders backward. At "I'm telling you," she stands up and steps toward O'Brien. With each "stink," she gets closer to him, and, on

Figure 5.1 Jayne Mansfield insists she cannot sing in *The Girl Can't Help It*

the last one, releases the tension in her back and arms: she snaps backward at the waist, places her knuckles on her hips, and throws her head back indignantly (Figure 5.1). Murdock isn't buying it: he insists that her speaking voice is fine, so her singing voice should be, too. "Talk, Jerri!" he insists. Jerri responds, "Stink, STINK, *STINK*, Mr. Murdock!" Mansfield accentuates the last "stink" not only by yelling it, but through facial and bodily gestures. Her face is the picture of comic anger, all frowning eyebrows and pouty lips. Mansfield thrusts her still-akimbo arms back, and sticks her chest so far out that O'Brien actually leans backward. The movement of her breasts adds bodily punctuation to the line.

This a far subtler and more refined performance than that in *Illegal*. It is also funny. Mansfield gets a good deal of comic mileage out of her many pronunciations of a single word, and she uses her body to accentuate the most humorous moments of her delivery. Mansfield's vocal intonations in this scene are a kind of sonic non-gag: her lines themselves are not particularly humorous, but her pronunciations of them are. Tashlin uses Mansfield's vocal skill for comedy, just as he did with Porky, Hope, and Lewis before her. In this case, however, vocalized comedy was not a part of his actor's performative repertoire—Tashlin coaxed it out of her.

Mansfield's breasts, strongly accentuated by a tight, brightly colored sweater, are used for comic effect: when she thrusts them at him, Fats

Figure 5.2 Mansfield acts the diva in *Will Success Spoil Rock Hunter?*

actually looks slightly scared. This single gesture serves numerous purposes. First, it is evidence of the dimension of self-mockery in Mansfield's persona, a facet of her image not exploited in film until *The Girl Can't Help It*. Here, Mansfield uses the most noticeable, talked-about feature of her anatomy for purposes other than sexual allure. Second, it demonstrates the ambivalent nature of Tashlin's sexual comedy, in that Mansfield's body is played for laughs, but so is its power over men. Finally, it is a moment of the integration of gag (or non-gag) and narrative. Jerri's actions here anticipate a moment later in the film when, after years of acceding to Fats's every whim, she finally stands up to him. The "stink" scene is a turning point in the story in that it demonstrates to Fats the unfeasibility of his plan to make Jerri a star. In no way is Mansfield's performance style so rich in her pre-Tashlin work.

Another fine example of the relative subtlety of performance that only Tashlin could coax out of Mansfield occurs in a key scene in *Will Success Spoil Rock Hunter?*, in which advertising executive Rock Hunter (Tony Randall) tries to convince starlet Rita Marlowe (Mansfield) to endorse Stay-Put lipstick. As the scene begins, Marlowe lies prostrate on a massage table, wrapped in a pink towel. She speaks by phone to her estranged boyfriend Bobo, observing that it's "simply divoon" to be apart from him; she raises her shoulders and angles her head and chin upward in a show of condescension (Figure 5.2). Throughout the film, Marlowe affects an air of importance in order to justify her unlikely stardom: Mansfield the self-mocking bombshell as Marlowe, the bombshell who merits mockery.

Mansfield uses her voice to great comic effect in this scene. It ranges from little-girl coy (when she hints at having a man in the room) to the mock outrage of a diva (when she gets upset that Vi, her assistant, refuses to talk like a man to keep up the ruse) to comic-book sultry (to Bobo: "It's room temperature now, but the room temperature's changing, if you get my cruder meaning"). In the examples below, Mansfield uses three very different vocal intonations for three subsequent sentences.

> To Vi, after learning Hunter's name: "Rockwell Hunter! Oooh! His name sounds very influential!" Spoken breathily, and at a high register: the voice of an easily impressed starlet.
> To Bobo: "His name only so happens to be Rockwell Hunter!" Spoken in an even higher register, a kittenish voice that Marlowe employs specifically to raise Bobo's ire.
> To Hunter: "What do you do?" Instantly, she shifts to a no-nonsense, even slightly harsh, businesswoman's voice. She uses no oohing or aahing—just direct, unemphasized, plain English, with no trace of seductiveness or airheadedness.

Each of the three tones of voice is, on its own, funny, but it is the differences and quick leaps between them that is the essence of the comedy here.

When she convinces Hunter to speak to Bobo, Marlowe sits eagerly on the edge of the table. She leans forward, grinning hugely, occasionally hunching her shoulders forward in girlish delight. She titters and twitches as Hunter embellishes her fabrications. The scene ends with Mansfield emitting her trademark high-pitched squeal and enveloping Hunter in a massive hug. She smothers him with sloppy kisses while running her left hand rapidly through his hair. ("You're hurting me," he sputters.) This over-the-top display of sex-kitten libido is made all the funnier by the differences between Mansfield's brashness and Randall's reserved manner.

This scene shows that Mansfield could be funny without having to resort to being the butt of jokes about her anatomy. Much of the comedy of the scene depends on the audience's knowledge of Mansfield's persona: that she is a starlet playing a starlet, and that Marlowe's actions are not totally removed from Mansfield's own. Tashlin makes the fullest possible comedic use of Mansfield's talents.

Equipped for Sexual Comedy

Both *The Girl Can't Help It* and *Will Success Spoil Rock Hunter?* contain a great deal of sexual humor, nearly all of it focused on Mansfield. In a scene in Miller's apartment, Mansfield clutches two bottles of milk to her chest, one squarely in front of each breast (Figure 5.3a). Obviously, this gag works on two levels. Another example from *The Girl Can't Help It* occurs when Mansfield "hides" behind a scraggly bush to change her clothes (Figure 5.3b). The thrust of this fine visual gag is that it would take a redwood to conceal Mansfield's figure; the sparseness of the shrub only highlights her ample dimensions. The joke is simply that Mansfield's body is on humorous display.

Much of the sexual humor in these films, though, is of a somewhat different order. In a scene in which Jerri prepares breakfast for Miller, Tashlin places Mansfield at the left edge of the CinemaScope frame so that her body is visible from just below her shoulders to the middle of her thighs. It is an especially blatant case of the objectification of the female form, and Tashlin gleefully employs it for laughs. Moments later, Jerri expresses her dissatisfaction that "everyone figures [her] for a sexpot!" She leans in, exposing ever more of her cleavage to Ewell, and says, "No one thinks I'm equipped for motherhood!" The scene ends with another shot of this same restricted view of Mansfield, her breasts jutting unmistakably into the frame. Ewell does his best not to gaze at them (Figure 5.4). Tashlin often uses Mansfield as an emblem of overheated sexuality who literally embodies his ambivalent approach to sex and satire. On one hand, her voluptuousness is itself an object of ridicule; but the object of even greater ridicule is Miller, who is confused and astonished by Jerri's body. Indeed, the more cutting sexual satire is reserved for Miller, whose speechlessness stands in for the befuddlement of the modern American male when he is confronted with self-assured femininity. This ambivalence is a strong mark of Tashlin's style.

The scene that immediately precedes the breakfast scene also taps into this current of sexual ambivalence. As Jerri walks down a city

Figure 5.3 *The Girl Can't Help It*: The famous milk-bottles gag, and Jayne Mansfield, inadequately hidden

Figure 5.4 Mansfield's breasts jut into the frame, and Tom Ewell does his best to avert his gaze

street, several men respond to her in physically impossible ways. Jerri raises the temperature of an ice-delivery man so much that his bare hands melt a huge block of ice, makes such an impression on a milkman that his bottle of milk ejaculates creamy spume into the air, and shatters an onlooker's glasses with a mere flash of her legs. As in the breakfast scene, the object of the gags here is doubled: Mansfield's voluptuousness in and of itself, and the ways in which her sexuality completely incapacitates these men.

In *Will Success Spoil Rock Hunter?*, Tashlin combines a sexual joke with a gag about offscreen space. Moments after Rita insists that she never wears a girdle, she and Rock kiss lustily while we look at Rock's associate Rufus watching them. As he looks on, we hear the sounds of fabric stretching and buttons popping, upon which Rufus says with a smirk, "She wears a girdle." This gag is a good example of the ways that Tashlin's Mansfield films combine and unify his aesthetic interests.

Did Censorship Spoil *Rock Hunter?*

It is unsurprising that the PCA expressed concern about the sex suggestiveness of *Will Success Spoil Rock Hunter?*.[7] The film's censorship documents offer some insight into the PCA's rationales for suggesting changes, as well as evidence of Tashlin's (and Fox producer Frank McCarthy's) refusal or neglect of those changes.

In 1957, Geoffrey Shurlock, director of the PCA, wrote two letters to McCarthy concerning *Will Success Spoil Rock Hunter?*: one on February 7 and the other on March 13; the latter was written six days before the start of principal photography.[8] Above all else, the first letter aims to eliminate ambiguous double entendres. Shurlock recommends changing fairly innocent-sounding phrases such as "see you about your endorsement" and "a night's work" that, in context, have potentially sexual meanings. He also warns of potential problems with scenes involving bathing suits and bathtubs — fairly standard concerns.

The letter of March 13 is more intriguing, for two reasons. First, its list of suggested changes and/or cuts is longer than that in the earlier letter: most of the eighteen specific suggested changes in the March letter are entirely different from the sixteen mentioned in the February letter. Of these eighteen suggestions, Tashlin or his producers elected not to abide by eleven. As with the mousetail joke in *Artists and Models*, some of these sexual gags — and they are, to a one, sexual in nature — could have been easily excised from the film without compromising continuity. A gag about a cardboard cutout of Rita Marlowe falling forward onto the sidewalk, then bouncing back up — the joke is that her breasts are so large and resilient that they bounce even when reduced to two dimensions — occurs at the tail end of a shot, and could very easily have been trimmed without affecting the continuity of the scene or the film. But this decidedly throwaway gag remains. In a letter to McCarthy of March 18, 1957 (five days after Shurlock's second letter), Tashlin writes of this scene, "I disagree completely on the cutout bouncing. It will be a flat cutout. I will shoot this, Frank, but in a manner that we can lose it in the final cut if we lose the hard fight we put up to keep it."[9] This letter reveals a great deal about Tashlin's strategies of negotiation with the PCA.

His counterargument is disingenuous: the *literal flatness* of the cutout is not the issue; the controversial part is the cutout's *implied elasticity*. Tashlin was as good as his word, though: the gag *was* shot in such a way that it could easily have been removed. Nevertheless, it remains.

Lea Jacobs writes, "[Censorship] negotiations concerning specific ideas or actions were generally resolved through the use of indirect modes of representation.... Offensive ideas could survive, but at the price of an instability of meaning."[10] Jacobs writes about the 1930s and early 1940s, but her arguments apply equally well to Tashlin's strategy in the 1950s. On March 13, 1957, the day Shurlock sent his second letter to McCarthy, McCarthy copied the letter and forwarded it to Tashlin, along with the following:

> No doubt you wish to argue about some of the points in this letter. I do. Probably, though, the best means of handling this would be for you and me to go through the letter, analyze and evaluate each of the points, make up our minds what we wish to do, and the shoot the picture without further reference to the Shurlock office. I have a pretty good idea of what they will and won't approve in a final picture, regardless of what they say in the letter.[11]

McCarthy's note indicates his willingness to work with Tashlin on developing creative responses to Shurlock's recommendations, and even indicates a disdain for the PCA in general. But the most significant part of the note is its last sentence, which gives a sense of the subtlety and deception inherent in the negotiation process.

Tashlin's response to McCarthy begins,

> After reading the Shurlock letter, I have come to the conclusion that had I made Rock Hunter a dope addict, [his girlfriend] Jenny Wells pregnant and momentarily about to lose her illicit child that of course had been fathered by either [Hunter's boss] Irving LaSalle, Jr. or Bobo Brannigan or both, the Shurlock office would have given my script unanimous approval. Anything that is cute, naughty, is unacceptable to these people. I doubt that the genius of Ernst Lubitsch could combat them.[12]

The thrust of this rather strangely phrased complaint is that Tashlin feels the PCA is focusing on the smallest details but overlooking the big picture. Tashlin goes on to discuss, item by item, his plans for responding to Shurlock's suggestions. In several cases, Tashlin makes minor dialogue fixes that keep the tone if not the original wording of the written line. For instance, Shurlock takes issue with a line about a mattress manufacturer who wishes to procure Hunter's endorsement for its product—the connection between "mattress" and "sex" being too obvious, apparently. Tashlin's response is to drop the word "mattress," changing the line to "A King Size Bed manufacturer wants me to endorse his King Size *Special*."[13] Shurlock also objects to the word "assets," presumably not only for its first syllable, but because the word is a vague euphemism for sexual anatomy. Tashlin's response is to have the relevant line trail off before the offending word is spoken: "But, honey, I love your . . ." Even when Tashlin agrees to make changes like these, he does not really do so in good faith. The sexual implications of these and other lines survive in Tashlin's reworkings of them—only the actual wording has been changed. Tashlin, apparently, knew how to operate within the gray areas opened up by the censorship process.

A line that Tashlin clearly intended as a double entendre is the subject of a different negotiation strategy. In the scene in which Rock, speaking to Bobo, pretends to be Rita's lover and business advisor, he says, "I'm president of Rita Marlowe Productions, Incorporated, but Miss Marlowe is the titular head of the company." Shurlock writes in his second letter, "Under the circumstances, the expression 'titular head' could prove extremely objectionable and we ask that it be changed."[14] Tashlin responds to McCarthy, "Frank, this particular line—'titular head'—was in the previous version of the script that was sent to the Shurlock office. They made no comment on it at that time one way or the other—why should they this time? I do not want to change this. I am not going to have this line read like a dirty line—it will just be thrown away."[15] Tashlin is correct that Shurlock's letter of February 7 makes no reference to this line. Whether this gives him the basis of an argument under the PCA strictures is arguable; nevertheless, the line appears in the finished film. Whether it is spoken in a lascivious fashion is entirely subjective—a fact that Tashlin surely knew and intended. Tashlin uses this same strategy to address several more of Shurlock's suggested changes, sometimes standing his ground, and sometimes agreeing to changes in spite of the first letter's incompleteness. In studying these documents, it emerges that Tashlin was a savvy negotiator. At times, for jokes that were less important to him, he acquiesces to Shurlock's wishes, even if

Shurlock raised criticisms about them in his second letter but not his first. This tactic provides him with a bargaining chip: he makes changes *even though* the items in question had passed muster in an earlier draft. He uses this ploy to preserve the jokes that were more important to him, such as the gag with the bouncing cardboard cutout.

Another small joke for which Tashlin fights occurs in the scene in which Rock is awarded the much-coveted key to the executive washroom. Shurlock, in the March letter, objects to the following dialogue on the grounds that it "goes too far in the area of toilet humor":

> Rufus: Now take that key—and go, boy, go!
> Rock: I wish Jenny was here to share this with me.
> Rufus: No women allowed . . . Go . . . boy, go.[16]

Tashlin's response to McCarthy is, "Frank, I'd like to make a fight on this. I will not do this in an offensive way and I have changed the line to: . . . I wish Jenny was here to share this moment."[17] In the film, the line comes off as anything but offensive: Randall's delivery conveys Rock's sincere wish to share an important moment with his fiancée.

Tashlin's negotiation strategy seems to have been almost entirely successful, as evidenced by a June 4, 1957, letter from McCarthy to Fox producer Buddy Adler, with copies sent to Tashlin, among others. McCarthy writes,

> I had to ask Earl Bright to take WILL SUCCESS SPOIL ROCK HUNTER? to the Shurlock Office. As you know, I was not worried about this picture from the Code point of view. . . . Here is Earl's comment on the screening: . . . "ROCK HUNTER was passed today by the Shurlock office without any objection whatsoever. The viewers chuckled and laughed virtually throughout the picture. They commented on the number of ingenious bits of business and thought it was perhaps the most enjoyable comedy they had seen in some time. They were pleased with the finesse with which were handled some of the lines which had worried them."[18]

The documentation of the censorship of *Will Success Spoil Rock Hunter?* tells us a great deal about Tashlin's negotiation strategy, as well as the state of censorship in the mid to late 1950s. Tashlin seemed to have the right combination of tact, bargaining skill, and not a little recklessness that allowed him to mount successful challenges to the PCA. By cleverly designing gags that were ambiguous enough to be read as either clean or dirty—and by, at times, insisting on the inclusion of easily removable gags—Tashlin found a way to preserve his films' robustly risqué humor.

Visual and Narrative Comedy in the Mansfield Films

Not all of the gags in the Mansfield films are sexual. Many of the films' most memorable sight gags are of the non-gag type that Tashlin favors. One of the most duly famous moments in all of Tashlin's *oeuvre* is the opening scene of *The Girl Can't Help It*, in which Tom Ewell appears on stage to address the audience. The first image in the film is an Academy-ratio, black-and-white shot of a tuxedo-clad Tom Ewell on the stage (Figure 5.5a). Right after he speaks to the viewing audience about the "grandeur of CinemaScope," he snaps his fingers, and the left and right edges of the frame extend outward to define the full 2.35:1 frame (Figure 5.5b). Ewell continues, "This motion picture was photographed in . . . gorgeous lifelike color by Deluxe," prompting the monochrome image to burst into gaudy blues, oranges, and golds that are, in truth, anything but lifelike. This famous moment is a fine gag about the state of film viewing in the mid-1950s, especially as it concerns Hollywood's first-line responses to the perceived threat of television. It is also, though, the type of gag at which we smilingly marvel rather than laugh. It demonstrates Tashlin's gift for *mise-en-scène*, but does not use color or space in a particularly *humorous* fashion.

Like many of the gags in these two films, this one serves more than one purpose. Not only is it a beautifully orchestrated and memorable sight gag, but it ruptures the diegesis in several ways. Ewell, in his monologue, says, "I play the role of Tom Miller in the film we're about to see": he speaks to us as Tom Ewell the actor, not Tom Miller the character. As well, Ewell "controls" the cinematic elements of color and aspect ratio, a superdiegetic power few film characters are granted. The metacinematic nature of this gag is the principal reason it is especially well remembered.

Will Success Spoil Rock Hunter? features two important scenes in which Tashlin uses sight gags to address a number of his other aesthetic concerns. The first of these is its famous opening, in which Tony Randall appears in a corner of the screen, dwarfed by the immense Twentieth Century-Fox logo (Figure 5.6). We hear the famous Fox fanfare, which Randall "plays" on drums, trumpet, and upright bass. ("Oh, the fine

Figure 5.5 The opening scene of *The Girl Can't Help It*

Figure 5.6 Tony Randall plays the Fox fanfare in *Will Success Spoil Rock Hunter?*

print they put in an actor's contract these days," he laments.) Seconds later, Randall identifies himself by his own — not his character's — name, and what starts as a sight gag (Randall dwarfed by the Fox logo) ends as a sly shattering of the diegesis. As well, Randall's one-man-band accompaniment deflates the bombast of the legendary Fox studio. This is *not* the manner in which Hollywood narratives typically commence.

Another scene in *Will Success Spoil Rock Hunter?* combines several of Tashlin's chief comedic interests. A little more than an hour into the film, Tashlin fades in on an empty stage. Randall appears from behind a curtain and, stepping out of his character, addresses the audience. "Ladies and gentlemen, this break in our motion picture is made out of respect for the TV fans in our audience, who are accustomed to constant interruptions in their programs for messages from sponsors." The large, color CinemaScope frame then shrinks to approximate a small, blurry, black-and-white television plagued with technical problems. As with the Ewell scene, this gag is, partly, a satirical comment on the state of viewership in the mid-1950s, when Hollywood was legitimately threatened by television's surging popularity. The gag is compelling because its satire and rupture are conveyed in visual terms: the moment at which the screen shrinks is the moment at which the scene's satire commences. This scene is one of the cleverest and funniest in all of Tashlin's work, and may in fact be *the* quintessential Tashlin joke.

Will Success Spoil Rock Hunter?'s lampooning of Hollywood is somewhat nonspecific, but assuredly present. As a purveyor of vapid diversions, Hollywood is the target of the film's barbed but generalized commentary on mass entertainment. Hollywood as an entity does not receive nearly as much satirical criticism as do the television and advertising industries.

The Girl Can't Help It, however, ridicules certain conventions of Hollywood storytelling. The film addresses a familiar Tashlin topic—the pat Hollywood ending—in a way that demonstrates the director's visual-comedy skill. In the film's denouement, Tom and Jerri, now happily married, appear on a stage—the same stage on which Tom appears in the prologue. At first, Tom stands on the stage alone (Figure 5.7a); in short order, he is joined by Jerri, and then four scampering children who emerge from frame right to stand in a line next to their parents. The left side of the frame is unoccupied for a few seconds (Figure 5.7b), and then Fats emerges from the wings, pushing a carriage in which lies the most recent product of Tom and Jerri's fruitful union (Figure 5.7c). It is a very fine joke: Murdoch's appearance is the topper to the extended gag about the couple's remarkable fertility, but it is also the final element in this clever use of the widescreen space: the gag and the composition are completed in a single stroke. Moreover, this gag satirizes the pat "Hollywood ending" in a way similar to that in the last scene of *Son of Paleface*. Tashlin challenges the formulaic nature of the happy ending by pushing it to extremes. Not only is the heterosexual union realized, but it is fruitful beyond any reasonable measure—so fruitful, in fact, that the couple seem to have reproduced for the very purpose of filling a CinemaScope screen with their progeny.

The Mansfield films are the ones in which Tashlin most fully integrates gag and narrative. The humor in these films derives largely from character and situation; rarely are gags made into stand-alone set pieces. These films contain numerous integrated gags that, were they performed by Hope or Lewis, would become isolated showcases. For instance, one sight gag in *Will Success Spoil Rock Hunter?* has Rock wearing one of Bobo's gigantic suits (Figure 5.8). Rather than plumb this setup for slapstick humor, as one could imagine him doing if Lewis were wearing the same suit, Tashlin uses it to emphasize a key narrative point: that Rock is not meant—he is literally ill-suited—to be Rita's lover.

In large measure, this greater integration of gag and narrative can be traced to the personae of the films' lead performers. As mentioned

Figure 5.7 Filling the frame and completing the story in the final scene of *The Girl Can't Help It*

Figure 5.8 A sight gag with narrative relevance in *Will Success Spoil Rock Hunter?*

above, Mansfield's persona is not one that lends itself to "showcase" moments of wild or impossible comedy, as Hope's and Lewis's do. Mansfield's less-developed persona as a self-mocking bombshell permitted no such performative capacity, and the same is true of the personae of Tom Ewell and Tony Randall. Ewell, like Robert Cummings, is a quintessential Everyman—he played similar characters in Tashlin's *The Lieutenant Wore Skirts* and Billy Wilder's *The Seven-Year Itch* (1955). Randall, who was a few years away from his signature roles as the scene-stealing comic relief in the Doris Day-Rock Hudson comedies, was arguably Hollywood's (and Broadway's, and television's) most talented Everyman, but he was still an Everyman; his persona was fairly nonspecific.

When the diegesis is broken in a Tashlin film with Hope or Lewis, it is Hope or Lewis who does the breaking: the wild comedians engaging in the most disruptive comedy. For both of these actors, this tendency to break the diegetic effect is built in to their personae. This tendency was not, however, part of Mansfield's persona. Rather than giving the rupturing gags to Mansfield, Tashlin assigned them to Ewell and Randall. His reasons for doing so were at least two: Ewell and Randall were not only more skilled performers in an absolute sense, but the roles they play in these films are, in both cases, the roles around which the narrative revolves. As central characters, they are far more rational, stable, and "straight" than those played by Hope or Lewis. In a sense, Tashlin has split the comic duties: Mansfield is assigned the outrageous, over-the-top humor (be it verbal or physical), and Ewell and Randall are assigned the humor that has more to do with the way in which the films' narratives unfold. The diegetic ruptures in *The Girl Can't Help It* and *Will Success Spoil Rock Hunter?* are of a different type than those in *Son of Paleface* and *Artists and Models*. In the earlier films, diegetic rupture usually takes the form of knowing glances into the lens, or wisecracks directed at the audience. In the Mansfield films, the ruptures carry stronger narrative functions: they introduce the story, bring closure to the story, and, in the "television screen" scene from *Will Success Spoil Rock Hunter?*, interrupt the narrative for the purpose of jokingly calling into question its complications and eventual resolution. Unlike the more scattered instances of rupture in the earlier films, Tashlin, in his films with Jayne Mansfield, uses diegetic breakage as a structuring device. The result of assigning the rupturing responsibilities to the more rational characters is that these pictures possess a greater degree of narrative unity than any other of Tashlin's films.

Sex and (Ambivalent) Satire

Despite the relatively weaker personae of his leads in both *The Girl Can't Help It* and *Will Success Spoil Rock Hunter?*, Tashlin does craft several satirical jokes in both films around a split between gag and narrative. *The Girl Can't Help It*, set in the milieu of New York's music industry, is packed with performances by some of the leading (and lesser) lights of 1950s rock music. In the course of the film, we see and hear performances by such top-notch acts as Little Richard, Fats Domino, Abbey Lincoln, and Gene Vincent, as well as such less-remembered artists as The Chuckles, Johnny Olenn, and Nino Tempo. In most cases, these performers do not interact with the other characters, and the performances themselves have little or no bearing on the characters' actions. These musical numbers are not, in themselves, gags, but they do break somewhat with narrative unity in that they do not advance the film's story.[19]

Nowhere is Tashlin's tendency toward satirical ambivalence more apparent than in the musical scenes in *The Girl Can't Help It*. These scenes are moments of aesthetic pleasure as well as moments of pop-culture satire. For Tashlin, such artists as Little Richard and The Chuckles embody the energy and authenticity of rock 'n' roll, but also the music's (and, even more so, the music industry's) inherent tackiness, exploitativeness, and ridiculousness. The Eddie Cochran number, "Twenty-Flight Rock," is perhaps the best example.

Cochran performs his song on Peter Potter's televised talent show, and the stage is dressed in spartan fashion: a blue-gray curtain as a backdrop, and no props save Cochran's suitcase-sized amplifier; the singer is lit by a single spotlight. He wears plain black shoes, loose blue pants, a blue collared shirt with white stripes, and a very large beige sportcoat with enormously padded shoulders. Besides his modest pompadour, the only thing that identifies Cochran as a rock star is his signature huge, cherry-red Gretsch guitar.

As Fats himself points out, Cochran's singing style is a strange one. His voice is fairly deep, and he sings in hiccup-like fits and starts. Cochran hunches his shoulders up to his ears as he darts his eyes rapidly from left to right and jerks his body back and forth. The arrangement of the song itself is quite spare, with Cochran's plucked, thick guitar shuffling atop a click-clack drumbeat. The lyrics of the song tell a humorous story of modern teenage love: a young man loves a woman who lives in a twentieth-floor apartment, but her building's elevator is broken, forcing him to climb the stairs. "When I get to the top," Cochran sings, "I'm too tired to rock," where "rock" carries the usual double sexual meaning. The song is a lament for misplaced physical activity: he climbs stairs when he should be having sex.

In many ways, Cochran's performance is presented as "authentic": the lyrics humorously address a "problem" of modern teenage life, the song's beat derives genuinely and unabashedly from the African-American blues tradition,[20] and Cochran is received warmly by both the TV audience and Fats himself. On the other hand, the very fact of the televised performance indicates the crass commercialization of a young and promising art form, and the show's host is little more than a modern-day carnival barker. Tashlin's treatment of rock and roll is complicated: it is both vulgar and authentic, appealing and cheap, genuinely exciting and already overhyped. It is precisely this kind of ambiguous cultural satire that marks Tashlin's mature style.

The theme of the corrupt and vacuous nature of the American culture industry recurs in numerous other scenes in *The Girl Can't Help It*. It is introduced in the film's opening scene, when Ewell's words "the music that expresses the culture, the refinement, and the polite grace

Figure 5.9 A memorable sight gag in *The Girl Can't Help It*

of the present day" are completely drowned out by Little Richard's sudden, high-volume rendition of the title song. Several other scenes also address this theme: Miller suffers a beating at the hands of Wheeler's music-industry goons; Jerri makes it to the top of the charts by imitating a siren's wail (a situation emphasized by one of Tashlin's finest visual gags: a shot of the sheet music Jerri uses in her recording session [Figure 5.9]); Fats's and Mousie's use of strong-arm tactics to drive Jerri's ridiculous song to the top of the charts. Such events do not portray the music industry in an especially favorable light. Tashlin himself worked within the very entertainment industry that he subjected to vicious satire, but this does not compromise his polemic.

A quasi-diegetic scene in *Will Success Spoil Rock Hunter?* addresses many of the same themes. The film's opening credits consist of a series of clever mock-commercials. A heavily bearded man tells us that the Handy Dandy Dandy electric razor can shave the fuzz off of an overripe peach, and then proceeds to lose the device in his extensive beard; a woman extols the virtues of Tres Chic Shampoo, but loses huge hanks of hair to a few brushstrokes; an overeager woman pitches Wow, a dishwashing detergent with Fallout, "the exclusive, patented ingredient," as her sink rapidly overflows with voluminous foam. The commercials are separate from the narrative proper, but the satire within them is of a piece with that of the body of the story. These inherently ridiculous advertisements dishonestly pitch useless or fraudulent products, but they are only slightly more dishonest, useless, and fraudulent than any advertisements for Stay-Put Lipstick. In the first scene of the narrative proper, Rock proposes to Rufus his latest idea for the Stay-Put campaign: three chickens that extol the product's virtues in song. Rufus himself proposes a number of absurd ad ideas: a Stay-Put-sponsored nationwide teen kissing contest, complete with "osculation booth"; a new line of lipsticks flavored with gin, scotch, and Manischewitz.

Presented, as they are, outside of the story, the mock-commercials are satirical barbs unencumbered by narrative association; they are fully unintegrated. Tashlin reserves his funniest and most vicious gags about the advertising industry for this quasi-diegetic scene.

Interestingly, the satire of the mock commercials scene (which attacks the advertising industry, the foolish people who believe its claims, the medium of television, and, most broadly, the fraudulent nature of the entire American consumer economy) is *not* ambivalent in the way that the rock 'n' roll numbers in *The Girl Can't Help It* are ambivalent. For Tashlin, rock music is a genuine form of creative expression, even if it is somewhat hollow and vulgar. Advertising, however, receives no such backhanded compliment: these commercials are shrill, vacuous, and dishonest, and the products they hawk are cheap and ineffective in the extreme: neither the ads nor the products have any redeeming qualities. Indeed, this is a recurring theme in Tashlin's work, stretching all the way back to his print cartoons in the early 1930s.

This ambivalent satire does exist in *Will Success Spoil Rock Hunter?*, but it is not aimed at consumerism. As he does in *The Girl Can't Help It*, Tashlin uses Jayne Mansfield as an object of aesthetic pleasure as well as an object of ridicule. Rita Marlowe, despite her shallowness, is a sympathetic figure. As the story progresses, we come to understand that Rita's misplaced love for Rock Hunter is a result of her being manipulated by her studio's publicity department. So thoroughly do they control every aspect of her life that even *she* begins to believe that "Lover Doll" is her one true love. Rita is the film's emblem of superficiality, but it is only because she doesn't know any better. Tashlin ridicules anyone foolish enough to buy into the empty promises of the advertising industry, and in many ways Rita is the ultimate dupe, since she has bought into the advertisements about herself. But Tashlin does not treat her cruelly.

When she is finally reunited with her long-lost love Georgie Schmidlapp, Rita is lifted from the world of artifice into a life of genuine happiness, and we feel happy for her.

However, Tashlin will not let us get off that easily, as a grim ambivalence permeates even Rita's reunion with Georgie, a scene that offers a summary of the state of Tashlin's fully formed style.

The film's penultimate scene (there is a brief epilogue) takes place during the Stay-Put Lipstick TV spectacular, hosted by Rita Marlowe, Stay-Put's new spokeswoman. At the start of the show, Rita emerges from behind a curtain to address the camera—ostensibly, the TV camera shooting the show. She says, in part,

> Because this is my first live television appearance, the sponsor has agreed to relinquish his commercial time. There will be no mention of Stay-Put Lipsticks, nor Stay-Put Lipstick's wonderful Stay-Put colors, such as Stay-Put Lipstick Red, Stay-Put Lipstick Pink, Stay-Put Lipstick Flame, Stay-Put Lipstick Crimson, Stay-Put Lipstick Magenta, Stay-Put Lipstick Devil Red. These are wonderful lipsticks I personally use for my oh-so-kissable lips—that you will not be hearing about.

Her rapid pronunciation of this ad-writer's copy serves three purposes. First, it impresses upon us that Tashlin could extract great talent from his performers, as these are difficult words to speak rapidly. A second, related purpose is that it demonstrates Tashlin's interest in sonic humor: the fast pace and repetitive nature of her dialogue is itself a source of comedy. Finally, her monologue is a satirical comment about the cheap, obvious ways that 1950s advertisers planted sales pitches within the body of television programs.

Before the show can begin, who should appear on the stage but Georgie Schmidlapp (Groucho Marx[21]), who, to Rita's surprise and delight, emerges from nowhere to say, "Rita—I love you!" Rita, astonished, says, "Oh, and I love you, Georgie, but why did you wait so long to tell me? You know, you never even tried to kiss me!" Georgie replies, "I never could get that close," and then looks into the camera and flashes his eyebrows. As Groucho turns his back to the camera to embrace Mansfield, we see that embedded in the back of his jacket is a glowing neon sign that reads "Stay-Put Lipstick."

A great many of Tashlin's aesthetic interests come together in this, the penultimate scene of his best film. With the appearance of Groucho Marx, Tashlin cements his fondness for both vaudeville humor and performance-based humor. Part of Groucho's familiar persona, and part of the vaudeville aesthetic, is direct address.[22] When Groucho looks into the camera and rapidly flashes his signature eyebrow-raising gesture, he is both shattering the fourth wall and acknowledging the comic lineage that runs from vaudeville through Tashlin, and on into the early days of television. The scene is also another important example of Tashlin's challenging of the conventional Hollywood ending.

Also present is the sexual humor for which Tashlin is so well known. The gag about not being able to get close to Rita refers to Jayne Mansfield's bust size. With this scene, Tashlin again skirts the censors. This time, he accomplished the task by manipulating his shooting schedule. According to Howard Prouty, the scene was filmed on June 10, 1957 — five days *after* the PCA issued its formal approval of the film in the form of Certificate #18548.[23] This was not a matter of shooting a scene in such a way as to make its replacement or censorship extremely difficult; here, Tashlin actually added a brief but very important scene to the film *after* PCA approval had already been granted. The Schmidlapp scene clearly contains potentially objectionable material. It is unclear exactly how Tashlin managed to obtain the approval to include the scene, but it is a mark of his boldness — and, perhaps, of his recklessness — that he included it at all.

Finally, the joke about the neon sign in Georgie's suit jacket synthesizes Tashlin's approach both to visual humor and to satire. The presence of the sign, in itself, is a fine sight gag, as it is completely unexpected. But the gag is richer than this. As argued above, Rita Marlowe is a sympathetic character who is rescued by Georgie's unexpected appearance from a publicist-planned life. We are pleased that Rita can now quit her manufactured life and be happy with her new love. But it is not so simple as that: even her first moment of true happiness in years is sponsored — in flashing neon — by the Stay-Put Lipstick Company. Rita is not truly able to free herself from her prefabricated life, since the love that redeems her is itself predicated on advertising, the film's ultimate symbol of tawdriness and corruption.

The "Stay-Put Lipstick Spectacular" scene epitomizes the coming together of the many facets of Tashlin's directorial style. This artistic convergence is the hallmark of the peak phase of Tashlin's style, of which *Will Success Spoil Rock Hunter?* is itself the high-water mark. Subsequent Tashlin features, detailed in the next chapter, tap into these same familiar features of Tashlin's style, but combine them to lesser degrees.

6 DISORDERLY CONDUCT TASHLIN IN THE 1960S

ashlin's films are strongly identified with the 1950s. Authors such as Ed Sikov, Dirk Lauwaert, and Robert Sklar see Tashlin as the embodiment of certain of that decade's sensibilities.[1] Curvaceous women, bold colors, rock music, a sexuality that bubbles just barely below the surface—these are often cited as the hallmarks not only of Tashlin's style but the American 1950s aesthetic.

However, the fact that certain mid-century aesthetic tendencies appear to crystallize in Tashlin's films has little to do with some 1950s zeitgeist. It relates to the arc of Tashlin's artistic achievements and the critical reception of his films. In *The Girl Can't Help It* and *Will Success Spoil Rock Hunter?*, Tashlin combines and permutes his many stylistic and comic interests in a richer, more compelling manner than any of his other films. Tashlin made thirteen features after *Will Success Spoil Rock Hunter?*, some of which are quite good, but none of which so creatively address the director's major aesthetic concerns as do the Mansfield pictures. Tashlin's best films have come to represent his style in general. It is a legacy in which he could take pride, but it is not a complete or accurate picture of the breadth of his style. This chapter looks in detail at two of Tashlin's later features (*The Disorderly Orderly* and *Bachelor Flat*), as well as several other 1960s Tashlin films, and compares them to the films he made at his creative zenith.

Dis/Integration:
The Man from the Diners' Club and *Cinderfella*

None of Tashlin's later films approaches the level of gag/narrative integration in *The Girl Can't Help It* or *Will Success Spoil Rock Hunter?*, but neither do they possess the disconnected nature of *Speaking of the Weather* or *Have You Got Any Castles?* (Such disjointedness is far easier to sustain in a seven-minute cartoon than in a feature-length film.) *The Man from the Diners' Club* and *Cinderfella* illustrate the range of narrative/comic strategies in Tashlin's late features.

In one scene in *The Man from the Diners' Club*, Ernie (Danny Kaye) impersonates a masseur and physically harasses his effete boss. This extended gag serves a crucial narrative purpose: Ernie administers an especially vigorous and messy massage in order to prevent his boss from realizing that Ernie is not at the office. The funniest part of the gag—Ernie liberally dousing his boss's face with baby powder and liniment (Figure 6.1a)—is also important to the story: if the man's eyes are caked over, he will be unable to recognize his assailant.

Tashlin uses a similar strategy in a scene in which Ernie attempts to retrieve a card from a room-sized, threatening computer. The scene is a showcase for the broad antics of Danny Kaye, former *tummler*: Ernie's tie gets caught in the gears of the machine, and he contorts his body to extricate himself. The climax of the scene occurs when the computer spews out thousands of punchcards, causing Ernie to gesticulate wildly in the vain hope of finding the one card he needs (Figure 6.1b). Again, though, the gag is not solely a forum for Kaye's skills: Ernie's failure to find the card is the event that sets the rest of the story in motion. These two scenes are the exceptions: most of the comic scenes in *The Man from the Diners' Club* do not advance the narrative.

Tashlin opts for a different method of gag/narrative integration in *Cinderfella*, possibly the most uneven of his films. This film relies heavily on showcase scenes: isolated moments of performative comedy that highlight a star's talents but have, at best, tenuous connections to the film's plot. In showcase scenes from earlier in his career, such as the massage-table scene in *Artists and Models*, Tashlin maintains a balance: he highlights his performer's special talents but still fits the scenes into the film's narrative matrix. The showcase scenes in *Cinderfella*, however, are representative of a trend in Tashlin's later films toward less integration of gag and narrative. Were they to be removed from *Cinderfella*, the film's plot would barely be affected. In fact, nearly all of the humor in the film is to be found in the showcase scenes; few of the scenes that advance the narrative are also comic. In other words, the showcase scenes serve a key generic function: without them, *Cinderfella*, already a strange hybrid of comedy and melodrama, could not properly be considered a comedy at all.

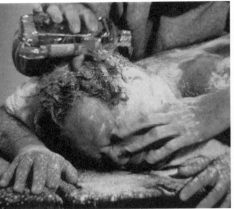 

Figure 6.1 *The Man from the Diners' Club*: Ernie torments his boss with talc and liniment; Danny Kaye in a hail of punchcards

One scene in particular illustrates the film's strategy of gag/narrative integration. By himself in the kitchen, Fella (Jerry Lewis) listens to a radio broadcast of the Count Basie Orchestra. The gag consists of Lewis's elaborate mimicry of the actions of nearly all the members of the band: with only his face, body, and vivid imagination, he plays drums, saxophone, piano, and other instruments. The "imaginary band" scene is one of the purest instances of a showcase scene in all of Tashlin's films, as it has precisely nothing to do with the rest of the film's story—the scene is plainly designed to highlight Lewis's gifts for timing and mimicry.[2]

Such performative skills have been fundamental to Lewis's comedy since his one-man shows as a teenager in the early 1940s. In his "record act," the young Lewis, billing himself, rather puzzlingly, as a performer of "satirical impressions in pantomimicry," would eccentrically lip- and body-synch along with recordings of popular tunes of the day.[3] Scenes of such pantomimicry appear in other Tashlin films (*Who's Minding the Store?* features a particularly inspired scene of Lewis musically tapping away on an imaginary typewriter), as well as Lewis-directed films, such as the scene in 1961's *The Errand Boy* in which Lewis plays at being "Chairman of the Board" while gesticulating musically. That we can find this Lewisian performative staple in Tashlin films strongly suggests a collaborative authorship, a concept especially relevant to understanding the director's 1960s films.

It is useful to compare the "imaginary band" scene from *Cinderfella* to the scene of Georgie Schmidlapp's appearance from *Will Success Spoil Rock Hunter?* I argue in the previous chapter that the Schmidlapp scene represents all of the essential elements of Tashlin's style coming together: performance-based comedy, sight gags, sonic humor, sexual humor, diegetic rupture, and ambivalent satire. Moreover, the scene is not only fully integrated into the film's narrative, but humorously ties up a number of loose ends in the story. The joke depends on the narrative, but the narrative also depends on the joke.

The scene of musical mimicry from *Cinderfella* is representative of Tashlin's late feature style in that it demonstrates the diminished presence of several of Tashlin's major aesthetic and comic concerns. Tashlin's emphases on comic performance, visual non-gags, and sonic humor come through very clearly in this scene, but it is not complicated or enriched by sexual humor, satire (ambivalent or otherwise), diegetic rupture, or, perhaps most crucially, the dynamic of narrative integration.

Authorship and "The Jerry Lewis Question"

Lewis himself is of vital importance to the latter period of Tashlin's career. But the Jerry Lewis whom Tashlin directed in *Artists and Models* and *Hollywood or Bust* was, in many ways, not the same performer he directed in *Rock-a-Bye Baby, The Geisha Boy, Cinderfella, It's Only Money, Who's Minding the Store?*, and *The Disorderly Orderly*. After his split with Dean Martin, Lewis altered his persona radically, bringing to the fore a latent sentimentality and combining it, occasionally awkwardly, with his trademark nutty behavior. This important change crystallized in Lewis's first solo film, *The Delicate Delinquent* (1957, Don McGuire), and crucially informs the six films he went on to make with Tashlin.

Frank Krutnik identifies the Martin-Lewis split in 1956 as the origin of the sentimental dimension of the Lewis persona, and Lewis's solo films, beginning with *The Delicate Delinquent*, do evince a pronounced sentimentality.[4] Lewis himself has said, "At heart I really belong to the old school which believed that screen comedy is essentially a combination of situation, sadness and gracious humility," and that he hoped to "capture the same warm, sympathetic quality which Chaplin and a few others had."[5] As Krutnik astutely notes, some of the Martin and Lewis films feature a put-upon Jerry who commands our sympathy. "Films such as *The Caddy, Scared Stiff, The Stooge*, and *Living It Up* teased with the Lewis figure's status as a harassed misfit, but the poignancy had always been trammeled."[6]

Lewis's biographer Shawn Levy writes, "[*The Delicate Delinquent*] is, in fact, a transitional film, and its varied tones and dependence on a variety of genres only proves its intermediate status."[7] This perception of the film was echoed by the popular press of the day; *Variety* called *The Delicate Delinquent* "slapstick blended with pathos and some straight melodrama tossed in,"[8] and Bosley Crowther of *The New York Times* referred to a "certain sobriety" in "the new Mr. Lewis," and remarked that the film's eccentric comedy might dilute the genuineness of its message.[9] The most plainly sentimental scene in *The Delicate Delinquent* occurs when Sidney (Lewis), in an alleyway at night, contemplates his existence and sings the hushed, melodramatic song of loneliness "By Myself." The film's romantic subplot, in which Sidney falls for Patricia (Mary Webster), is handled with none of the flailing immaturity that typically marks Lewis's characters' infatuations with women.

In losing Martin, Lewis lost a straight man (with fine comic timing), a singer of songs, and a performer who could carry a romantic subplot. As early as *The Delicate Delinquent*, Lewis assumed these responsibilities himself, with, generally speaking, a diminished degree of success. The "handsome man and a monkey"[10] dynamic that made Martin and Lewis so successful was reduced to a less conventional and less successful "melodramatic monkey" model, which had significant structural implications for Lewis's post-Martin films. Lewis's assuming of both the comic and the romantic/melodramatic roles is a root cause of the modular structures of such later Tashlin films as *Cinderfella*, *The Disorderly Orderly* and *Who's Minding the Store?*

The success of *The Delicate Delinquent* proved the viability of Lewis's new persona. The film was made for $460,000 and eventually grossed about $7 million—a fifteen-fold return on investment.[11] So important was Lewis to Paramount that, by 1959, he was the only A-list performer to remain under exclusive contract, and was guaranteed $10 million for fourteen films over seven years.[12] The sentimental dimension of his persona was further developed in three Tashlin films: *Rock-a-Bye Baby*, *The Geisha Boy*, and *Cinderfella*.[13] *Cinderfella* once again provides a useful example of the ways in which the two artists influenced each other.

For every one of Lewis's comic scenes in *Cinderfella*, he appears in at least one sentimental scene. Just as he does in *The Delicate Delinquent*,

Lewis's character often laments his insignificance, and performs a lachrymose musical number about the same subject. The last scene in the film, in which Fella and the princess (Anna Maria Alberghetti) finally fall for each other, contains no elements of comedy. Rather, both Lewis and Alberghetti play the scene with misty eyes and forlorn expressions—a far cry from the satirical romantic ending of *Artists and Models*.[14]

Cinderfella is a complicated example, since questions about its authorship remain. Howard Prouty cites Lewis's oft-repeated version of the story: *Cinderfella* was slated for release in the summer of 1960, but Lewis insisted that, as a family film, it should be released at Christmas. Writes Howard Prouty, "Paramount agreed to the rescheduling after [Lewis] promised to deliver another picture to fill their summer slot."[15] The picture Lewis delivered was *The Bellboy*, his first directorial effort (and a fascinating film). *Cinderfella* was the first film made under the aegis of Jerry Lewis Pictures Corp., and it was Lewis's first real opportunity to formally exercise a sizable degree of creative control over one of his projects. Anecdotal evidence suggests that Lewis seized this opportunity, making *Cinderfella* a locus of the debate over the authorship of the Tashlin-Lewis films. Prouty writes that Lewis "appears to have cut about nine minutes" from the film; Claire Johnston and Paul Willemen assert that Lewis "drastically altered the structure of Tashlin's script by cutting most of Tashlin's gags. In this way, the film might perhaps better be regarded as belonging to the Jerry Lewis oeuvre than to Tashlin's."[16] David Ehrenstein makes a similar claim, adding that Lewis made the changes against Tashlin's wishes.[17] The exact nature of Tashlin's and Lewis's on-set responsibilities remains obscure (Ehrenstein admits that "separating Frank Tashlin from Jerry Lewis once and for all is just about impossible"[18]), but the anecdotal evidence suggests that Lewis, at the very least, used *Cinderfella* as a dry run for his directorial début.

Lewis's transition from star to director/star is the other major change in his post-Martin film career. His first star was himself, a fact that allowed him to further develop his sentimental persona. Moreover, with the important exception of *The Nutty Professor* (1963), the first half-dozen of Lewis's films as a director are modular in structure, like a vaudeville performance, or like one of Tashlin's "Fox and Crow" cartoons. *The Bellboy* (1960), *The Ladies' Man* (1961), *The Errand Boy* (1961), *The Patsy* (1964), and *The Family Jewels* (1965) are each primarily composed of a series of blackout gags, augmented somewhat uneasily by sentimentalism. These films are minimally concerned with the integration of gags and narratives.

Before proceeding to a discussion of the films themselves, it is important to note that Jerry Lewis is one of the principal reasons that Tashlin occupies a marginal place in the scholarly literature on American film comedy. Lewis's undeniable performative and directorial talents make him a perfectly reasonable candidate for auteur status. The problem is that, in his eight Tashlin films, Lewis was the star (or costar), not the director, and it is the director who is typically anointed the auteur. Lewis's directorial career began squarely in the middle of his career collaboration with Tashlin: by the time of his 1960 directorial debut *The Bellboy*, he had already made four films with Tashlin. For the next four years, Lewis alternated between directing himself and starring for Tashlin; for the latter half of their shared film career, Tashlin was directing a fellow member of the Directors' Guild. By making auteurist exceptions for Jerry Lewis, critics have diminished Tashlin's creative role in the Tashlin/Lewis films. By the early 1960s, Tashlin was known largely as a director of subpar, highly sentimental Jerry Lewis films. As a result, Tashlin's critical reputation has suffered.

The problem gets more complicated. When Jerry Lewis was a popular, bankable movie star, and when his reputation among critics was at its zenith—a period from, approximately, the early 1950s through the mid-1960s—his talent and presence often overshadowed those of Tashlin, the man who, Lewis freely admits, taught him much that he knows about directing. "[Tashlin's] knowledge of comedy far surpassed that of any director I had ever worked with," Lewis writes. "What I learned from him couldn't be bought at any price, because there is no college in the world where they can teach you how to think funny."[19] But when Lewis's reputation started its lengthy nosedive in the mid-1960s in both America and Europe, Tashlin went down with him.

Andrew Sarris has written, "What little Tashlin cult interest there was has now [in 1968] shifted almost entirely to Jerry Lewis, actor-director extraordinary."[20] This shift is nowhere more apparent than in Sarris's own milestone book *The American Cinema*, in which Tashlin merits but a page in the "Expressive Esoterica" section, and warrants little more than an oblique dismissal: "Tashlin sounds better than he plays. One can approve vulgarity in theory as a comment on vulgarity, but in practice all vulgarity is inseparable."[21] On the other hand, Sarris's detailed, appreciative essay on Lewis (in the "Make Way for the Clowns!" section) is over five pages long.[22] Though he is not explicit in answering the multiple-author question, Sarris comes down pretty obviously on the side of Lewis. He argues that, to the critics who matter most, a Jerry Lewis film is a Jerry Lewis film, regardless of who was behind the camera. When Tashlin directed Lewis, the film belonged to Jerry the auteur.

The Disorderly Comedian

To return to the subject of Lewis's relatively small interest in the integration of gags and narrative, *The Errand Boy* provides an excellent illustration. The film's premise is that the board of directors of Paramutual [sic] Pictures assigns Morty S. Tashman (Lewis, in a nod to his mentor) the job of going undercover within the studio, assuming various studio jobs with the purpose of studying the efficiency of Paramutual's many departments. Once mentioned in the first scene, however, this premise is effectively abandoned, and the film becomes a vehicle for a string of unrelated, isolated gags concerning the goings-on at a movie studio. In a representative nine-minute span, Morty disrupts the filming of a musical number, then angers his boss in the studio mailroom, then finds himself trapped in an elevator packed with cigar-smokers and gum-chewers. None of these gags has anything to do with any of the others; as they occur, not even the smallest mention is made of the studio's efficiency. As a director, Lewis pushed to extremes the use of a modular, gag-based narrative structure.

Tashlin, more than Lewis, was interested in exploring the relationship between gag and narrative. However, Tashlin was a less important player for Paramount than was his star. The clout Lewis had accumulated as a star and a director, coupled with his interest in modular gags and sentimentality, may partially explain the fact that at least three of his Tashlin films — *Rock-a-Bye Baby*, *Who's Minding the Store?* and *The Disorderly Orderly* — resemble fairly strongly the films Lewis directed. These films unfold as if pulled by two divergent forces: Lewis's interests in sentimentality and modularity, and Tashlin's interests in bawdy humor and creative explorations of the gag/narrative axis. These films are hybrids, the most vexing cases in the Tashlin/Lewis authorship question.

Modular structures were by no means unfamiliar to Tashlin. However, by the time of his Mansfield films, he had generally moved away from narrative modularity. Lewis, in fact, gives a particularly zany performance in *The Disorderly Orderly*, demonstrating once again that no one—not even Lewis himself—knew how to direct him better than Tashlin. The film is both modular in structure and somewhat sentimental, but is not without its moments of madcap comedy. For these and many other reasons, *The Disorderly Orderly* is an important film of the latter portion of Tashlin's feature career.

The Disorderly Orderly concerns, among other things, unrequited love and suicidal despondency; a synopsis of its plot does not play out as that of a comedy. In fact, the film's plot is an ideal vehicle for Lewis's reconfigured persona. Though Lewis is assuredly the film's central comic figure, he is also the center of its pathos. Many scenes have a distinctly non-comic tone: in a flashback, Jerome (Lewis) cries at seeing Susan (Susan Oliver), the object of his affections, embrace another man; when he learns that Susan will recover from a suicide attempt, Jerome looks heavenward and whispers, "You did good." Most prominently, Jerome undertakes many acts of anonymous personal sacrifice for the benefit of Susan—a story device plucked from the plot of many a melodrama. Curiously, these pathetic scenes alternate fairly regularly with the film's comic scenes, in which Lewis's performance is, often, unusually unrestrained.

An analysis of a comic scene from *The Disorderly Orderly* demonstrates the ways in which its comedy and pathos coexist somewhat uncomfortably; indeed, the scene discussed below immediately precedes one in which Jerome breaks his date with his girlfriend, Julie, so he may stay at Susan's bedside. It also stands in comparison to the massage table scene from *Artists and Models* (as well as to the barbershop scene from Taurog's *You're Never Too Young*), discussed in Chapter Four, on the grounds that they both present comic set pieces in which the Lewis character unintentionally subjects a man to numerous physical indignities. This time, the victim is Milton M. Mealy (Frank J. Scannell), a patient at the hospital at which Jerome is an orderly. The scene begins with Jerome entering Mr. Mealy's room to wake him for breakfast.

Opening the door to Mr. Mealy's room with a loud "GOOD morning, Mr. Mealy!," Jerome bursts in and begins talking a mile a minute; Mr. Mealy remains asleep and immobile. Lewis's voice is childish and patronizing: he speaks like a nine-year-old know-it-all talking down to his classmates. "Up, up, up!" says Lewis, as he claps his hands manically at each word. "Sandman working overtime last night?" Lewis wears a genial smile and walks with a deliberate spring in his step to convey enthusiasm.

Lewis continues the baby-talk: "Look what we have for Mr. Mealy this morning! We have num-nums! Isn't that goody-good-good? Num-nums!" Finally awakened by this overbearing orderly, Mr. Mealy reaches for a coffee cup. This simple action prompts Lewis to burst into a fit of manic — if not maniacal — energy. He looks like nothing so much as a lunatic performing seal as he slaps Mealy's hand away, claps his own hands vigorously five times, and loudly cries, "Ah-ah-ah-ah-ah-ah-ah-ah-AAAH!," meaning, "Don't you touch that cup!" As he caws, Lewis's mouth hangs agape, and he rolls his eyes up into his sockets and lowers his head. The clapping involves his entire upper body: his elbows flap every which way, and he shakes his head from side to side; the last two claps are emphasized by Lewis raising one leg, then the other, to jump in place. This is an inspired bit of madness, and it involves nearly every comic tool Lewis has as a performer: facial gesture, upper and lower body movement, vocal intonation, comic nonsense words. It is Lewis at his most unhinged.

The reason Jerome so emphatically denies his patient a cup of coffee is that he is insistent that Mr. Mealy brush his teeth first. As he singsongily chants, "Not before we brush our teeth," Lewis walks jauntily around the bed, prepares a toothbrush, and sits down on Scannell's right side. Singing, "This is the way we brush our teeth," Lewis proceeds to create a foamy mess all over the face of the still-silent but visibly agitated Mr. Mealy. Moments later, Lewis pauses, confused. He stares into Mr. Mealy's mouth, looks around the room, and says, "All right, where are they?": he can't find his patient's teeth.

The moment at which Jerome discovers Mr. Mealy's dentures in a glass of water on the nightstand marks a shift in Lewis's performance technique. Upon realizing his embarrassing error, Lewis looks directly into the camera (Figure 6.2) and exaggeratedly mouths the following words to the audience: "They're in the glass. [pause] They're in the glass. I didn't know they were in the . . . Did you know? [to Mealy] Did you know they were . . . ? [to camera] He didn't know they were . . ." Lewis contorts his face and scratches his head to denote confusion.

For the rest of the scene, Jerome slowly hunches his way out of the room and offers lame apologies to Mr. Mealy. With a voice rendered soft by shame, Lewis blathers, "Your face contour was such a handsome-

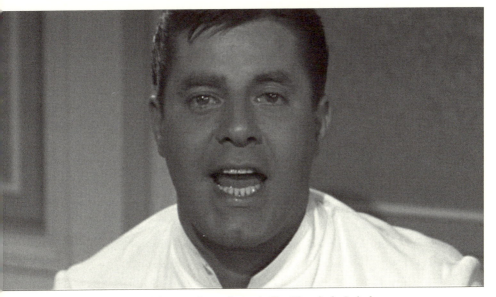

Figure 6.2 Jerry Lewis addresses the audience in *The Disorderly Orderly*

ness, you were dream-adorable, and I never imagined . . . But you could try some of this. It's soft. Lumpy-lump-lump oatmeal. That's very soft to chew." The scene ends when Mealy hurls the bowl at Jerome, who ducks at just the right moment. Offscreen, the bowl hits Jerome's long-suffering foil, Nurse Higgins (Kathleen Freeman), smack in the face.

The scene is a fine example of Lewis's skill at playing off of a straight man. Scannell's utter silence offers humorous counterpoint to Lewis's all-over-the-map yelping. Tashlin has used this type of contrast for comedy before, in, for instance, the breakfast-table scene in *Nasty Quacks*. But the vocal comedy runs even deeper. Early in the scene, Lewis speaks in high-pitched, condescending tones; when he puzzles over the missing teeth, he reverts to a version of his own fairly thick New Jersey accent, so that his line sounds like, "Awright, where ah dey?" The contrast is striking: when his enthusiasm is finally challenged, Jerome drops the act and reverts to his true nature, a change signaled by his speech patterns. (A similar moment occurs in the barbershop scene in *You're Never Too Young*.)

A comparison between the Mr. Mealy scene and the massage table scene from *Artists and Models* is germane, as it points to some of the changes that Tashlin's and Lewis's comic styles had undergone. In both scenes, Tashlin avails himself of Lewis's gift for peculiar phraseology, nonverbal utterances, and the comedy of vocal timbre. As well, in both scenes, part of the comedy derives from the quick change in attitude that the Lewis characters undergo. In *Artists and Models*, Eugene progresses rapidly from humbled to manic to sheepish; in *The Disorderly Orderly*, Jerome progresses from effervescent to puzzled to humiliated. The humor of both scenes derives largely from these quick shifts.

The most telling similarity between the two scenes occurs on the level of the rupture of the diegesis. In *Artists and Models*, Lewis looks into the camera for the briefest of moments, just so that it is noticeable. The Mr. Mealy scene is a model of audience address: Lewis speaks to and asks questions of the film's viewers. In the earlier film, the diegetic rupture is minimal; in the later film, it is pronounced.

Further differences between the two scenes are even more revelatory. The scenes' soundtracks differ in at least one important respect: whereas the massage table scene uses a whimsical musical theme to cue viewers that something humorous has occurred, the Mr. Mealy scene uses no music whatsoever. In fact, the soundtrack is unusually spare: just Lewis's dialogue and the diegetic sounds of walking, hopping, and toothbrushing. Tashlin uses sound effects only at the end of the scene: a *whoosh* accentuates the oatmeal bowl's flight, and is immediately followed by a loud, wet crash to indicate that, beyond the frame edge, it has hit Nurse Higgins. The absence of all other sounds—coupled with Scannell's utter silence—highlights the importance of Lewis's vocalized comedy to this scene. That Tashlin allows Lewis to carry the Mr. Mealy scene with no sonic assistance indicates, perhaps, an increased comfort with and confidence in the actor's abilities—a plausible situation, as this was Tashlin's and Lewis's eighth (and final) film together. Just as plausibly, it may indicate Lewis's increased creative control: by now, he was a director himself, and might have seen fit to give himself a showcase scene that made the most of his talents.

For most of the massage-table scene, Lewis is prevented from moving his lower body; in the Mr. Mealy scene, his comic gesticulations involve nearly every part of his anatomy. Lewis is both literally and figuratively far more unrestrained in this scene than in the massage table scene, a fact partly attributable to the different narrative situations. However, the increased clout Lewis had attained by this point in his career may have had something to do with it, as well. With more creative control, Lewis could have given himself showcase scenes in which he was able to push his physical comedy to extremes.

As is the case with all but one of the comic scenes in *The Disorderly Orderly*, the Mr. Mealy scene is devoid of sexual humor. This change is rooted in the new, "clean" star image that Jerry Lewis had been cultivating since shortly after making *Artists and Models*. Tashlin downplays impossible humor, too, in the Mr. Mealy scene, whereas it is one of the most important dimensions of the humor in the massage table scene. The only semi-impossible gag occurs when the toothless Mr. Mealy uses his "strong gums" to snap off the head of the toothbrush. Tashlin uses a fair amount of impossible humor elsewhere in the film—Jerome's thumb catches on fire from an especially vigorous snap, another character's broken ankle swells in seconds to three times its girth—but does not do so here. Lewis's performance is very clearly the focus of the scene's comedy.

The two most important things about the scene with Mr. Mealy are that Lewis's performance is so unrestrained, and that the scene could be removed in its entirety without affecting the film's narrative. (Recall that the massage table scene derives its humor from a key story point: Eugene's obsession with comic books.) The Mr. Mealy scene is a classic showcase scene, and could be removed wholesale from the film without affecting narrative events whatsoever.

With a few key exceptions (two scenes with a hypochondriacal patient whose every ailment also affects Jerome, the ankle-breaking scene, the climactic chase) none of the film's many comic scenes advances the narrative in any significant way. The film is full of stand-alone comic scenes, in several of which Tashlin crafts sonic gags. At one point, Jerome dons a stethoscope and listens to his own heartbeat, which *boings* and pops like a malfunctioning alarm clock when a pretty nurse walks by—the only mildly sexual gag in the entire film. Another comic set piece has Jerome approach a fountain bearing the sign "Pure Mineral Water." He takes a drink, and we hear what sounds like rocks rattling around in a metal can—an audio pun on "mineral." (Tashlin shoots this gag in a single forty-two-second take: the epitome of the stand-alone joke.) Another stand-alone sonic gag occurs when Jerome, while in one of the hospital's quiet zones, bites into an apple, and the ensuing crunch is so outrageously loud that it brings all nearby activity to a halt.

In one unusual gag, Tashlin presents four shots of sets of wind chimes, swaying in the wind and clinking musically. The fifth shot is of a medical skeleton hanging from a hook, its bones rattling musically. Tashlin is not "saying anything" about the wind chimes or the skeleton; he simply draws a mildly humorous association. A number of other stand-alone scenes feature impossible comedy. In one, Jerome is dispatched to repair the television in a patient's room: its screen shows only static, or "snow." When Jerome opens up the TV, a blizzard erupts from within it, filling the room with blinding snow of the frozen-water variety (Figure 6.3a). A later set piece has Jerome tending to the unfortunate Mr. Bryant, a man in a full-body cast who Jerome figures would benefit from some fresh air. As he is setting up a lounge chair for his patient, Jerome bumps into Mr. Bryant, sending him rolling down a grassy hill. Disrupting picnickers and sunbathers, Mr. Bryant's journey only comes to a halt when he crashes into a tree: the cast shatters, revealing absolutely nothing inside. Mr. Bryant has somehow vanished, leaving only an empty, shattered shell. Jerome is understandably perplexed (Figure 6.3b).

Tashlin also uses the film's comic set pieces as occasions for diegetic ruptures. The first scene in the movie is a prologue that, like those in *The Girl Can't Help It* and *Will Success Spoil Rock Hunter?*, stands partially outside of the diegesis. In this three-minute scene, Jerry Lewis appears in three different vignettes: first, he is a spineless soldier, then an acrophobic alpinist, and finally a squeamish surgeon. Each of these characters, when faced with a difficult situation, runs screaming for his mother. Assembled moments later on a stage, the three characters await their inclusion in the upcoming narrative: a voiceover narrator says, "Will the real hero of this movie please fall down?" Jerry the would-be doctor collapses, thus commencing the story of this particular disorderly orderly. The funniest diegetic rupture in the film may be the simplest. In an attempt to bandage a bedridden patient, Jerome manages to wrap surgical tape around the patient, himself, and the nurse who assists him. His bewildering incompetence prompts the nurse to stare, deadpan, directly into the camera, as if to ask of the audience, "Can you believe this idiot?" (Figure 6.4a).

On only one occasion in the film does Tashlin break diegetic unity in a non-comic scene. Dining in a restaurant with Jerome, Julie gets upset

Figure 6.3 Sight gags in *The Disorderly Orderly*

Figure 6.4 *The Disorderly Orderly*: Acknowledging the audience; product placement and self-referentiality

about his affection for Susan. She leaves the restaurant and runs across the street, where there happens to be a travel agency. Jerome joins her, comforts her, and they go back inside, but the camera lingers on the display in the plate-glass window. We see an advertisement for TWA's in-flight movies, one of which is *The Disorderly Orderly* (Figure 6.4b).[23] This moment of self-referentiality is the only one in the film, rendering it, arguably, out of place.

The fact that the great majority of Lewis's comic set pieces in *The Disorderly Orderly* are not integrated into the narrative is the principal reason that the film resembles one directed by Lewis himself. By the late 1950s, it appears that Tashlin's interest in this particular narrative option had run its course, but Lewis's strong personality and directorial interests probably had a great deal to do with *The Disorderly Orderly*'s lesser degree of integration. The film possesses a distinctly modular structure, thus more closely resembling *Son of Paleface* than *Will Success*

Figure 6.5 A visual non-gag in *The Disorderly Orderly*

Spoil Rock Hunter? Other Tashlin comedies of this period that do not star Lewis do not feature modular narratives; that he seemed to reserve this strategy for his most famous star is telling, indeed.

Many of the visual gags in *The Disorderly Orderly* are of the same types that Tashlin used throughout his career. One example uses offscreen space: we see an ambulance drive into a tunnel, and hear a screech and a bump; in the next shot, Jerome is perched atop the vehicle's hood. Tashlin uses a very similar joke in *Porky's Road Race*, described in Chapter One. A good example of non-comic visual play occurs in a scene in which an administrator addresses the hospital's board of directors. In a particularly Tati-like cutaway, four of the board members raise cigarettes to their mouths simultaneously (Figure 6.5): a moment of clever *mise-en-scène*, if not out-and-out comedy. Another non-gag occurs when Jerome loads heavy laundry bags onto a cart. As he hefts one of the bags, a man carrying a tray of beverages passes just beneath its arc, narrowly missing getting clobbered but not batting an eye. The gag, which depends purely on blocking and timing, is enhanced by the fact that a laundry cart obscures the man's approach: his very appearance is unexpected, and the near-miss with the bag cleverly accentuates our surprise.

The Disorderly Orderly, along with most of his post-1957 Lewis comedies, deviates significantly from Tashlin's style in that it contains minimal amounts of two of his most important stylistic calling cards: sexual humor and satire. Once again, the lack of these features can be partially explained by the presence of Jerry Lewis.

At this point in his career, the peculiar sexuality of Lewis's persona had been downplayed significantly. His characters were still sexually immature and afraid of women (a tendency crystallized in *The Ladies' Man*), but, in such films as *It's Only Money*, his roles increasingly come to comprise elements of the conventional romantic leading man. The sexually immature man-child of films such as *Artists and Models* had been replaced, by 1957, by gentler, more normal—albeit inexperienced— characters who are genuinely interested in attaining romantic love.

Lewis's persona at the time of *The Disorderly Orderly* afforded Tashlin few opportunities for sexual humor. One small exception is mentioned above: the attractive nurse who makes Jerome's heartbeat race. Interestingly, the concept behind this gag is essentially identical to that behind the gag in *The Girl Can't Help It* in which Jayne Mansfield inspires in three male onlookers all manner of physically impossible displays of lust. Here, however, Lewis's response is far tamer than those of the three onlookers, and the elaborate sight gags have been replaced by a simple sound-effect gag.

Tashlin *could* have designed gags around the sexualities of the film's other performers, but he did not. With the tiny exception of the stethoscope gag, *The Disorderly Orderly* does not even contain the gratuitous nubility for which Tashlin's films are known. It is a very "clean" film, a fact reflected in the film's PCA negotiations, which were entirely unproblematic and do not suggest any difficulties over blue material.[24]

The film is free not only of sexual humor, but of satire. If *The Disorderly Orderly* attacks anything, it is a healthcare system that denies treatment to seriously ill but impoverished patients. But this idea is not important to the film's humor; rather, it is little more than a plot point that sets up Jerome's plan to pay Susan's hospital costs. Other late-period Tashlin-Lewis films, however, do employ this comic mode.

One of the characters in *Rock-a-Bye Baby* is an elderly woman who not only cannot tear herself away from the television, but who purchases every one of the ridiculous products whose advertisements she views. Though she has no genuine need or fondness for Old Chicory-Flavored

Brand Coffee ("No coffee—just flavor!"), Superbo Cigarettes ("Now with a cork tip at one end and a filter tip at the other!"), Burperex tablets ("One little Burperex tablet will keep your tum-tum from going on the dum-dum!"), or Gookum hairspray, she buys them anyway, and uses them the very instant their ads appear. "You know, I believe in loyalty to the sponsor," she says. The two scenes with this character are very similar to the mock commercials in *Will Success Spoil Rock Hunter?*, in that both employ shrill, ludicrous ads to ridicule the American consumer economy, but reserve special distaste for the hapless consumers who fall for these pitches.

The White Virgin of the Nile, the movie-within-the-movie in *Rock-a-Bye Baby*, provides Tashlin with several opportunities to poke fun at his own industry. The wittiest of these is the scene in which a bevy of "Egyptians" performs the film's title number. The men sing in forced baritones, and all of the women, including Marilyn Maxwell (in the title role), sing in exaggerated, high-pitched nasal tones. The song contains such deliberately asinine lines as "Neither Cleo or Bathsheba / Has her tactics to beguile / You can bet your fez / There would be no Suez / Without the White Virgin of the Nile." The dancers are clad in bright-colored loincloths and absurd gold-lamé headdresses, and their dance consists of little more than bent-arm "Egyptian" strutting. Tashlin uses this musical number to ridicule the insipid nature of popular entertainment; more incisively, he uses it to satirize Hollywood's shallowness and cultural insensitivity.

The most extended and effective use of satire in any Tashlin film of the 1960s is that in *Who's Minding the Store?* In its modular structure, it resembles the films Lewis directed, while its continued attacks on consumerism are a Tashlin hallmark. Here, the very device that permits the modular structure is the one that permits the satire. The film is set almost entirely within a department store, and Tashlin uses each successive department—sporting goods, household appliances, and so on—as another opportunity to satirize American consumerism.

But *Rock-a-Bye Baby* and *Who's Minding the Store?* are the exceptions to the rule. Most of Tashlin's 1960s films have few such barbs. Even the isolated scenes of consumerist satire in *Rock-a-Bye Baby* are heavily diluted by the many sentimental scenes of the Jerry Lewis character raising infant triplets. Generally speaking, the humor in Tashlin's 1960s features is less *challenging* than in his earlier features, in that sexual and satirical comedy are less important. These later films contain little of the compelling ambivalence that characterizes the sexual and satirical humor of the Mansfield films. The humor in the 1960s films is gentler and less ribald than that in *Son of Paleface*, *Artists and Models*, and the Mansfield films.

Bachelor Flat: Dachshunds and Dinosaurs

The chief exception to the general claim about the diminished ribaldry in Tashlin's late films is *Bachelor Flat*, one of a small handful of sex farces that Tashlin directed late in his career. A film with nearly no cultural currency, thanks to its nonexistence on video and negligible presence on television, *Bachelor Flat* is an odd film that plays something like an attempt by Tashlin to recapture his earlier comic form.

The plot of *Bachelor Flat* is unusually thin: very little actually *happens*; film time is mostly given over to scenes of bedroom farce and broad comedy. Moreover, certain plotlines peter out without closure or are dropped entirely: its cause-and-effect structure is weak. We never learn whether either of two characters lands the research grant that they speak of often, for instance. Entire characters possess no narrative function whatsoever: the key example here is Paul, a former lover of Helen, one of the principal characters. Paul half-heartedly romances Helen while she is in Paris, but she never takes his advances seriously. He follows her to California, but when Helen reconciles, for reasons unclear, with her fiancé Bruce (Terry-Thomas), Paul simply vanishes from the film.

Certain would-be recurring gags do not pay off. At one point, in an ostensible attempt at a self-reflexive joke, Jessica, a dachshund around whom several gags are crafted, is poised seaside, barking repeatedly. Just before rushing out to the beach, her owner, Mike (Richard Beymer), says to himself, "Four barks? Gotta be Jayne Mansfield!" Presumably, this was intended as but one iteration of a gag that acquires humor only through repetition: the greater the number of barks, the more attractive the woman. But the gag never recurs, leaving the comic premise dangling; this is but one of the more noticeable hints that a fair portion of the film may have been rudely excised. The reference to Mansfield comes off as near-tragic: a forced joke that all but concedes that the director's best years are behind him.

The small degree of gag/narrative integration in *Bachelor Flat* may be

Figure 6.6 *Bachelor Flat*: Female anatomy in widescreen

attributed in part to the relative incohesion of the narrative itself. The film's narrative is so thin as to be more properly called a *premise*: women find Bruce irresistible, a condition that causes him no end of problems. Characters in *Bachelor Flat* have no plain goals. Mike, for instance, is a layabout with no narrative arc of his own; Bruce's "goal" is to marry Helen, but they are already engaged at the beginning of the film and remain that way at its end. *Bachelor Flat*'s gags are seldom integrated with its narrative, precisely because the film's central comic premise supplants the narrative almost entirely. The story is very thin indeed.

On occasion, Tashlin does construct gags with both narrative and visual significance. Perhaps the best of these occurs during the film's opening title sequence, in which credits play over shots of Bruce driving to campus. Tashlin shows Bruce's effect on young women in a series of cleverly composed gags that yoke together the director's interest in sight gags, widescreen comedy, and sexual humor (Figure 6.6). The shots of the lissome appendages of the young women who line these campus avenues are fine examples of Tashlin packing every inch of the widescreen frame with a visual non-gag that is mildly racy and entirely germane to the film's central gag-premise.

Alas for the viewer, the cleverness of these early shots appears very seldom in the film's remaining eighty-three minutes. The film does have its visually witty moments, but they are unintegrated into the film's story, flimsy though it may be. The film's finest comic moment involves a series of shots in which Jessica Dachshund hauls a prized dinosaur bone to the Santa Monica surfside, and there buries it. Tashlin delights in framing these shots (Figure 6.7) so that they humorously emphasize the sausagelike proportions of dog, bone, and CinemaScope frame. This fine gag does not, however, do much in the way of altering the course of the narrative. Moments after Jessica makes off with the bone, Bruce

Figure 6.7 Suitable subjects for scope in *Bachelor Flat*

sees the tracks in the sand and figures out what has happened; moments after that, he recovers the bone. Since the subplot of the dinosaur bone itself has no impact on the outcome of the story, the gags with Jessica Dachshund can hardly affect any narrative events.

Diegetic rupture is simply not present in *Bachelor Flat*. Despite Tashlin's apparent willingness to construct gags—such as the dog-and-bone joke—that would interrupt or otherwise stand apart from narrative, he does not push it any further than this.

Just as it exhibits a diminished degree of gag/narrative integration, *Bachelor Flat*'s quotient of integrated sexual comedy is quite low. This is not to say that there are no sexual gags in the film—there are several—but they, too, are mostly unintegrated, and generally relatively tame compared to some of Tashlin's earlier work. One of the more prominent sexual gags occurs when Bruce, in a show of exasperation, clutches to his chest two breast-shaped dishes as he calls out to Mike to get him a couple of quarts of milk: "You know ... the large size" (Figure 6.8). This somewhat lewd gag is less outrageous than its counterpart, the gag in *The Girl Can't Help It* in which Jayne Mansfield holds two milk bottles in front of her breasts, which is funny on a visual, verbal ("jugs"), associational, and narrative level (Jerri's vain attempts to shed her "sexpot" image). The dishes gag in *Bachelor Flat* possesses only a certain level of visual comedy and a deflected, oblique element of verbal humor. Even if we consider that Bruce's exasperation has been brought about by the youthfully threatening sexuality of Libby (Tuesday Weld), a young boarder he has reluctantly taken in, the film makes it exceedingly clear that Bruce is in no way attracted to Libby. Indeed, when he dreams of her, his thoughts run to worries about her safety and her future. The dishes gag, in other words, possesses no particular sexual *meaning* beyond its obvious visual comedy.

Figure 6.8 *Bachelor Flat*: Terry-Thomas evokes Jayne Mansfield

For a film about sex, *Bachelor Flat* contains a surprisingly small amount of Tashlin's trademark racy humor. Most such gags have simply to do with the amply proportioned Gladys Schmidlapp (Francesca Bellini), who at one point jiggles near-manically as she attempts to eat a slab of cake while lying across a vibrating massage table. Most of the film's sex jokes are about sex without being especially bawdy. Many women throw themselves at Bruce, but these moments are not so much gags as reiterations of the film's central premise. In the film's two extended comic set pieces (one in which Bruce hides both Libby and Gladys in his bedroom, another in which Bruce drunkenly chases a number of women around the beach), the humor arises from sight gags, and from clever *mise-en-scène* manipulations. Though concerned with sexual impropriety, neither scene contains any moments of Tashlinian ribaldry.[25] Within the context of Tashlin's style, these scenes are most notable for their evocation of the clever blocking and farcical situations of vaudeville and silent-film comedy.

In *Bachelor Flat*, none of Tashlin's familiar targets—consumer culture, pop culture, Hollywood glitz, sexual mores—receives any of the brickbats that he had earlier hurled with such gusto. Even one of Tashlin's very favorite victims, the all-too-pat "Hollywood ending," gets off unscathed. Indeed, the abruptness with which the film ends—and the utter lack of ambiguity with which all parts fit into place—shows that

Bachelor Flat is, precisely, the kind of film whose pat ending would formerly have been the object of Tashlin's satirical jibes.

In its dearth of bawdy humor and satire, and its nonexistent sonic humor, and in its relative disintegration of gag and narrative, *Bachelor Flat* is some distance removed from Tashlin's mid-1950s peak. It demonstrates, perhaps better than any other of his films, that for Tashlin's style to flourish, he needed a solid narrative structure onto which he could fasten his gags. Considered alongside some of his other 1960s features, *Bachelor Flat* suggests one of several ways in which Tashlin's style underwent a period of disintegration.

The Declining Career of Director Tashlin: The Last Films

I have argued that Tashlin's 1960s features generally evince somewhat gentler comedy: lesser amounts of ribaldry and Tashlin's customarily ambiguous satire. This is not to say, however, that these films do not bear the marks of his authorship. The following section uses selected examples from several of Tashlin's 1960s features to determine which elements of the Tashlin style rise to the surface, and which become somewhat submerged. Rather than go through each film in chronological order, this section moves among these later films freely, treating them as a unit unto themselves. The films addressed in this section are the last ten of Tashlin's career, from *Cinderfella* (1960) to *The Private Navy of Sgt. O'Farrell* (1968).[26]

Another reason for the diminishing comic returns of the later features is related to Tashlin's leading comic performers. As was the case with Jerry Lewis, several of the stars in the late Tashlin features—Tony Randall, Doris Day, Danny Kaye, Terry-Thomas, even Bob Hope—posed challenges to Tashlin's performer-centric style. By observing the ways in which Tashlin's principal aesthetic and comic interests unfold in the films of the latter portion of his career, we may understand the ways his style changed, as well as the reasons for the changes.

In Tashlin's late features, his stars were either on the wane (*The Man from the Diners' Club* was Danny Kaye's last film as a comic leading man; *The Private Navy of Sgt. O'Farrell* was Bob Hope's third-to-last starring role), ill-suited for Tashlin's style of comedy (Doris Day, most notably), or simply misused or miscast (Tony Randall is far less effective in *The Alphabet Murders* than he is in *Rock Hunter*; Terry-Thomas, after a decade and a half of portraying cads and petty bureaucrats, was significantly offcast in *Bachelor Flat* as the kindhearted, effete Bruce Patterson). In the 1960s, the match between star and director, even in the Lewis films, was never perfect.

Kaye should have been an excellent fit for Tashlin, as he emerged from the same Borscht Belt circuit that produced Jerry Lewis and, like Lewis, excelled at both physical and vocal humor. In fact, numerous comedy historians regard Kaye as the single most talented comedian to emerge from the Borscht circuit.[27] But Tashlin seems less comfortable with Kaye than with Lewis, giving him only one showcase scene in which to display his formidable verbal and physical comedy skills. This is the massage scene discussed above, and it is the only one in the film to make use of the full range of Kaye's comic talents. In other comic scenes, Kaye merely flails about or stutters his lines of dialogue. Though his set of comic skills was not immensely different from that of Jerry Lewis, Tashlin seemed less able to take advantage of it.

Tashlin uses Bob Hope to much lesser effect in *The Private Navy of Sgt. O'Farrell* than in *Son of Paleface*. Though he always looked younger than his years, Hope was sixty-five when he made *The Private Navy of Sgt. O'Farrell*, a fact that dimmed the sexual deviance of his screen persona. In *The Private Navy of Sgt. O'Farrell*, Hope's title character is mildly wolfish, but his gender preference is never in question; neither does Tashlin craft any jokes around the difference between O'Farrell's sexual boasting and his sexual abilities.

Terry-Thomas begins his autobiography with as concise and complete a summary of his star image as could be written:

> I've been called any number of things in print. T-T with his permanent air of caddish disdain ... bounder ... aristocratic rogue ... upper-class English twit ... genuine English eccentric ... one of the last real gentlemen ... wet, genteel Englishman ... high-bred idiot ... cheeky blighter ... camel-haired cad ... amiable buffoon ... pompous Englishman ... twentieth-century dandy ... stinker ... king of the cads ...
>
> All those descriptions added up to my public image as Terry-Thomas.[28]

But Bruce Patterson, Thomas's character in *Bachelor Flat*, is mild, friendly, and rigorously monogamous—not exactly a recipe for eccentric comedy. A truly funny man such as Thomas should have been a great comic boon to Tashlin, but, as Thomas himself writes, "Tashlin had been a number-one director . . . but by the time we met he had fallen by the wayside a bit."[29]

Doris Day presents the most curious case of all of the stars of Tashlin's later features. Day's persona had long been established by 1966, the year of her first Tashlin film, *The Glass Bottom Boat*. (The two collaborated on *Caprice* the following year.) Day specialized in light romantic comedies with a trace of good-natured sexual humor, epitomized by the films she made with Rock Hudson, *Pillow Talk* (1959), *Lover Come Back* (1961), and *Send Me No Flowers* (1964). In these and other films, Day's character type did not vary; Katz's *Film Encyclopedia* aptly characterizes her as "the virginal heroine of a succession of pseudosophisticated bedroom farces."[30] *The Glass Bottom Boat* does not change this persona too greatly, though the film does at least acknowledge that Day, then forty-two, was no longer young enough to plausibly play the eternal virgin. In the film, Day plays a widow who unexpectedly finds love again. *The Glass Bottom Boat* represents a small shift in Day's persona, but *Caprice* is a major attempt at off-casting. In this spy movie spoof, Day plays a sophisticated secret agent, a character quite far removed from her girl-next-door image.

The Glass Bottom Boat contains a fair amount of sexual humor. Day herself, however, is involved in no sex gags—they are farmed out to supporting players; in this way is she associated with racy humor without actually participating in it.[31] Paul Lynde spends the last third of the film in drag, and his poor attempts at femininity are repeatedly played for laughs (Figure 6.9a).[32] A slightly naughty visual joke has a young Dom DeLuise attempting to hide behind the breasts of two women (Figure 6.9b). In the bawdiest gag of the film, two men are tricked into getting into bed together. When the lights are suddenly turned on, the bottle of champagne in one man's hand ejaculates fizz all over the other's face (Figure 6.9c).

By far, the raciest films of Tashlin's late career are *Bachelor Flat* and *The Glass Bottom Boat*. In films such as *Cinderfella, It's Only Money*, and *The Alphabet Murders*, sexual humor is almost entirely absent. This is not to say that *sexuality*, in its typically Tashlinian form of voluptuous women, is not present in these and other late features. In fact, Tashlin's camera lingers on the bodies of Anita Ekberg in *The Alphabet Murders*,

Figure 6.9 Sexual humor in *The Glass Bottom Boat*: Paul Lynde in drag, Dom DeLuise "hiding" between two sets of breasts, an ejaculating champagne bottle, and a phallic rocket

Cara Williams in *The Man from the Diners' Club*, Irene Tsu in *Caprice*, and Gina Lollabrigida in *The Private Navy of Sgt. O'Farrell*. The key difference is that these women and their bodies are not used for comic purposes. (Given Tashlin's sense of humor, it is hardly necessary to say that, if women are not subjected to comic sexualization in these films, neither are men.) As his career progressed, Tashlin relied less and less on sexual comedy.

Diegetic rupture maintains only the smallest presence in the late features. Before the opening credits of *The Alphabet Murders*, Tony Randall addresses the audience as himself, not as his character, Hercule Poirot. This situation is similar to the pre-credits sequence of *Will Success Spoil Rock Hunter?*, but telling differences distinguish the two scenes. In *Will Success Spoil Rock Hunter?*, Randall makes a series of quips and jokes (one of which is sexual in nature); in *The Alphabet Murders*, he merely introduces himself. In the earlier film, he makes a joke of being unable to remember the film's title; in the later film, he merely points to the film's title on the screen. The prologue in *The Alphabet Murders* is diegetic rupture for its own sake, not for the sake of comedy.

When Tashlin does break the diegetic effect in his later films, the joke is often isolated and, arguably, at odds with the rest of its film's humor. For instance, about halfway through *Caprice*, Patricia (Day) enters a movie theater that is showing . . . *Caprice*. This self-referential joke is the only one of its kind in the film. It *does* shatter the diegesis, but the effect is puzzling rather than comic, since this type of reflexivity and rupture has not been established as a part of the film's comic strategy. Similar problems afflict the one and only instance of diegetic rupture in *The Private Navy of Sgt. O'Farrell*. In this gag, a Japanese soldier speaks in English and has his words subtitled in Japanese, and then speaks in Japanese and has his words subtitled in English; moreover, the character can "see" the subtitles and responds to the mistranslations. Because it is the only instance of diegetic rupture in the film, this clever joke breaks the comic unity of the film.[33] A variation of this type of gag occurs in *The Glass Bottom Boat*, a film that commences with Leo, the MGM lion, emitting a foghorn's bellow as well as his traditional roar, thus allowing a bit of the diegesis (the film's milieu is nautical) to permeate this conventionally nondiegetic moment. However, this gag does not establish a precedent: at no other point does Tashlin break the diegesis for comic effect. Tashlin appears to have had trouble maintaining the comic unity of his later features.

Like his earlier films, Tashlin's later pictures rely on sight gags and non-gags; he doles them out sparingly, however. One of the most inventive occurs in a scene in *The Alphabet Murders* in which Poirot, inside a steam cabinet, converses with Inspector Hastings (Robert Morley). Atop the cabinet is a small mirror, which Tashlin uses as the crux of the gag. In a shot/reverse-shot setup, Tashlin frames the actors and a mirror in such a way that the upper half of Randall's face appears atop the grotesquely magnified lower half of Morley's, and vice versa (Figure 6.10). This clever, odd joke is one of the comic highlights of the film.

A scene at the beginning of *Cinderfella* contains a number of small sight gags. Fella (Lewis) sets two large bowls, one inside the other, on an offscreen ledge outside a kitchen window. He yanks the branch of an orange tree inside, and makes several random slashing movements with a large knife. Seconds later, he retrieves the bowls, both of which now brim with neatly halved oranges, despite the fact that the smaller bowl was fully inside the larger. A short while later, Lewis makes a quick loop around the kitchen, calling out, "Paper!" just before passing the window. He is thrown a newspaper by an unseen paperboy, catches it without

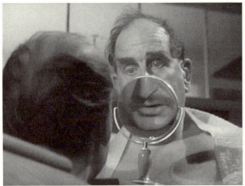

Figure 6.10 Bizarre visual humor in *The Alphabet Murders*

breaking stride, and exits the kitchen. The humor here derives from the smoothness of Lewis's movements and the seamlessness of the blocking. It is just barely a gag.

Perhaps the greatest consistency between Tashlin's early and late work is his continued reliance on sonic humor. Though in his 1960s features Tashlin uses sonic jokes somewhat less frequently than he did earlier in his career, the drop is not as precipitous as those of diegetic rupture and performance-based humor.

Some gags involve the humorous use of music. Examples include the scene in *The Man from the Diner's Club* in which Ernie gets his tie stuck in the gears of a massive computer, a moment accompanied by flamenco music that accentuates the weird dance he must do to extricate himself. A later scene uses Irish jig music as Ernie again dances oddly, this time to cover with his foot a piece of condemning evidence. In several scenes in *The Alphabet Murders*, the rotund Robert Morley is accompanied by a loping tuba theme that comments on his size and gait. These humorous uses of music strongly resemble those in the Carl Stalling soundtracks to the Warner Bros. cartoons, as well as the many musical gags in such earlier films as *Marry Me Again*.

Other films employ humorous sound effects. In *The Glass Bottom Boat*, Dom DeLuise plucks an item from between his teeth, and we hear a tiny but distinct *plink* that in no way reflects the actual sound of such an action. Later in the film, when Jennifer (Day) has a bright idea, we actually hear a chime sound effect. In the opening moments of *Caprice*, a man extends a radio antenna, and we hear a *bloooooop*-like stretching noise.

Just as, in his early films, Tashlin used the vocal talents of Mel Blanc (as Porky Pig), Bob Hope, Jerry Lewis, and even Jayne Mansfield, he often employs his performers' vocal skills for comic effect in his late features. Examples include Danny Kaye's stuttering in *The Man from the Diners' Club*, Tony Randall's mock-Belgian accent in *The Alphabet Murders*, and Jerry Lewis's doubletalk in *It's Only Money*. An inspired, illustrative scene from the last example is one in which Lester (Lewis) orates on the innovations of Charles P. Albright, the putative inventor of television:

> Mr. Albright created a density lock, visually, so that in the event there was an impaired vision front and back, you wouldn't apply yourself and then get caught with one eye shook off. He locked them, so that the fusion of the electronic cathode tube would advance itself, deteriorate, and then the one look from the one eye would create, at least, an abundance of sight.

We can trace the arc of Tashlin's artistic development by observing the emergence, complication, and combination of the essential components of his style. In his cartoons and early features, the elements of Tashlin's directorial style emerge, and he begins to combine them. The full and thorough combination of most or all of these elements is the very thing that marks Tashlin's creative peak. In the features of his later career, the elements of Tashlin's style are still present, but they are present in smaller quantities and in weakened states. Moreover, these elements no longer interact with each other as richly or fully as in Tashlin's best films; these films have no moments equivalent to the Eddie Cochran scene in *The Girl Can't Help It* or the George Schmidlapp scene in *Will Success Spoil Rock Hunter?*

It is not the elements of Tashlin's style that change over time. His central aesthetic and comic interests remain fairly consistent. Rather, the relative emphases these elements receive, and the degrees to which they interact with one another, are the key indices by which we may understand the changes to his style.

7 THE MAN IN THE MIDDLE
TASHLIN, AUTEURS, AND PROGRAMMERS

Frank Tashlin's cinematic style has never really been taken on its own terms, nor considered within the contexts of genre and authorship in mid-twentieth-century Hollywood. To that end, this chapter investigates the mechanics of Tashlin's style in comparison to several of his contemporaries in live-action Hollywood comedy between 1951 and 1968. American film comedy during Tashlin's tenure as a feature director was dominated by two loosely defined types of directors: auteurs and programmers, or those who made "A" pictures and those who made program or genre pictures, respectively. Comparing Tashlin's style to members of each group reveals a great deal not only about Tashlin's method, but about his place on the totem pole of the Hollywood studio system.[1]

The renowned comic stylists Howard Hawks and Billy Wilder made numerous comedies that helped them achieve auteur status.[2] Tashlin has generally been considered in the company of auteurs since the critics of *Cahiers du Cinéma* and *Positif* recognized his authorship in the late 1950s; Claire Johnston and Paul Willemen's 1973 English-language volume *Frank Tashlin* cemented this assessment. But Tashlin is an unusual auteur in that he worked almost entirely within a single genre; the auteurist reputations of Wilder and Hawks are staked partially on the fact that their stylistic and thematic hallmarks are evident in films of several genres. Joseph McBride in his book *Hawks on Hawks*, for instance, describes Hawks as "the most versatile of all great American directors, [who] worked with equal ease in screwball comedies, westerns, gangster movies, musicals, private-eye melodramas, and adventure films."[3] That Tashlin differs from Hawks and Wilder in this regard and yet is still generally considered an auteur is one sign of his liminal status.

Programmers, as an entity, are somewhat harder to define, precisely because their "regular" films are often seen to be exemplars of Hollywood's so-called invisible style. Brian Taves defines the program film within the context of the 1930s, but elements of his definition apply just as well to comedies of Tashlin's time. The program film, Taves writes, is neither a prestige picture (a big-budget, heavily advertised film whose success is crucial to its studio) nor a "B" picture (a low-budget film with no "name" stars, designed to fill out a double bill). A program picture usually had some trappings of higher-budget films, such as "reasonably elaborate sets" and "one or two well-paid performers"; however, such films are also formulaic vehicles designed to test the box-office potential of new or specialized performers.[4] Program comedies often downplay narrative in favor of irreverent humor that derives from vaudeville and is used to showcase the talents of a particular star. Nearly all of Bob Hope's and Jerry Lewis's films are program pictures.[5]

The group of programmers is here represented by Norman Taurog, Norman Z. McLeod, and Hal Walker, directors who maintained a presence—albeit a somewhat anonymous one—in Hollywood comedies for many years. Walker, though he made only nine films, directed both Bob Hope and Jerry Lewis multiple times. McLeod directed forty-three pictures—most of them comedies—between 1928 and 1959. Taurog made an incredible 127 films—comedies, musicals, short subjects—between 1920 and 1968.[6]

One key link between Tashlin and the programmers is in the realm of casting. Simply put, the auteurs' films do not usually star comedian comics. Hawks made four comedies with Cary Grant, and Wilder made six with Jack Lemmon,[7] but these performers are of a different kind than Bob Hope, Jerry Lewis, Danny Kaye, Red Skelton, or any of the other comedians who are the focus of Steve Seidman's monograph. Films that star comedian comics are less likely to have large budgets, less likely to garner critical praise, and are generally seen as less prestigious films. Such films were made to fill the "comedy" slot in a studio's release schedule; by definition, they were the domain of the programmers. In this key regard, Tashlin is a program director.

That comedian comics generally have the lead roles in Tashlin's features is one of his clearest links with the programmers, but neatly slotting Tashlin into one category or the other is usually not so simple. Indeed, the argument for auteurism holds that a director who exhibits a consistent artistic signature has some claim to auteur status; the previous chapters are largely concerned with identifying the stylistic consistencies among Tashlin's films. Though the elements of his style appear with varying frequency and effectiveness across his career, Tashlin remained concerned with many of the same aesthetic and comic interests for as long as he directed film. To say that Tashlin is an auteur who directed program pictures is not totally inaccurate, but neither is it especially precise. By observing how the key dynamics of Tashlin's style play out in the films of both auteurs and programmers, we can observe the ways in which Tashlin blurs the line between the two groups.

Sex and the Single Auteur

Sexual comedy does not appear to be a major interest of the programmers. Between 1951 and 1968, Walker's, McLeod's, and Taurog's films make only minor use of sexual humor, relying almost entirely on the preestablished sexual dimensions of the personae of their stars. In Walker's *Road to Bali*, for instance, Hope's character's humorous, leering lust for Lala (Dorothy Lamour) is fully congruent with his well-established sexual persona; in Taurog's *The Stooge*, Jerry Lewis's character's first kiss is accompanied by a "woo woo woo" sound effect that merely accentuates the sexual immaturity that was, by 1953, an established facet of the actor's screen image.

In this regard, Tashlin's films differ from those of the programmers in two respects. First, they go beyond actors' personae in creating their sexual humor; second, Tashlin's films are far bawdier than those of the programmers. The jokes in *The First Time* about bananas and prostitutes illustrate this. The film's leads, Robert Cummings and Barbara Hale, have nonspecific sexual personae, so Tashlin compensates by involving them in unmistakably bawdy gags. Film scholar Denise Mann singles out *The First Time* as an exemplar of the then-popular "realist-domestic" strain of comedy, noting that the film's satirical approach to gender and social roles further distinguishes it from other, "safer" comedies.[8]

Tashlin's films with Hope and the pre-1957 Lewis contain a great many more sexual gags than do these actors' films with other directors: the difference in sheer quantity points to Tashlin's enthusiasm for this type of humor.

If program films are more inclined to use comedian comics and their personae for sexual humor, auteurs' films are much more likely to use plotting and situational contrivances for this purpose. In Hawks's *Mon-*

key Business, for instance, a miracle formula causes several rational adults to revert, both intellectually and sexually, to the behavior of their youth — a situation that is the basis of nearly all of the film's humor. The premise of Wilder's *Some Like It Hot* is that two male musicians, in order to escape from the mob, dress as women so they may hide amid the female musicians in Sweet Sue's Society Syncopators. This comedy of the sexes is at its most ribald when "women" fall in love with women, and men fall in love with "women."

Tashlin made a few films of this type: both *Susan Slept Here* and *The Lieutenant Wore Skirts* are built around premises, not performances, that invite sexual humor. In *Susan Slept Here*, an unhappily engaged thirty-five-year-old man is "given" a seventeen-year-old girl as a Christmas present; their forbidden but obvious love for one another is the source of nearly all of the film's comedy. In *The Lieutenant Wore Skirts*, a man acts the part of an army wife when his spouse is drafted by the WACs, and this reversal of gender roles is the film's main wellspring of humor. But the fact that Tashlin made such films does not necessarily make him an auteur trapped in the body of a programmer. What *is* a mark of his authorship is the pronounced bawdiness of the humor not only in the comedian comedies, but in such films as *Susan Slept Here* and *The Lieutenant Wore Skirts*, which depend more heavily on plot-based sexual comedy. Regardless of whether it is character or situation that provides Tashlin with an opportunity for sexual comedy, he seizes it; both cases give him the chance to push the limits of blue humor. *Susan Slept Here* is one of Tashlin's most risqué films.

A major hallmark of Tashlin's style is that his sexual gags are both extremely blue and creatively and thoroughly ambiguous. We have seen numerous examples of such gags: the bananas in *The First Time* (Figure 3.2), for instance, and the explosive burst of champagne in *The Glass Bottom Boat* (Figure 6.9). *Susan Slept Here* and *The Lieutenant Wore Skirts* rely on ambiguous sexual humor as well. In *Susan Slept Here*, Susan remarks on the blonde hair of Mark's fiancée, opining that she has gotten a "dye job"; Mark insists that she's a natural blonde. "You sure?" asks Susan, to which Mark says, "We're very good friends. [*pause*] She told me." Clearly, the "She told me" was added to ward off the censor; without it, the verbal double entendre is inescapable.[9] In *The Lieutenant Wore Skirts*, Gregory Whitcomb (Tom Ewell) acquires a gaudy lamp that features a gyrating hula girl as its base. In one shot, Whitcomb positions

Figure 7.1 Tom Ewell enjoys his new lamp in *The Lieutenant Wore Skirts*

the lamp right in front of his crotch, so that it appears he is, in some strange way, having sex with the hula girl (Figure 7.1). This gag, too, can be read innocently, but the sexual undertones are unavoidable.

Satire as a Mark of Authorship

With regard to satire, Tashlin's films again provide a kind of liminal example. The films of both the auteurs and the programmers employ satire, but the *objects* of their satire differ significantly. Broadly speaking, the auteurs set their sights on major social issues, such as gender roles, politics, and consumerism, while the satire found in program films is of a more localized variety, lampooning genre conventions and Hollywood itself. (This distinction, indeed, is an implicit part of the method Mann uses to distinguish between the various tiers of Hollywood films in the decade and a half following the 1948 Paramount case.) Tashlin satirizes *both* of these types of targets, a fact that points to his intermediate status as a director.

Howard Hawks, in *Monkey Business*, *Gentlemen Prefer Blondes*, and *Man's Favorite Sport?*, satirizes gender roles and relations; Billy Wilder does the same in *Some Like It Hot*. Wilder also attacks consumer culture and globalism in *One, Two, Three*, and reveals the corrupt nature of the American corporation in *The Apartment*. These films address broad social problems or situations, and offer humorous critiques thereof. More often than not, they hit their marks; the important point is that the aim and scope of their satire is broad.

In a great many of his films (as discussed in previous chapters), Tashlin fairly viciously attacks consumerism, mass entertainment, mob mentality, advertising, and the complicated sexuality of the American male, to name a few. The polemics of these films link them with those of the auteurs. It is not necessarily a defining characteristic of an auteur that his films engage in social satire; rather, social satire seems to be a common link among the films of auteurist comedy directors. Tashlin shares this tendency with the members of that group.

Social satire of this kind is simply not a component of the programmers' films. What satire exists in program pictures rarely extends beyond the world of the films themselves: they may lampoon genre conventions, the nature of Hollywood storytelling, or even the institution of Hollywood itself, but they almost never address broader social concerns. In at least two films, Norman McLeod ridicules the Hollywood ending. *Casanova's Big Night* ends with Pippo Popolino (Hope) on the executioner's block, but the frame freezes just before the axe connects. The voiceover tells us that, instead, we shall see an ending directed by "Bob 'Orson Welles' Hope." In this "alternate ending," Hope addresses the camera and surveys the audience about whether they wish his character to live; the film ends as Hope cracks wise about the audience's lack of compassion. McLeod has it both ways: he rejects the happy ending (nothing can stop the axe's descent), but also adheres to it (Pippo lives, anyway). The ending of McLeod's *Alias Jesse James* satirizes the generic convention of the happy heterosexual union. The film's final gag is that Milford (Hope) has fathered five children in the brief span of time between the plot's end and the denouement. The ending satirizes the convention of the heterosexual union by making the union out to be successful beyond all reasonable expectations. The ending of *Son of Paleface* is nearly identical.

Endings, in fact, are special sites of satire in many program pictures. In the last scene of *The Caddy*, Norman Taurog has Joe (Dean Martin), Harvey (Jerry Lewis), Kathy (Donna Reed), and Lisa (Barbara Bates) meet their *doppelgängers*: another set of aspiring performers played by Martin and Lewis with girlfriends played by Reed and Bates. By this point in the story, the real Joe and Harvey have become successful performers, while their doubles are at the very beginning of their careers. In its peculiar way, this ending satirizes the nature of Hollywood narrative. Walker's *Road to Bali* also wages an assault on the conventional Hollywood ending. The end of the film has George (Crosby) walk off into the sunset with not one but two women, leaving Harold (Hope) alone. Harold does all he can to prevent the film from ending, including "pushing" the "The End" credit off of the screen—to no avail.

Tashlin's films satirize not only broad social concepts but also generic conventions, Hollywood filmmaking, and Hollywood itself. Examples of this smaller-scale satire can be found in the endings of *Son of Paleface*, *The Girl Can't Help It*, and *Artists and Models*, among other films. Tashlin had an interest in satire itself as a tool of comedy, no matter whether its scope was broad or narrow. His films use the satirical strategies of both the auteurs and the programmers.

Broken Diegeses and Narrative Integration

In the above examples from McLeod, Taurog, and Walker, the sites of satire are also sites of diegetic rupture. To a large extent, the presence of these ruptures can be traced to the presence of the comedian comics who star in the films, as these comics' personae carried with them a sense of irreverence, disrespect for tradition, and diegetic breakage—the very qualities Steve Seidman identifies as hallmarks of the comedian comedy.[10] Again, key differences between the auteurs and the programmers can be traced, in part, to the types of performers with whom the directors usually worked. Because they so often star comedian comics, and because comedian comics are figures of rupture, the films of the programmers break much more frequently with diegetic unity than do those of the auteurs. Many if not most of the comedian comedies Seidman cites in his monograph are program comedies that break diegetic unity.

The presence of comedian comics is not the only way to break the diegesis, of course, and their absence from the auteurs' films does not prevent these films from occasionally breaking the fourth wall. However, the auteurs' films break diegetic unity less often, less thoroughly, and less effectively than do the programmers' films. In *Monkey Business*, for instance, only once does Howard Hawks suggest a world beyond the diegesis. This occurs in the famous opening credits sequence, in which Cary Grant, in character as absentminded scientist Barnaby Fulton, walks through a door "too early," and the voice of Hawks himself says, twice, "Not yet, Cary."[11] Once the narrative proper gets underway, Hawks does not break story unity at any point. The one moment at which Billy Wilder breaks diegetic unity in *The Seven Year Itch* occurs so deep into the narrative and with so little warning that the gag comes off as inappropriate. The situation is that a woman (unnamed in the script) played by Marilyn Monroe is hiding in the kitchen of Richard Sherman (Tom Ewell). A visitor drops by, hears a noise coming from the kitchen, and asks who it is. Sherman replies, "Maybe it's Marilyn Monroe." Another scene is jokingly intertextual, referring comically to the famous scene from *From Here to Eternity* in which Burt Lancaster and Deborah Kerr writhe romantically in the surf. But these are *The Seven Year Itch*'s only gags calling the diegesis into question. The very sparseness of such gags (and, in the case of the Monroe joke, its awkward occurrence a scant five minutes before the film ends) render them ineffective: they challenge the diegesis in the most cursory way.[12] The fact that diegetic rupture is less common and thorough in the films of Hawks and Wilder is related to the fact that their films' humor derives heavily from story and situation. Story, plotting, and diegetic unity are extremely important to the comedy of the auteurs; gags that depend on the violation of conventional methods of storytelling are not often appropriate to these films.

One of the distinguishing marks of Tashlin's style is his success in designing gags of diegetic rupture. As discussed in previous chapters, Tashlin's interest in breaking the frame extends from his early cartoons through his late features, giving him ample opportunity to refine it. Among directors of Hollywood comedies in the 1950s and 1960s, he may be the most consistent and fluent user of this device.

It is unsurprising that, on the whole, the auteurs are far more invested in the integration of gag and narrative than are the programmers. The films of the auteurs are marked by a heavier reliance on story and situation; a strategy of near-total gag/narrative integration is suited for films of this kind. Wilder's films are models of this type of integration: nearly every joke serves a narrative purpose. Twice in *The Seven Year Itch*, Sherman trips over the roller skates left behind by his son, a gag that is not simply a slapstick moment but a painful reminder to Sherman, who has designs on his attractive neighbor, that he has a wife and son. Even tinier gags have narrative implications: Sherman, carrying a boat paddle left behind by his son, accidentally catches it in the blades of a ceiling fan, a moment that barely qualifies as lightly humorous. The paddle is in fact a major motif: Sherman repeatedly forgets to ship it to his family's summer home because he spends all his time dallying with his neighbor. Wilder calls attention to the significance of the paddle by having Sherman bump it into the fan. When, at film's end, Sherman finally leaves New York City to join his family, he runs out the front door carrying the paddle, the symbol of his faithfulness. Wilder's underrated *One, Two, Three* is perhaps the ultimate example of this integrative tendency: the film bursts with comic motifs (balloons, Brian Hyland's song "Itsy Bitsy Teenie Weenie Yellow Polka Dot Bikini," crossdressing, cuckoo clocks), all of which serve, at every iteration, key narrative functions. Indeed, such motifs fairly *constitute* the narrative structure of this film.

The integration of gag and narrative in Hawks's *Gentlemen Prefer Blondes* is crystallized in a visual joke in which gold digger extraordinaire Lorelei Lee (Monroe) imagines that the head of her prospective sugar daddy, Sir Francis "Piggy" Beekman (Charles Coburn), is a gigantic, glowing diamond (Figure 7.2). This joke summarizes the film's narrative, which concerns Lorelei's quest to marry a wealthy man. The gag is one of the few moments of impossible humor in the film, and yet its comedy still depends on narrative situation. In fact, it is probably a stretch to dub this moment an impossible gag, as it likely represents Lorelei's vision of what Piggy "actually" looks like.

In Tashlin's best films, gags and narrative are tightly integrated—this is one of the principal ways in which his comic style resembles those of the auteurs. Gags in the Mansfield pictures that would, in other films, come off as unintegrated instead derive much of their humor from narrative situations. An important story point in *The Girl Can't Help It*, for instance, is Jerri's sex appeal and star potential; when she walks down the street and causes a cake of ice to melt, a milk bottle to erupt, and a man's glasses to shatter, we receive confirmation of her celebrity potential. When Tashlin is able to marshal all of his major aesthetic interests and combine them in compelling ways, his style is that of an auteur. It is no coincidence that his Mansfield films are the ones for which he is best known, and on which his auteurist reputation is largely staked. The Mansfield films are the exceptions in his body of work, however: most of Tashlin's films make frequent use of one-off, unintegrated gags, a fact that links his style to that of the programmers.

In the programmers' films, the relationship between gag and narra-

Figure 7.2 An unusual moment of impossible comedy in Howard Hawks's *Gentlemen Prefer Blondes*

tive is far looser. One of the most extreme cases is Hal Walker's Martin and Lewis film *At War with the Army*. Walker almost never permits a comic scene to advance the narrative, or a narratively important scene to be funny. The film's first fifteen minutes contain very few important story events, bogged down as they are in the ostensibly humorous interactions of several soldiers. A later scene exists only as an excuse to put Lewis in drag; at this point, the story stops completely. It is a key distinction between *At War with the Army* and *Some Like It Hot*: in the former, cross-dressing is used solely to showcase the comedian's performance; in the latter, it is the root of all narrative complications.

The clearest testament to Walker's lack of interest in gag/narrative integration is his use of a tactic quite common in program comedies: the inclusion of an autonomous scene of performance within the narrative. Martin and Lewis perform what appears to be a self-contained, cleaned-up portion of their popular nightclub act; the pretext is that their characters are rehearsing for an army revue. *My Friend Irma Goes West*, another Walker film, uses the same device.

The films of Norman Taurog exhibit a somewhat greater degree of gag/narrative integration than Walker's, but not nearly so strong as Hawks's or Wilder's. Taurog devotes large portions of the running times of both *The Caddy* and *The Stooge* to self-contained scenes of comic performance—again, apparently, portions of Martin and Lewis's nightclub act. However, these scenes are better integrated into the narrative than those in Walker's films in that, in both *The Caddy* and *The Stooge*, Martin and Lewis play performers.[13] Taurog integrates gags and narrative in only the most perfunctory way. The scenes of performance advance the narrative—especially in *The Caddy*—because the narrative concerns the rise to fame of the performers; each performance, therefore, is a relevant step in their advancement. This narrative structure and its concomitant gag/narrative dynamic are common in program comedies: it is logical that films expressly designed to showcase a comedian's talents include scenes of his performance. Just as he does in his nine Elvis Presley films, Taurog integrates scenes of performance with scenes of narrative advancement in only the most cursory of ways.

The entirety of Tashlin's style cannot be explained away by comparisons to those of the auteurs and the programmers. Certain facets of Tashlin's style have no equivalents in the styles of his contemporaries. The most prominent of these is his frequent use of the non-gag. Such gags demonstrate Tashlin's essential connection to the genre of comedy, as their pedigree extends back to silent film, vaudeville, and their antecedents. In Hollywood, Buster Keaton, for one, employed non-gags regularly. To cite but one famous instance, in *The General* (1927), Johnnie Gray (Keaton) sits on a locomotive's cowcatcher and uses one railroad tie to clear the tracks of another, and we marvel at his quick thinking and the physical design of the setup, but the situation is not funny *per se*.[14] Outside the Hollywood tradition, the films of Jacques Tati make frequent use of such humor. In American feature comedies of the 1950s and 1960s, no director uses non-gags so thoroughly as does Tashlin. The importance of non-gags to Tashlin's style is demonstrated by their presence in nearly every one of his films, from the long-take tracking shot of the fire hose in *Porky the Fireman* to the suggestion of the similarities between wind chimes and a skeleton in *The Disorderly Orderly*. In fact, the only Tashlin films that lack non-gags are *The Way of Peace* and *Say One for Me*—his only non-comic films. Tashlin's contemporaries were, for the most part, simply not interested in this type of comedy; that Tashlin *was* speaks to his deep connections with American comic tradition.

More broadly, Tashlin is extremely interested in sight gags, visual comedy, and jokes that depend in a general way on visual design. Programmers such as McLeod occasionally craft gags out of elements of composition or color, such as the scene in *Casanova's Big Night* in which Casanova (Vincent Price) throttles his tailor, the insolent Pippo Popolino (Hope), thereby turning the latter's face a rich indigo. "That's the exact color I want in my new jacket!" declares Casanova. But this is a rarity among program comedies, whose humor depends almost entirely on performance. Neither are the auteurs' films likely to rely heavily on visual comedy; they are far more reliant on situational comedy. Neither Hawks nor Wilder relies so heavily on sight gags as does Tashlin. Tashlin's commitment—even devotion—to visual comedy is another distinguishing mark of his style.

Tashlin and the Politics of the Studio System

Unlike those of Taurog, McLeod, and Walker, Tashlin's program pictures evince a distinct style—the mark of authorship. On one hand, this distinction is largely academic, as "auteur" and "programmer" are merely tools of analysis. On the other hand, the fact that most of Tashlin's films are essentially very well-directed program comedies speaks to his marginal status within the studio system. Hawks, by the 1950s, was a powerful producer at Fox; Wilder co-produced fourteen of the films he directed, many under the auspices of The Mirisch Corporation. Other auteur contemporaries of Tashlin, such as Robert Aldrich, formed their own independent production companies. Tashlin, however, did not, and was thus unable to take full advantage of the relative creative and economic freedom that such a move would have afforded him.[15] In fact, the only live-action films on which he served as his own producer are *The Girl Can't Help It*, *Will Success Spoil Rock Hunter?*, and *Say One for Me*. (Tashlin produced all of his Columbia cartoons, and assumed supervisory responsibilities as a Looney Tunes director, as well.[16]) The fact that he wrote, directed, and produced his two Jayne Mansfield pictures suggests that this unusual degree of creative control is a major reason for the films' success. *Say One for Me*, as always, is an exceptional case, for it is probably the *least* Tashlinian of all his films; however, we may probably take Tashlin at his word that his original vision of the film was severely diluted and distorted by the PCA and Martin Quigley.

It is unclear precisely why Tashlin did not establish his own film production company, or whether he was even interested in doing so. Frankly, Tashlin's career decisions are often a bit puzzling: he often seemed to make choices that could not possibly have had any positive impact on his career. Indeed, Tashlin moved with such frequency from studio to studio and from one production company to another that it would have been difficult for him to establish roots anywhere. (In the full span of his career, considering the studios for which he made both his cartoons and his features, Tashlin moved from one employer to another *thirty-eight* times.[17]) It is telling, however, that program directors such as Taurog and McLeod never formed their own production companies, either: the genre pictures that were their bread-and-butter were not the typical fare of the independent production company.

A director's establishment of his own production company is not the definitive indication of whether he should be regarded as an auteur or as a programmer. It is, however, a mark of a certain degree of economic and artistic autonomy. That Tashlin did not establish an independent company made him more beholden to his distributors than a director like Hawks, who had a great deal more authority over his projects. It appears that Tashlin's studios treated him like the journeyman program director that, on many levels, he was—a fairly strong argument for Tashlin's status as an unusually talented director of program pictures.

8 WHO'S MINDING THE STORE?
TASHLIN'S INFLUENCE

his book begins on a note of surprise—could we truly be in the middle of a Tashlin renaissance? Such a notion is as implausible as ... a Tashlin gag.

Perhaps I spoke too soon: Tashlin's work remains underrepresented on DVD and in recent scholarly literature; despite the online resurfacing of some of his more arcane titles, it appears that such events as the 2006 Tashlin retrospective were little more than one-off occurrences.

This is not to suggest that Frank Tashlin's films have been uninfluential, or that they carry no cultural currency. Tashlin's legacy may not be as strong or as palpable as those of Howard Hawks or Billy Wilder, but the influence of his style is demonstrable in at least a small handful of very interesting filmmakers. This final chapter discusses the ways in which Tashlin influenced two of those filmmakers: Jean-Luc Godard and Joe Dante. If these two directors appear as disparate in artistic temperament as Martin and Lewis circa 1956, then perhaps Tashlin may usefully be considered as the bridge between them. The very fact that such a director has influenced filmmakers as dissimilar as Godard and Dante suggests that his style is more complex than it may appear at first blush.

Bad Education: Tashlin and Almodóvar

Before addressing Tashlin's influence on Dante's and Godard's styles, though, it is worth mentioning briefly another director to whose films the adjective "Tashlinesque" has often been applied: Pedro Almodóvar. I have not included a more thorough discussion of the Tashlin influence on Almodóvar because, frankly, I do not think it particularly strong. Nevertheless, Tashlin's name is invoked with some frequency in a fair bit of the literature on Almodóvar, so it seems worthwhile to investigate the associations between the two.

The grounds for the connection between Tashlin and Almodóvar have never been particularly well explained. Color, for instance, is seen as one avenue of linkage: Emanuel Levy, for one, writes that Almodóvar "borrows from Tashlin a cartoon-like abandon and color delirium."[1] But this putative hue-based connection between the two filmmakers is as ill-sketched as the assertions that the whole of Tashlin's style is his "vibrant" use of color and his live-action films' cartoonlike nature. Many directors make excellent use of color: Jacques Demy, the Wachowski Brothers, and Yasujiro Ozu all come immediately to mind. But to say that these filmmakers are therefore similar is to pass over the stuff of analysis—we must posit ways in which these directors' *uses* of color are similar to or different from each other. Though both Tashlin and Almodóvar are doubtless skillful directors of color, a comparison of their respective talents in this area needs to be considered in context—in particular, in the context of comedy. Almodóvar does not use color for the same reasons or purposes as does Tashlin.

In a similar vein, while it is certainly true that both Tashlin's and Almodóvar's films brim with sexuality, the functions and uses of these cinematic sexualities are not particularly congruent—due in part to the differing economic and cultural environments in which the directors worked. Paul Julian Smith alludes to this fact in his book *Desire Unlimited: The Cinema of Pedro Almodóvar*: "Much has been made of Almodóvar's avowed debt to the Hollywood sex comedies of Doris Day and Frank Tashlin. If we seek a Spanish context for such accounts of femininity, however, it may be in representations of women current in the 1960s at the time of Almodóvar's adolescence."[2] Even if Smith is off the mark, Tashlin's and Almodóvar's films reveal entirely different attitudes toward sex and sexuality. Almodóvar, working in a more liberal era, makes sex the subject of many of his films, and has since the beginning of his career. His first feature, *Pepi, Luci, Bom and Other Girls on the Heap* (1980); mid-period films such as *Law of Desire* (1987) and *Tie Me Up! Tie Me Down!* (1990); and more recent films such as *Bad Education* (2004) are all explicitly about sex and sexuality, and are at times explicit in their depictions of these subjects. But while Tashlin tends to use sex as a means to satirize popular culture or social mores, Almodóvar—true to his preferred genre, the melodrama—tends to depict sex as problematic at best, and destructively divisive at worst. The sexual uncertainty and impropriety found in most Almodóvar films is at the root of his characters' anguish and (self-) destructiveness; sex may produce great pleasure, but it also leads to irrevocable pain, and sometimes death. In Tashlin, sex, like everything else, is played for laughs. This disparity is not small.

In Almodóvar's otherwise un-Tashlinian *oeuvre*, one scene, from *Women on the Verge of a Nervous Breakdown* (1988), merits mention. The situation is that Pepa, a television actress who plays the mother of a notorious killer, watches television in her apartment and happens to catch a commercial in which she appears. The ad is for "Ecce Omo" laundry detergent, and it appears to be a reference to one of the mock commercials from the opening credits sequence of *Will Success Spoil Rock Hunter?* In the mini-narrative of the commercial, Pepa uses Ecce Omo to completely eradicate the blood and gore from the clothing of her murderous son; even the detectives who appear at her door are impressed by the stain- and odor-free garments. "Ecce Omo," Pepa says. "It's unbelievable." Almodóvar's use here of a mock television advertisement to comment on the vacuity of popular culture is indeed a Tashlinian gesture (the only such gesture in the film), and all the more so for resembling so closely the "EZ Kleen Washing Machine" commercial in *Will Success Spoil Rock Hunter?*, in which a housewife perkily praises the product's abilities to eliminate the aroma of her "big, filthy husband."

Almodóvar himself maintains that, when he made *Women on the Verge of a Nervous Breakdown*, he had Tashlin on his mind, but he is not very specific about it. In an interview with Vito Russo, Almodóvar remarks,

> The aesthetics of the film are purely Frank Tashlin, but at the same time it's my vision of what I loved about those films twenty years later.... I remember Frank Tashlin movies with a certain kind of housewife, who I didn't know if she actually existed, but was a kind of artificial and false image that has a powerful truth for me, which I can't explain. I look at it with humor, but it very much belongs in my sensibility. They don't belong to my fantasies, those movies, they belong very much to my reality.[3]

Almodóvar has elsewhere said, "I use cinema in a very active way, never as a pastiche or homage, because for me, a film is something that once I have seen it, it has become part of my experience."[4] And Russo has written, "So it's not a copy, and it's not an homage. It's more that in

Figure 8.1 A deliberately artificial set in Almodóvar's *Women on the Verge of a Nervous Breakdown*

a very real sense [Almodóvar has] incorporated into his work what the movies of his adolescence looked like."[5] Russo's observations seem accurate; see Figure 8.1, in which the artificiality of the setting is emphasized by Almodóvar's choices in colors, lighting, props, and, especially, the background. These directors share few, if any, specific stylistic methods or intentions; rather, any connections that may exist between the two occur at the somewhat indeterminate level of "outlook" or "sensibility." Generally speaking, the two directors seem more dissimilar than similar. This is not to say that the one director had absolutely no influence on the other, but that, if the connection exists, it would seem to be fairly attenuated.

J-L. G. and F. T.

Like Almodóvar, both Jean-Luc Godard and Joe Dante have gone on record multiple times about their admiration for Tashlin's films. Unlike Almodóvar, however, these directors' films resemble those of Tashlin in several ways: in visual style, in comic style, in their irreverence for classical Hollywood storytelling, and in a particular deployment of caustic satire and parody. Godard is one of the most important and written-about filmmakers in history; Dante is the subject of far fewer column inches but the creator of several challenging and inventive films. Despite their differences, Godard and Dante have created large and varied bodies of cinematic work, only the surfaces of which may be scratched in this brief, Tashlin-centric comparison.

If Jean-Luc Godard underwent a "Tashlin phase," it most likely occurred early in his career, before his turn to a more heavily politicized, polemical cinema in the late 1960s.[6] This was the period in which Godard's love/hate relationship with Hollywood is most apparent, and the one that offers the most compelling comparisons with American comedies of Tashlin's time.

The Introduction briefly addresses Godard's enthusiasm for Tashlin, which he professed in various pieces for *Cahiers du Cinéma* in the late 1950s and early 1960s. Another of his reviews is worth citing, if only to show the fervent accolades that Godard heaped upon Tashlin. In his double review of *Artists and Models* and *The Lieutenant Wore Skirts*, Godard compares Tashlin to both Voltaire and Hitchcock in the same sentence, pronounces him better than Billy Wilder, and suggests that he has inherited the mantle of Ernst Lubitsch.[7] Other *Cahiers du Cinéma* writers were perhaps not quite so effusive, but the journal's praise for Tashlin was fairly consistent.

But does one filmmaker's evident admiration for another's work necessarily manifest itself in cinematic form? While nearly all of Godard's films from the period 1959–1967 refer in some way to Hollywood cinema, there seem to be fairly few direct nods to Tashlin. What stands out, rather, is that some of Godard's techniques of diegetic rupture and gag construction are of types very similar to those employed by Tashlin. While Godard does not seem to directly invoke Tashlin at any particular point, he does employ stylistic and narrative practices that evoke American comedian comedies, and that suggest a strong kinship between such films and the films of the French New Wave.

On a simple level, Godard's films contain a fair number of sight gags that would by no means be out of place in a Tashlin film. For instance, in *Weekend* (1967), a "hidden" cut depicts a vacant field that instantaneously fills with baaing sheep. Another highly Tashlinian gag occurs in *Les Carabiniers* (1963), when three characters look at a photo of the Leaning Tower of Pisa, and simultaneously tilt their heads to the side. More notably, *A Woman Is a Woman* (1961) employs a gag/topper/

topper-topper structure to highlight a small bit of impossible humor. The joke is that the film's characters, merely by passing behind a vertical support beam inside of a nightclub, may undergo an instant change of attire. The first time it happens, a woman asks Angela (Anna Karina), "Have you seen my new act?" and proceeds to pass behind the beam, thereby changing from her everyday attire to the raiment of an Indian chief; the second time, Angela says, "Look, I'll try it," and, wrapped in a towel, passes behind the support beam. She emerges, after the deliberately ill-hidden cut, fully dressed, coat and all. The third instance—the topper-topper—stands out for the fact that it does not actually occur. Godard sets us up to expect that, when Angela passes behind the post yet again, the instant clothing change will occur one more time, but it does not. In a clever undermining and re-undermining of audience expectations, the topper-topper is replaced by a subversive non-gag: no change of clothes occurs—a fine example of a filmmaker subverting his film's intrinsic norms. Later in the film, Angela, while frying an egg, tosses it from the pan into the air, walks out into the hallway for a moment, and then, upon reëntering her apartment, catches the egg in the pan just as it falls from above. This gag is nearly identical to the egg-tossing gag in the barbershop scene in Norman Taurog's Martin and Lewis film *You're Never Too Young* (discussed in Chapter Four).

Godard's films are also exceedingly rich in the type of referentiality and self-reflexivity that characterizes so many anarchic Hollywood comedies. *Bande à part* (1964) includes snippets of the music from *The Umbrellas of Cherbourg*, (1964) whose composer, Michel Legrand, also composed the score for *Bande à part* itself; the film also contains references to the Nouvelle Vague (in the name of a nightclub which the characters pass), and Loopy de Loop, the lupine, ostensibly French-Canadian cartoon character that represents Hanna-Barbera's sole foray into theatrical animation.[8] *A Woman Is a Woman* refers to *Breathless*'s (1960) airing on television, as well as to *Jules and Jim* (1962) and *Shoot the Piano Player* (1960). *Masculin féminin* (1966) cites Amiri Baraka's play *Dutchman* as well as Godard's own *Pierrot le Fou*, (1965) a film that itself refers to *Breathless* and Nicholas Ray's *Johnny Guitar* (1954), the latter apparently a favorite Godard reference, as it shows up again in *Weekend* as well as *La Chinoise* (1967). *Made in U.S.A.* (1966) is so rich in intertextual references that subtitle translator Lenny Borger compiled a brief "glossary" to accompany the film's recent restoration.[9]

Godard frequently name-checks films and directors he loves, the films of his friends, and films he has made, just as many American comedies refer to themselves as well as to other comedies. A few of the countless examples: Bob Hope's films make frequent reference to the actor's previous pictures, to his putative rivalry with Bing Crosby (even to the point of shattering spatial and temporal unity, as in the insert shot of Crosby in a modern automobile that occurs at the beginning of *Son of Paleface*, a film whose story takes place no later than the 1910s), and even to other Paramount comedy duos: Martin and Lewis appear in a dream sequence in *Road to Bali* (1952); as if in response, Hope and Crosby appear in gag cameos in the subsequent year's Martin and Lewis film *Scared Stiff*. (And, again in *Son of Paleface*, Hope's character refers to two buzzards as "Martin and Lewis.") This kind of intertextuality is exceedingly common in anarchic Hollywood comedies, and not just those made by Frank Tashlin. Indeed, of all Hollywood genres, comedy is the one that most readily lends itself to such techniques as diegetic rupture and (self-)reflexivity, techniques also frequently found not just in Godard films, nor just in the films of the French Nouvelle Vague, but in art cinema films in general. The same devices may be found in films by directors as disparate as Ingmar Bergman, Rainer Werner Fassbinder, and Michael Haneke.

One of the densest of Godard's intertextual gags occurs in *Les Carabiniers*, in which a naïve young man goes to the cinema for the first time. He views crudely remade versions of the Lumière films *L'Arrivée d'un train à la Ciotat* (at which the man hides his face in terror; 1896) and *Repas de bébé* (complete with the expletive "Son of a fascist bitch!"; 1895), as well as a film made to resemble one of the many "through the keyhole" exploitation films of cinema's first decades. The character also takes part in a gag that deliberately invokes Buster Keaton's *Sherlock, Jr.* (1924). During the "keyhole" film, the young man becomes so entranced by the woman on the screen that he tries to jump "into" the screen, thereby tearing it down. It's a terrific gag: a reflexive reference to one of the definitive statements of cinematic self-reflexivity, and a further strengthening of the bond between anarchic Hollywood comedy and the works of the French Nouvelle Vague.

Godard's films routinely break their own diegeses, a fact that offers one of their strongest linkages to the type of Hollywood comedy on which Tashlin built his career. In fact, some of the techniques Godard uses for diegetic breakage are similar if not identical to Tashlin's. *Bande à part*, for instance, concludes with Franz and Odile, two of its central characters, adrift on an ocean freighter; moments later, a voiceover informs us that an upcoming film will detail, in Cinemascope and Technicolor, the characters' "tropical adventures." *A Woman Is a Woman* makes similar gestures, referring to both comedy and Eastmancolor in its opening credits; Godard, in this, his first widescreen film, also has his characters make note of the aspect ratio that ostensibly surrounds them. The opening of *The Girl Can't Help It* and the "television" scene in *Will Success Spoil Rock Hunter?* come immediately to mind. Later in *A Woman Is a Woman*, Jean-Claude Brialy says, to the camera, "It's hard to tell if this is a comedy or a tragedy, but either way, it's a masterpiece." The film ends with a shot of a neon "FIN" sign through an apartment window — a gesture very similar to Tashlin having his characters interact with the titles in cartoons such as *Under the Shedding Chestnut Tree* and features such as *Son of Paleface*. In *Le Petit Soldat* (1963), one of the characters makes reference to "cameraman Raoul Coutard" — the name of the great cinematographer who shot that film as well as thirteen other Godard films of this period. *Les Carabiniers* at one point uses the very same stock-standard "howling wolf" sound effect found in, for instance, Universal's 1930s horror films (and countless cartoons) — a sonic gag used to denote a highly subtle rupture, one perhaps meant only for dedicated cinephiles (or scholars). Multiple shots in *La Chinoise* reveal to the viewer the slate used for sound-synchronization purposes, on which are visible both Godard's and Coutard's names. In *Weekend*, the main characters feel no pity for a woman they kill on their journey, dismissing her as merely a fictional character. In the same film, the diegesis and the intertitles interact in curious ways. Not only does the "WEEKEND" intertitle recur at various points in the story, but, at one point, Corinne asks aloud what time it is, only to be "answered" by an intertitle that reads, "Samedi, 15 heures."[10] This is not an exhaustive list.

The technique of direct address, mentioned above, is of special significance for Godard, as he uses it in most of his films of this period. It occurs in *Breathless, Bande à part, Masculin féminin, Contempt* (1963), *Pierrot le Fou, Weekend, Les Carabiniers, Le Petit Soldat, Un Femme Mariée* (1964), *La Chinoise*, and even in *Alphaville* (1965), a film that little resembles Godard's other films from this time. A list of Godard's uses of this technique would be very long, so one particularly rich example will suffice. In *Le Petit Soldat*, the main character, Bruno Forestier, says to another character, "You look at me but you don't know what I'm thinking," a line made significant by his delivering it directly into the lens of the camera. The line becomes not just a point in the diegetic argument Bruno is making, but an indictment of the film's audience, and indeed of the very act of spectatorship. Direct address is so common in Godard's films that it must be identified as one of the primary components of his style during this period. Moreover, it should be identified as one of the strongest links between Godard's films and American anarchic comedies in general, if not Tashlin's films in particular.

Another trait directly links Godard to Tashlin with some force: their skilful anticonsumerist satire. The directors' shared distaste for the more vapid and corrupt products of consumer/capitalist culture is one of the strongest connections between them; in fact, several of Godard's more acerbic jabs at consumer culture have a distinctly Tashlinian flavor. Godard, at one point a highly committed Marxist, is well-known for his disapprobation of the mercenary nature of modern consumer society; this is the director who famously suggested, in an intertitle, that *Masculin féminin* might also be titled "The Children of Marx and Coca-Cola." Nevertheless, highly committed Marxists are certainly not spared Godard's satirical barbs. In the films of the 1959–1967 period, most of the politically aware, radical left-wing characters are depicted as hopelessly naïve, idealistic, and ineffectual, if not downright foolish, dangerous, and corrupt — no better than the capitalists, in other words. This is certainly true of the young ideologues of *Masculin féminin*, *Les Carabiniers*, *Made in U.S.A.*, *Weekend*, and especially *La Chinoise*. This ambivalence further strengthens the connection to Tashlin, whose consumer satire (and even his political satire: see the Cold War subplot of *Artists and Models*) is marked by just such an attitude. Godard may have found in Tashlin a kindred spirit, albeit one whose anticonsumer satire was produced under the aegis of the largest consumer entertainment industry in the world. Indeed, the commercial nature of Tashlin's satire was, in a way, a guarantee of its essential ambivalence.

It was surely this romantic notion of Tashlin as the termite (to use Manny Farber's famous term) eating away at "The System" from the inside, that at least in part attracted Godard, and the rest of the *Cahiers du Cinéma* filmmaker-critics, to Tashlin's films. Jacques Rivette, for instance, wrote with great admiration of such "macho" filmmakers as

Anthony Mann and Robert Aldrich, precisely because they do not aspire to make "high art" but because they use bold stylistic choices to depict the grim ambivalence of the modern world.[11] Eric Rohmer, for another, wrote in praise of the refreshingly modern gestures of American comedy,

> Notwithstanding its classicism of form and inspiration, American cinema is more modern, in a certain sense, than American literature, which is too turned in on itself to open its eyes to the evolution of the natural or the social environment. . . . If there is one genre where America has shone with an incomparable brilliance, to a point no one else can even approach, it is comedy, ever since the days of Mack Sennett. And what is it that makes its satire so virulent? The denunciation of a bourgeois conformity caving in on itself? Much more that of new constraints which are more topical and more acute.[12]

Bernard Eisenschitz astutely summarizes the *Cahiers du Cinéma* writers' general position on Tashlin himself: "Tashlin not only identified and denounced the contradiction of American cinema, but also embodied it, since the ambivalence of his films makes it impossible to say which side he is taking, or to be sure that he is not exploiting the very thing that he is denouncing. The *Cahiers* group did not only see Tashlin as radically destructive, they also appreciated the sheer beauty of what he showed."[13]

For the *Cahiers du Cinéma* critics (and, to an extent, the critics at *Positif*, as well), Tashlin represented a fresh, modern talent who embodied the gloss and top-notch craftsmanship of the studio system while at the same time subtly critiquing it from within. It was surely a heady combination of associations for these brash *cineaste*-critics, and it is worth noting that certain Godard films evince similarly ambivalent preoccupations. *Contempt*, perhaps Godard's most flat-out gorgeous film, is also a critique of high-gloss Hollywood (and European) productions. The beautiful, almost impossibly saturated colors of *La Chinoise* are used to bring into relief the film's characters' political naïveté: here, vivid primary colors (especially Mao's favorite color, red) are aligned with faux-intellectual dogmatism.

Godard's films from this period brim with gags (and non-gags) whose targets are advertising and other excesses of consumerism. *Masculin féminin* uses an intertitle to introduce an upcoming segment, a "dialogue with a consumer product." The "consumer product" turns out to be "Miss Nineteen," the winner of a national teen beauty contest; in a single, uncomfortable, six-and-a-half-minute take, Paul, the film's protagonist, interviews, from offscreen, this young woman about matters political, and her responses are unerringly vacuous. The scene has no relationship with any other element of the film's diegesis. The joke here is not just that the vaunted representatives of modern French youth culture are politically uninformed (a point made all the more clearly by the scene's ostensible use of documentary technique), but that this scene itself is a further interruption of the already scattered narrative about Paul and his romantic pursuits. In other words, Godard here uses a diegesis-rupturing non-gag to satirize consumer culture—a highly Tashlinian gesture. And, while the "Marx and Coca-Cola" reference has been duly celebrated, a similar line, delivered into an interviewer's microphone by aspiring pop star and willing shill Madeleine, is just as thorough an indictment of the ever-blurring line between entertainment and advertisement: "J'adore Pepsi-Cola!"

The mordantly funny *Weekend* is perhaps Godard's definitive statement on a consumer culture that he views as not just empty, but lethal. When Corinne and Roland, the film's protagonists, crash their car and it bursts into flames, Corinne worries not for herself or her lover, but for her Hermès handbag; later, she dives into another of the many wrecked cars in the film not to save an injured person, but to steal her *très chic* pants. (Even this pales in comparison to the film's final joke, in which Corinne, having taken up with a roving gang of cannibal hippie Marxists, unflinchingly eats the flesh of her executed lover.) One of *Weekend*'s best gags is very similar to the final joke in the climactic "Stay-Put Lipstick Spectacular" scene at the end of *Will Success Spoil Rock Hunter?* In one of the film's many digressions, a man incongruously plays a Mozart sonata in a barnyard. Amy Taubin offers a concise description of this scene's central gag: "In a ludicrous parody of the product placement just then gaining a foothold in Hollywood movies, Godard has painted 'Pianos Bechstein' in large white letters on the side of the concert grand."[14] Even Mozart cannot escape the taint of commercial crassness, just as Rita Marlowe's "true love" is sponsored in neon by Stay-Put Lipstick. Furthermore, the gag bears some resemblance to, for instance, the joke in *The Disorderly Orderly* in which a travel agency's window display advertises TWA's in-flight movies, which include *The Disorderly Orderly*. Tashlin plugs TWA (and his own film) while still making a joke about the ubiquity of advertising. Godard does much the same thing: Bechstein is in fact a manufacturer of pianos, and, though they probably did not pay for the advertisement, Godard provides it, albeit in a sardonic manner.

While Tashlin is hardly the only filmmaker with a distaste for the ugly side of commercial culture, this theme runs throughout his work, from the print cartoons to the children's books to the animation and through to the features. Given Godard's professed admiration of Tashlin's work, and the general tendency of New Wave filmmakers to celebrate as auteurs those Hollywood filmmakers who appeared to subvert the studio system from within, it seems plausible that this satirical, anticonsumerist tendency in Godard's films may be traced in part to Tashlin.

Of the three directors briefly surveyed here, Almodóvar seems to have the least direct connection to Tashlin: his films contain elements that may also be found in Tashlin's work, but that are not used in similar ways. Godard's films have a closer, albeit somewhat slippery, relationship to those of Tashlin: he employs techniques that Tashlin used, and for similar if not identical purposes, but cannot be said to definitively refer to or evoke Tashlin specifically. Rather, as discussed above, the films of Godard's 1959–1967 period evoke the irreverence and the disregard for narrative cohesion that characterizes many Hollywood comedies of the studio era. Tashlin's films are one possible benchmark here — one made all the stronger by Godard's avowed appreciation for them. But diegetic rupture, impossible gags, and the like do not belong exclusively to Tashlin; indeed, the finest examples of such anarchic comedy may be found in such ardently madcap films as *Hellzapoppin'* and *Never Give a Sucker an Even Break*. As discussed above, the consumerist satire evident in both directors' films does, however, suggest a somewhat stronger linkage between them: the targets of their bitter humor were similar, if not identical, even if Godard tended to season it with more overtly political content. Indeed, one of the many reasons that Godard is such a superb and important filmmaker is that he is able to synthesize the influences of so many of the directors he admires and, in so doing, produce something entirely original. His praise for Tashlin was not empty: the cinematic evidence bespeaks the fascinating connections between these two filmmakers.

The Heir Apparent: Joe Dante

Jean-Luc Godard is as mercurial a filmmaker as has ever been; his Tashlin phase, if indeed he can be said to have had one, was early in his career, and fairly brief. For Joe Dante, however, Tashlin's films have been a constant point of reference. Dante is almost certainly the most Tashlinian director since Tashlin's time—with the exception of Jerry Lewis. More than Godard's, Dante's films demonstrate clear stylistic, thematic, comic, and "attitudinal" similarities with those of Tashlin. The Tashlin influence on Dante is more direct and palpable than it is on either Almodóvar or Godard, partly because the two directors worked in the same industry as well as the same genre.

As discussed in the Introduction, Dante has professed admiration for Tashlin's skill with diegetic rupture, as well as with anarchic comedy in general. The example cited in the Introduction is *Gremlins 2*, but these devices may be found in many other Dante films as well, even those such as *Piranha* (1978) and *The Howling* (1981), which are not marked as comedies. The Introduction also notes the difficulty in singling out Tashlin as the standard-bearer of anarchic comedy, for, though he excelled at this mode of humor, he was by no means its only practitioner. An investigation into some of Dante's films, however, reveals that the Tashlin influence runs deeper than this. Dante's films are not only anarchic comedies, but they are, more often than not, *Tashlinian* anarchic comedies.

A good, if unusual, place to begin investigating the similarities between Tashlin and Dante is the 1989 omnibus film *Amazon Women on the Moon*, the directorial credit for which is shared by Dante, John Landis, Peter Horton, Carl Gottlieb, and Robert K. Weiss. The film is an assemblage of scattershot gags that are presented as if the viewer were "changing the channel" on the putative television on which he or she watches the film. The structure of the film, in other words, is akin to that of a vaudeville performance; moreover, the film's humor itself is decidedly rooted in the vaudeville tradition. One of Dante's segments, for instance, presents a "roast" of a recently deceased man presided over by none other than Rip Taylor, Slappy White, Jackie Vernon, Henny Youngman, Charlie Callas, and Steve Allen, comedians with strong links to the vaudeville tradition. Dante clearly favors this type of comedy, allowing the segment to overstay its welcome so that all the comedians (save Vernon) may perform brief bits. If nothing else, Dante's directing of this segment (and, indeed, his very participation in *Amazon Women on the Moon*) indicates that his comic roots are similar if not identical to Tashlin's.[15]

Dante's other contributions to *Amazon Women on the Moon* are Tashlinian in the sense that they are rife with sight gags and consumer satire. The segment "Hairlooming" capably employs both of these comic techniques: it takes the form of a low-budget mock advertisement for a company that offers a unique solution to baldness: a swatch of custom-cut carpet affixed to the skull with a nail gun. The central sight gag is the deep-pile toupée itself (as well as a shot of a satisfied customer lathering it up in the shower). The ad itself is a parody of cheap late-night hucksterism, and its target is the insecure, foolhardy viewer who would purchase the Hairloom. Another segment, "Bullshit or Not?," a parody of such shows as "In Search of . . .," puts forth the notion that perhaps the true identity of Jack the Ripper was, in fact, The Loch Ness Monster. The segment builds up to, and is entirely justified by, a single sight gag: that of a large, crudely made Nessie prop attired like a Victorian Londoner.

A final Dante sketch from *Amazon Women on the Moon* is worth noting: "Reckless Youth," a parody of the "social guidance films" to which countless unwitting mid-century American children were subjected. This segment contains a number of Tashlinian gags. In one, a man who has been blinded by his unnamed "social disease" scorches his offscreen coworker with a blowtorch; in another, a point-of-view shot of infectious germs through a microscope's lens shows a small swarm of cartoon mice scampering into their mousehole. But the best gags in "Reckless Youth" are those in which Dante uses cinematic devices themselves for comic purposes, much as Tashlin does: stuttering, decentered camera framings and movements; pointedly mismatched shot/reverse-shot exchanges; the deliberate revelation of the actors' chalked marks on the floor of the set. Each of these examples uses film technique itself to parody not only the form but also the message of these preposterously disinformational films. Moments of subtlety in *Amazon Women on the Moon* are rare, but, here, Dante contributes a nice handful, all of which resemble Tashlinian visual non-gags.

Another Dante film with a direct connection to the sources of Tashlin's humor is *Looney Tunes: Back in Action*, a somewhat misunderstood film that, as its title proudly declares, was an attempt by Warner Bros. to further capitalize on its renowned animation.[16] The film is Tashlinian in a number of ways. First, and most obviously, it uses some of the very same characters and gags that Tashlin used as a Warner Bros. animator: many of the jokes in the film are either lifted from or are references to jokes in the Looney Tunes and Merrie Melodies that are such an important influence on Dante's style. The film is thereby that much closer to the vaudeville and anarchic comedy traditions. Second, the film makes constant, joking reference to its identity as a product designed to exploit the Looney Tunes "brand"—indeed, this idea, which offers numerous opportunities for Tashlinian consumerist satire, is built into the film's narrative. Finally, *Looney Tunes: Back in Action* repeatedly breaks its diegesis and refers, both overtly and subtly, to other Hollywood comedies and other Dante films.

The film's zany plot resembles that of an archetypal Looney Tune, in the ways in which one character routinely uses "reverse psychology" to impel another to act foolishly (a nod to Chuck Jones's *Rabbit Fire* [1951], *Rabbit Seasoning* [1952], and *Duck! Rabbit! Duck!* [1953]), and in its essential impossibility: the characters' goal is to prevent nefarious forces from acquiring a device that can turn humans into monkeys. Moreover, the plot actually incorporates narrative strains from Warner Bros. cartoons into its own narrative, making *Looney Tunes: Back in Action* simultaneously a pastiche, an homage, and a kind of meta-narrative. The film's villain, for instance, is Mr. Chairman (Steve Martin), the goofily sinister head of the Acme Corporation, the company that, in the cartoons, provides all of Wile E. Coyote's ill-built roadrunner-catching devices. All of the familiar cartoon heavies—Yosemite Sam, Elmer Fudd, Nasty Canasta, Wile E. Coyote, Marvin the Martian, and the Tasmanian Devil—turn out to be agents of the Acme Corporation, a fact that retrospectively justifies their antagonistic activities in countless cartoons. The film's story itself is motivated by Daffy Duck's desire to break free of being typecast as second banana to Bugs Bunny, a narrative situation found in countless Warner Bros. cartoons. The film's excerpting from the narratives of the cartoons is near-totalizing, in fact. To observe that the film uses these cartoons for purposes of inspiration, commentary, and *Ur*-reference point is to note that it also, on some level, uses many of Tashlin's films for these same purposes.

One of *Looney Tunes: Back in Action*'s strongest parallels to Tashlin's work is in the various ways in which the film somewhat grimly acknowledges its identity as a consumer product. On several occasions, the film refers to the corporate forces that inevitably play a major role in shaping any work of modern popular art—the kind of shrugging admission that permeates both Dante's and Tashlin's work. The decision to "fire" Daffy Duck, for instance, is undertaken by committee, in the boardroom of the Warner Bros. corporate offices. In subsequent scenes, numerous Warner Bros. properties make appearances: the 1989-vintage Batman and Batmobile (which Daffy steals), for instance. Later, in a multilevel gag, Dante stages a scene in the Warners commissary in which two-dimensional cartoon versions of Scooby-Doo and Shaggy (who appear in a cartoon that runs nearly constantly on Time-Warner's Cartoon Network) converse with Matthew Lillard, the actor who plays Shaggy in Warner Bros.' two live-action/animated *Scooby-Doo* movies (the first of which was released in 2002, and the second of which would be released four months after the premiere of *Looney Tunes: Back in Action*). It is a cross-platform, intra-studio plug that also fits precisely into the film's ironic combination of live-action and animation.

In a later scene, the film's main characters, wandering aimlessly in the southwestern desert, come across, of all things, a Wal-Mart, shimmering like an oasis in the heat—and, indeed, this is the gag: not only that Wal-Mart has colonized even the most desolate reaches of the desert, but that our modern vision of paradise is little more than low, low prices. Before they enter, DJ (Brendan Fraser) asks Kate (Jenna Elfman), a Warner Bros. executive, "Was this your idea?" She responds, "The audience expects it. They don't even notice this kind of thing anymore," at which remark Fraser disappointedly looks directly into the lens. Moments later, when the characters leave the store, Bugs Bunny remarks, "Nice of Wal-Mart to provide these Wal-Mart beverages in return for us saying 'Wal-Mart' so many times." Such moments are clever meta-fictional gags that greatly enhance the film's comedy, but are also tacit, somewhat defeated admissions that modern American filmmaking is more concerned with "branding" and corporate synergy than it is with entertainment. It is no coincidence that a ™ emblem is appended to the film's title.

Diegetic rupture in this film, in fact, is so pervasive that it may be dubbed a structuring device. Dante has said,

> The concept of breaking the fourth wall, which is very difficult to talk people into doing today, is, I think, just great. If you love the act of watching movies, and you love watching movies, then what's

wrong with referring to the fact that you're doing something that you like? Studio executives more often will say, "Well, it takes me out of the picture." I got a lot of that on . . . [*Looney Tunes: Back in Action*]. It was like, "Well, if they turn and talk to the audience, then it takes me out of the movie." My reaction is: You're not in the movie. You're *watching* the movie. It's different.[17]

Nearly every gag in this film refers either to a Warner Bros. cartoon, to the uncanny and impossible combination of live action and animation, or to one of many other films, thereby breaking or commenting on the filmmaking process. For example, Timothy Dalton, who played James Bond in two films, here plays Damian Drake, an actor who plays a Bond-like figure in a successful film series and who, it turns out, actually *is* a spy. Similarly, Brendan Fraser plays DJ, a stuntman who, in the world of the film, doubles for Brendan Fraser; not only does DJ remark that he is onscreen more often than Fraser in *The Mummy* films, but he actually punches and knocks out Fraser (playing an insufferably smug version of himself) at the end of the film. Daffy Duck quotes from *A Few Good Men* (1992); Bugs Bunny overdramatically reënacts the shower scene from *Psycho* (1960), complete with Hershey's-syrup blood; actor Kevin McCarthy (digitally rendered in black and white), star of the original *Invasion of the Body Snatchers* (1956) and a Dante regular, appears at one point clutching a gigantic seed pod; and our heroes are set upon by the villainous monsters and aliens from such films as *This Island Earth* (1955) and *Fiend Without a Face* (1958). A self-referential double gag occurs as DJ gets behind the wheel of an AMC Gremlin, an action underscored by composer Jerry Goldsmith's lifting of a few bars from his own score to Dante's film *Gremlins* (1984).

All of the devices and gags described above are entirely in keeping with the aesthetic of anarchic Hollywood comedy (a category that encompasses Warner Bros. animation), and, more specifically, demonstrate certain pronounced similarities with the films of Frank Tashlin. Such examples exist in vast quantities in Dante's work. A great many of the gags in a great many of his films bust through the diegetic wall (see above), or use sound in incongruously humorous ways (as in the "tweet tweet" sound effect we hear when a creature gets knocked out in *Gremlins*), or highlight the vapidity of some element of popular/consumer culture (the dismantling of the toy industry throughout *Small Soldiers*

[1998]), or comment on their own status as products of a spend-crazy society (the knowing references in *Piranha* to the film's identity as a knockoff of *Jaws* [1975]). The Tashlin connections, if outlined in full, would run to book length.

Jean-Luc Godard and Joe Dante, dissimilar though they may otherwise be, are nevertheless united in their specifically Tashlinian mode of ambivalent, anticonsumerist satire.[18] This tendency seems stronger in Dante than in Godard; it is a feature of nearly all of his films, just as it is a feature of nearly all of Tashlin's. This particular form of satire is not only one of the defining elements of Dante's style, but one of the strongest links between his films and those of Tashlin.

As in Tashlin's films, the satire in Dante's pictures often takes on a bitter flavor; like Tashlin, his real target is not the advertiser, nor even the culture that permits advertising to reach such levels of pervasiveness as it has. Rather, Dante sets his satirical sights on the individual consumer who buys, buys, buys, often at the cost of his or her own freedom or identity. This is the essence of much of the satirical humor in Tashlin: he uses Jayne Mansfield, for instance, not just as a lampoon of modern femininity, but as a means of exposing the real chump: the male consumer who has been taken in by such overblown, disingenuous attempts to commandeer his sexual impulses. The sadness behind such comedy pervades Dante's films, as well.

The plot of *The 'burbs* (1989) concerns a group of suburbanites who convince themselves that their peculiar new neighbors, the Klopeks, are murderers, and, furthermore, that their basement is an abbatoir. *The 'burbs* skewers the paranoia, territoriality, and intolerance of the suburban American. It is when the residents of Mayfield Place finally realize their increasingly mistrustful behavior and stop haranguing their unusual but otherwise untroublesome neighbors that *The 'burbs* cuts somewhat more deeply. The ultimate punchline of the film is that their reactionary suspicions about their neighbors turn out to be justified: the Klopeks really *are* murderers, a fact upheld by a car trunk full of human bones. The confirmation of such seemingly foolish suspicions lends *The 'burbs* a mordant tone: the film leaves none of the characters blameless or honest, and, Dante suggests, the American suburbs are hotbeds not only of sameness and closed-mindedness, but of paranoia and deceit—not to mention large-scale butchery.

The Second Civil War (1997), made for HBO, is one of Dante's most bitter satires. Set in the near future, the film depicts an America so massively multicultural that unexpected racial enmities have entirely squelched any possibility of rational political dialogue. In response to the governor of Idaho shutting his state's borders to a planeload of child refugees from the India-Pakistan nuclear war, federal forces face off against several state National Guard units (as well as libertarian militia members); members of a local Sioux tribe suspend their recognition of the federal government; a hot-headed congressman who is also the leader of the Nation of Islam chides a well-respected African-American reporter for not being black enough; an all-powerful lobbyist weighs minority groups' relative electoral capabilities against their expendability in armed combat; members of Los Angeles's African-American gangs open fire on their city's Latino mayor; the Chinese governor of Rhode Island, home to the nation's largest Chinese population, follows Idaho's lead and closes *his* state's borders . . . to other Chinese citizens; and the deadline for military action is determined by the airtime of "All My Children." The event that eventually triggers the titular armed conflict is the mishearing of a single word: "succession" mistaken for "secession."

Intriguingly, *The Second Civil War* suggests further similarities between Dante and Godard, in that it signals a mid-career turn from satirizing consumer culture to satirizing political culture. This film, as well as Dante's two entries in the "Masters of Horror" series, marks a palpable shift in the objects of his satire. (Notably, all three of these films were made for cable television.) It was only in his book *The World That Isn't* that Tashlin approached the kind of political satire found in both Dante's and Godard's films, suggesting, perhaps, that both of these directors may have drawn on the satiric skills they learned from Tashlin to tap into a subject that their teacher barely scratched.

Gremlins 2: The New Batch (1990), as argued in the Introduction, is a wholeheartedly anarchic comedy which is, in many ways, Dante's most Tashlinian film: a thorough discussion of it would be quite lengthy. Here, instead, I wish to discuss one final Dante picture: *Explorers* (1985), an overlooked film that unexpectedly contains some of Dante's most acerbic satire.

Explorers concerns three teenage boys who realize that, in their dreams, they have each been receiving messages from a distant planet that, when decoded, can help them assemble their own small spacecraft, which they proceed to construct out of a Tilt-a-Whirl car, a home computer, and materials scavenged from a junkyard. Devoted science-fiction fans and full of youthful curiosity, the boys are immensely excited about the possibility of discovering new worlds. But they are tremendously disappointed when they finally manage to make contact with Wak and Neek, the aliens who had been sending them the dream-messages. These new, weird, life forms have no life-changing revelations, no new insights, or anything of the sort. All they can offer the boys is an endless, meaningless barrage of quotations of and references to American popular culture. The aliens have been receiving television and radio signals from Earth for years, and have become so consumed with their wondrous variety that they have devoted their lives to studying, quoting, and aping these transmissions, albeit without the benefit of any sort of context.

Upon their first encounter with the aliens, Ben (Ethan Hawke, in his first role), in a blanket reference to the 1950s sci-fi films that Dante adores, says, "I've waited all my life to say this," holding up his right hand, palm outward. "We come in peace." Wak, after a pause, replies, "Ehh, what's up, Doc?" in perfect imitation of Bugs Bunny, a cultural touchstone of obvious importance to Dante. "It's probably not English," Ben rationalizes in the subsequent scene. "It's probably just an alien language that *sounds* like English." Wak responds by singing the theme song to "Mr. Ed."

The exchange continues in this vein, culminating in Wak's performance of a series of one-liners, celebrity impersonations, and advertising copy in front of a gigantic screen, on which flash fragments of old movies, TV shows, commercials, and assorted bits of broadcast ephemera. The aliens are unable to distinguish the entertainment from the commercials. For them, it's all equally enjoyable, just as it is, Dante is thereby arguing, for the undiscriminating American viewer, manifestations of whom appear in many Tashlin films, perhaps most notably in *Rock-a-Bye Baby*. Wak's one-alien show ends with his lip-synching to "All Around the World" by Little Richard, the very artist whose songs stand in so cleverly, in *The Girl Can't Help It*, for both the joyousness and the emptiness of modern popular culture. (During the song, the massive video screen even flashes a clip of Little Richard performing "Ready Teddy" in that selfsame film.) "They don't make any sense," says Ben, crestfallen and visibly ill at ease.

The boyish wonder so earnestly expressed by the three main characters in *Explorers* is absolutely crushed by their realization that the most vacuous elements of popular culture have preceded them, and have thus rendered impossible any attempt at interstellar communication. The very cultural artifacts that the boys themselves enjoy—their bedrooms teem with movie posters, comic books, and the like—take on new and disappointing meanings when co-opted by ostensibly superintelligent alien beings. But these elements of popular culture are not entirely malevolent: they provide Wak and Neek with genuine amusement and entertainment, which, after all, is what they were designed to do. Herein lies the film's Tashlinian ambivalence: the aliens, in all earnestness, celebrate popular culture, yet *Explorers* depicts that popular culture as capable of nothing less than the shattering of youthful idealism. It is a truly bitter ending, and one that strongly echoes Tashlin's ambivalent stance on the very same subject.

Executives at Paramount Pictures, the studio that released *Explorers*, may have picked up on this bitterness, and were perhaps responsible for the film's tacked-on ending. In this last scene, the boys, somehow united in a dream, fly through the air as they receive another coded alien message. They swoop and dive joyously, and Ben is even joined—and kissed—by the girl on whom he has a crush. Apparently, then, the film ends not bitterly but hopefully. This hopeful tone is undercut, however, by the fact that the scene is unmistakably fantastical: it exists only in the boys' minds. They are not able to fly, and their spacecraft has long since crashed and sunk in a local harbor, thus ending their adventures. Indeed, the film's last word goes not to the boys but to Wak, who tells a hoary old vaudeville-type joke directly to the camera, and is then blasted off the screen by a three-second, multi-shot barrage of images from cartoons and commercials. Such an ending is entirely similar to those of such Tashlin films as *Son of Paleface* and *Will Success Spoil Rock Hunter?*, in which typically pat, romantic finales are destabilized by the suggestion of further disintegration or satire. As argued in previous chapters, Tashlin is especially keen on and good at such endings; so, too, is Dante, who employs them here as well as in *The 'burbs*, *Gremlins 2*, *The Second Civil War*, and *Homecoming* (2005), among others.

Generally speaking, we can trace a more direct line from Tashlin's work to Dante's than we can from Tashlin's to Godard's, partly because the two directors worked in the same industry, and, generally, in the same genre. Though Dante has made several films that might show up in the "Horror" or "Science Fiction" section of the local video store, in truth his films are hybrids that blend comedy with one or more other genres. There are no Dante films that are not at least partly comic, a fact that links him to Tashlin all the more strongly. Indeed, Dante's comedy track record is better, in some ways, than Tashlin's, for he has never made the equivalent of *Say One for Me* or *The Way of Peace*.[19]

Though the American studio system underwent a great many economic changes in the years between the end of Tashlin's career and the beginning of Dante's, both directors have been, to some extent, victims of their adherence to the genre of comedy. As discussed in Chapter Seven, Tashlin appears to have been regarded within the studio system as a capable programmer but never as an auteur: he bounced from studio to studio and, unlike several of his colleagues, never formed or was given the chance to form his own film production company, a move that might have granted him greater creative freedom and economic independence. Dante has had his own production company for some time, but since *Looney Tunes: Back in Action* in 2003, has not directed a feature film for theatrical release, concentrating on and distinguishing himself in television, where he has directed, among other works, two critically acclaimed entries in Showtime's "Masters of Horror" series: "Homecoming" and "The Screwfly Solution" (2006).[20] These somewhat similar career trajectories further the connections between Tashlin and Dante, and suggest that their approach to both content and style may have a particular niche in mainstream Hollywood filmmaking that may not be looked upon with favor by those running the show.

Did (Comic) Success Spoil Frank Tashlin?

Investigating the legacy of Frank Tashlin is a curious task. For one thing, few directors have cited him as an influence, a condition seemingly unlikely to change any time soon, even with the recent, mildly increased awareness of his work. Of Hollywood directors in the studio era, Tashlin will never be as large an influence as, say, Alfred Hitchcock or Howard Hawks, but neither is he a nearly forgotten man like Norman Z. McLeod or Melville Shavelson, both of whom had long, successful careers in comedy.

The fact that he worked nearly exclusively in comedy is one of the principal reasons that Tashlin's legacy is not especially pronounced. Not only do comic films rarely garner the accolades heaped upon films of the "serious" genres, but the fundamentals of Tashlin's style are entirely rooted in traditions of American comic performance and filmmaking. Without the framework of anarchic, vaudeville-derived comedy, Tashlin would barely have *had* a style.

The most significant of the several ironies of Tashlin's career is that, while the genre of comedy afforded him ample opportunity to express his artistic voice, it also placed limits on his status and reputation. Tashlin was a very good comedy director, and understood the genre as well as or better than any other Hollywood filmmaker of the 1950s and 1960s. However, his success within that genre, and the fact that he was not able to assert his economic and artistic independence, assured that his studios would deem his style appropriate only for program comedies. Jerry Lewis films were reliable moneymakers for Paramount, but directing them likely prevented Tashlin from becoming a name above the title, like Hawks and Wilder were. More than this, Tashlin's association with low comedy has dimmed his reputation within film history. Tashlin's single-genre career, his strong kinship with directors of program comedies, as well as the Jerry Lewis Question, have compromised his status as an auteur. Comedy was Tashlin's home and the best fit for his talents, but it was also, in many ways, a curse.

APPENDIX FRANK TASHLIN'S CREATIVE WORK

Unless otherwise noted, Tashlin is the director (or, in the case of some of the animated films, "supervisor," which means essentially the same thing) of all of the films listed below. The films' release dates are in parentheses.

The sections on Tashlin's recorded, radio, and television work are not incorporated into the chronological order of the rest of the filmography.

The essays that are the indispensable sources for the following information are all by Howard Prouty: "Filmography," "Bibliography," "Radio," and "Recordings," all in Roger Garcia, ed., *Frank Tashlin* (London: British Film Institute Publishing, 1994), pp. 197–238.

ANIMATED FILMS

VAN BEUREN CORPORATION PRODUCTIONS
Hook & Ladder Hokum (as codirector, with George Stallings; April 28, 1933)

LEON SCHLESINGER PRODUCTIONS
Buddy's Beer Garden (as animator, with Jack King; November 11, 1933)

UB IWERKS PRODUCTIONS/TAT'S TALES
There is some uncertainty about exactly which films Tashlin worked on at Iwerks's company. He claims to have worked on more than one of the "Flip the Frog" cartoons, but Leonard Maltin argues that it is more likely he worked on the "Comicolor" and "Willie Whopper" cartoons series.

LEON SCHLESINGER PRODUCTIONS
(as Frank Tash)
Porky's Poultry Plant (August 22, 1936)
Little Beau Porky (November 14, 1936)
Porky in the North Woods (December 19, 1936)
Porky's Road Race (February 6, 1937)
Porky's Romance (April 3, 1937)
Porky's Building (June 19, 1937)

(as Frank Tashlin)
Porky's Railroad (August 7, 1937)
Speaking of the Weather (September 4, 1937)
The Case of the Stuttering Pig (October 30, 1937)
Porky's Double Trouble (November 13, 1937)
The Woods Are Full of Cuckoos (December 4, 1937)
Porky at the Crocadero (February 5, 1938)
Now That Summer Is Gone (May 14, 1938)
Porky the Fireman (June 4, 1938)
Have You Got Any Castles? (June 25, 1938)
Porky's Spring Planting (July 25, 1938)
The Major Lied 'Til Dawn (August 13, 1938)
Wholly Smoke (August 27, 1938)
Cracked Ice (September 10, 1938)
Little Pancho Vanilla (October 8, 1938)
You're an Education (November 5, 1938)

WALT DISNEY STUDIOS

Tashlin did no directing at Disney, but served as a writer on numerous cartoons. Studio policy held that writers received no on-screen credit, so the list below is necessarily incomplete.

(as writer and/or story director)
Mr. Duck Steps Out (June 7, 1940)
Donald's Vacation (August 9, 1940)
Pluto's Dream House (August 30, 1940)
Mr. Mouse Takes a Trip (November 11, 1940)
Pluto's Pal Bobo (This unproduced cartoon may have evolved into *Pluto's Playmate* [1941], but animation historian Michael Barrier believes that Tashlin had nothing to do with this film.)
Peter and the Wolf (produced 1946) (In the early 1940s, Tashlin allegedly filmed pencil tests of a portion of this film, which later showed up in the compilation feature film *Make Mine Music* in 1946, and was released as a stand-alone short in 1955.)
Mickey and the Beanstalk (produced 1947) (In the early 1940s, Tashlin contributed story and joke ideas to this film, which was eventually released in 1947.)
Lady and the Tramp (produced 1955) (Tashlin is given sole writing credit for a 1940 draft of the screenplay for this film; the script

went through numerous revisions before being made into a feature in 1955. Additionally, there is some uncertainty about Tashlin's possible contributions to the scripts of *Pinocchio* [1937], *Fantasia* [1940], and/or *Cinderella* [1949]. Disney was in the habit of soliciting gags and situations from its staff writers, so it is possible that Tashlin, like many others, can take some small degree of credit for the scripts to these films.)

SCREEN GEMS, INC.
The Great Cheese Mystery (as writer; October 27, 1941)
The Fox and the Grapes (December 5, 1941)
The Tangled Angler (December 26, 1941)
A Hollywood Detour (January 23, 1942)
Under the Shedding Chestnut Tree (as supervisor/producer; February 22, 1942)
Wacky Wigwams (as supervisor/producer; February 22, 1942)
Dog Meets Dog (as supervisor/producer; March 6, 1942)
Concerto in B-Flat Minor (as supervisor/producer; March 20, 1942)
Wolf Chases Pigs (as supervisor/producer; April 20, 1942)
Cinderella Goes to a Party (as supervisor/producer; May 3, 1942)
A Battle for a Bottle (as supervisor/producer; May 29, 1942)
Woodman, Spare that Tree (as supervisor/producer, July 2, 1942)
The Bulldog and the Baby (as supervisor/producer; July 3, 1942)
Song of Victory (as supervisor; September 4, 1942)

Tashlin left Screen Gems in June 1942, citing differences with Dave Fleischer, who had been hired as executive producer two months earlier. The production of the following five cartoons was begun under Tashlin but completed under Fleischer; the extent of Tashlin's contributions to these films is uncertain.
Old Blackout Joe (August 27, 1942)
The Gullible Canary (September 18, 1942)
The Dumbconscious Mind (October 23, 1942)
Tito's Guitar (October 30, 1942)
Toll Bridge Troubles (November 27, 1942)

LEON SCHLESINGER PRODUCTIONS
Porky Pig's Feat (July 17, 1943)
Scrap Happy Daffy (August 21, 1943)
The Goldbrick (September 1943) (a "Private Snafu" cartoon)

Corny Concerto (as writer; September 18, 1943)
The Home Front (November 1943) (a "Private Snafu" cartoon)
Puss 'n' Booty (December 11, 1943)
I Got Plenty of Mutton (March 11, 1944)
The Swooner Crooner (May 6, 1944)
The Chow Hound (June 1944) (a "Private Snafu" cartoon)
Censored (July 1944) (a "Private Snafu" cartoon)
Brother Brat (July 15, 1944)
Plane Daffy (September 16, 1944)
Booby Hatched (October 14, 1944)
The Stupid Cupid (November 25, 1944)
The Unruly Hare (February 10, 1945)
Behind the Meat-Ball (April 7, 1945)
A Tale of Two Mice (June 30, 1945)
Nasty Quacks (December 1, 1945)
Hare Remover (March 23, 1946)

MOREY & SUTHERLAND PRODUCTIONS, "DAFFY DITTIES"
The Lady Said No (April 26, 1946)
Choo Choo Amigo (July 5, 1946)
Pepito's Serenade (August 16, 1946)

EAST WEST PRODUCTIONS
The Way of Peace (April 23, 1947)

LIVE-ACTION FILMS

MOVIES
Delightfully Dangerous (as story consultant; dir. Arthur Lubin, Charles R. Rogers Enterprises, 1945)
Double Rhythm (as cowriter; dir. George B. Templeton, Paramount, 1946)
A Night in Casablanca (as uncredited cowriter; dir. Archie Mayo, UA, 1946)
Monsieur Beaucaire (as uncredited cowriter; dir. George Marshall, Paramount, 1946)
Ladies' Man (uncredited cowriter; dir. William D. Russell, Paramount, 1947)
Variety Girl (as cowriter; dir. George Marshall, Paramount, 1947)

The Paleface (as cowriter; dir. Norman Z. McLeod, Paramount, 1948)
The Fuller Brush Man (as cowriter; dir. S. Sylvan Simon, Columbia, 1948)
One Touch of Venus (as cowriter; dir. William A. Seiter, Universal, 1948)
A Southern Yankee (as uncredited cowriter; dir. Edward Sedgwick, MGM, 1948)
Red, Hot and Blue (as uncredited cowriter; dir. John Farrow, Paramount, 1949)
Love Happy (as cowriter; dir. David Miller, Artists Alliance, 1949)
Miss Grant Takes Richmond (as cowriter; dir. Lloyd Bacon, Columbia, 1949)
The Good Humor Man (as writer; dir. Lloyd Bacon, Columbia, 1950)
A Woman of Distinction (as cowriter; dir. Edward Buzzell, Columbia, 1950)
Kill the Umpire (as writer; dir. Lloyd Bacon, Columbia, 1950)
The Fuller Brush Girl (as writer; dir. Lloyd Bacon, Columbia, 1950)
The Lemon Drop Kid (as cowriter and codirector; Paramount, 1951) (This Bob Hope comedy was originally directed by Sidney Lanfield, but previews in August of 1951 were unfavorable. Producer Robert Welch turned to screenwriter Tashlin, who wrote and directed additional scenes that ultimately comprised about 33 minutes of the film's 91-minute running time.)
My Favorite Spy (as uncredited cowriter; dir. Norman Z. McLeod, Paramount, 1951)
The First Time (as cowriter and director; Columbia, 1952)
Son of Paleface (as cowriter and director; Paramount, 1952)
Marry Me Again (as writer and director; RKO, 1953)
Red Garters (as uncredited cowriter; dir. George Marshall, Paramount, 1954)
Susan Slept Here (RKO, 1954) (Tashlin received no screen credit for cowriting this film's screenplay.)
Artists and Models (as cowriter and director; Paramount, 1955)
5 against the House (as uncredited cowriter; dir. Phil Karlson, Columbia, 1955)
The Best Things in Life Are Free (as uncredited cowriter; dir. Michael Curtiz, Twentieth Century-Fox, 1956)
The Scarlet Hour (as cowriter; dir. Michael Curtiz, Paramount, 1956)

The Lieutenant Wore Skirts (as cowriter and director; Twentieth Century-Fox, 1956)

Hollywood or Bust (Paramount, 1956) (Tashlin received no screen credit for cowriting this film's screenplay.)

The Girl Can't Help It (as cowriter, producer, and director; Twentieth Century-Fox, 1956)

Will Success Spoil Rock Hunter? (as writer, producer, and director; Twentieth Century-Fox, 1957)

Rock-a-Bye Baby (as writer and director; Paramount, 1958)

The Geisha Boy (as writer and director; Paramount, 1958)

Say One for Me (as producer and director; Twentieth Century-Fox, 1959) (Tashlin received no screen credit for cowriting this film's screenplay.)

Cinderfella (as writer and director; Paramount, 1960)

Snow White and the Three Stooges (as uncredited cowriter; dir. Charles Lang, Twentieth Century-Fox, 1961)

Gigot (as uncredited cowriter; dir. Gene Kelly, Twentieth Century-Fox, 1962)

Bachelor Flat (as cowriter and director; Twentieth Century-Fox, 1962)

Something's Got to Give (as uncredited cowriter; dir. George Cukor, Twentieth Century-Fox, 1962) (This Marilyn Monroe–Dean Martin film was never completed.)

It'$ Only Money (Paramount, 1962) (Tashlin received no screen credit for cowriting this film's screenplay.)

The Man from the Diner's Club (Columbia, 1963)

Who's Minding the Store? (as cowriter and director; Paramount, 1963)

The Disorderly Orderly (as writer and director; Paramount, 1964)

The Alphabet Murders (MGM, 1966)

The Glass-Bottom Boat (MGM, 1966)

The Bear That Wasn't (as producer; 1967) (In 1967, Tashlin produced one more animated film, an adaptation of his book *The Bear That Wasn't*. Despite Chuck Jones's direction, Tashlin was quite displeased with the film. I've placed it here, with the live-action films, to maintain chronology.)

Caprice (as cowriter and director; Twentieth Century-Fox, 1967)

The Shakiest Gun in the West (as source of adapted material; dir. Alan Rafkin, Universal, 1968) (This Don Knotts feature was based on the screenplay for *The Paleface*, cowritten by Tashlin and Edmund Hartmann.)

The Private Navy of Sgt. O'Farrell (as writer and director; UA, 1968)

TELEVISION

"Sleepyheads" episode (pilot) of the NBC series *Oops, It's Daisy* (as cowriter and director; aired August 5, 1953)

Pilot episode of the NBC series *The Great Gildersleeve* (as producer and director; aired September 12, 1954)

"The Face Is Familiar" episode of the CBS General Electric Theater series (aired November 21, 1954)

"The Honest Man" episode of the CBS General Electric Theater series (aired February 19, 1956)

"The Big Shooter" episode of the CBS *General Electric Theater* series (as cowriter and director; aired February 17, 1957)

"New Girl in His Life" episode of the CBS *General Electric Theater* series (as story consultant; aired May 26, 1957)

"The Frances Langford Show," an NBC Rexall TV Special (as writer and director; aired May 1, 1960)

RADIO

The Eddie Bracken Show (staff writer; CBS, September–December, 1946)

"The Boy Who Sang for the King" (as cowriter; NBC, December 19, 1946)

"The Voices of Walter Schumann" (as cowriter; NBC, July 13, 1950)

"Mr. Moonseed" (as writer; NBC, 1951)

RECORDINGS

"Frank Tashlin's *The Bear That Wasn't*" (as writer; MGM Records, 1947)

"The Boy Who Sang for the King" (as story consultant; RCA Victor Records, 1949)

"How the Circus Learned to Smile" (as story consultant; RCA Victor Records, 1949) (Tashlin also illustrated the 11-page story book that accompanied this two-record set.)

The Voices of Walter Schumann: "Romance in the Air!" (as cowriter; Capitol Records, 1952)

NOTES

PREFACE: TASHLIN RESURGENT

1. See http://archive.elca.org/archives/film/wayofpeace.html (last accessed 16 September 2010).

2. See http://www.filmforum.org/films/tashlin.html (last accessed 16 September 2010). *The Lieutenant Wore Skirts*, it is true, has been resuscitated somewhat by semi-frequent showings on Turner Classic Movies, but *Bachelor Flat* has virtually no cultural currency whatsoever.

3. I refer specifically to, respectively, Sam Wasson, *A Splurch in the Kisser: The Movies of Blake Edwards* (Middletown, CT: Wesleyan University Press, 2009); Remi Fournier Lanzoni, *Comedy Italian Style: The Golden Age of Italian Film Comedies* (London: Continuum Publishing, 2009); Rimgaila Salys, *The Musical Comedy Films of Grigorii Aleksandrov: Laughing Matters* (Bristol, UK: Intellect Books, 2009); Mel Watkins, *On the Real Side: A History of African American Comedy* (Chicago: Lawrence Hill Books, 1999); Elizabeth Kendall, *The Runaway Bride: Hollywood Romantic Comedy of the 1930s* (New York: Cooper Square Press, 2002); James Harvey, *Romantic Comedy in Hollywood: From Lubitsch to Sturges* (New York: Da Capo Press, 1998); Maria Di Battista, *Fast-Talking Dames* (New Haven, CT: Yale University Press, 2003); Imogen Sara Smith, *Buster Keaton: The Persistence of Comedy* (Chicago: Gambit Publishing, 2008); Noël Carroll, *Comedy Incarnate: Buster Keaton, Physical Humor, and Bodily Coping* (West Sussex, UK: Wiley-Blackwell, 2009); Edward McPherson, *Buster Keaton: Tempest in a Flat Hat* (New York: Newmarket Press, 2006).

4. See the Internet Movie Database's "All Time Worldwide Box Office" rankings at http://www.imdb.com/boxoffice/alltimegross?region=world-wide (last accessed 1 August 2011).

5. See the Internet Movie Database's "Full cast and crew for *Mama Mia!*" at http://www.imdb.com/title/tt0795421/fullcredits (last accessed 1 August 2011).

6. Incidentally, *The Girl Can't Help It* is, tangentially, the source of the working title for this book, "Cheerful Nihilism," which comes from a line in Jean Domarchi's article "D'une pierre trois coups" (*Cahiers du Cinéma* 72, June 1957, p. 45). Speaking of the final scene in *The Girl Can't Help It*, Domarchi writes, "Tashlin, the ultimate connoisseur of the failure of illusions, has crafted a rigorous conclusion that perfectly jibes with his cheerful nihilism." This semi-oxymoron (so rendered by my admittedly patchy French) seems to me to capture much of the ambivalent humor in Tashlin's films, and offers

astute commentary, whether intentional or not, on the somewhat tragic career of this very funny man.

INTRODUCTION: THE DIRECTOR WHO WASN'T

1. Howard Prouty speculates that anti-German sentiment during World War I led Tashlin to drop the *von* and, eventually, the *c* and *e* from his surname. (Howard Prouty, "Chronology," in Roger Garcia, ed., *Frank Tashlin* [London: British Film Institute Publishing, 1994], p. 187.) Prouty's article was indispensable in compiling this career overview.

2. Ibid. These cartoons were signed "Tashlein," but were later altered in Tashlin's scrapbooks, to "Tash"—a *nom de dessin animé* he occasionally used later in his career; "Tish Tash" is another.

3. On this last title, see http://www.compedit.com/whiz_bang.htm (last visited 3 August 2011) for a solid summary of the magazine's sense of humor, which, according to author William Coyle, was quite sexual.

4. Curiously, it is "Van Boring," one of Tashlin's earliest professional creative efforts, that has given him perhaps his strongest presence on the internet: "Van Boring" has a Facebook page, updated daily! http://www.facebook.com/pages/Van-Boring-He-Never-Says-a-Word/108739165850755?v=wall (last visited 3 August 2011).

5. Quoted in Prouty, in Garcia, ed., p. 188.

6. On The Internet Movie Database, Tashlin is noted for his uncredited contributions to three Laurel and Hardy films, all from 1935: *Thicker Than Water*, *The Fixer Uppers*, and *Tit for Tat* (http://us.imdb.com/name/nm0850895/; last visited 3 August 2011).

7. Howard Prouty, "Filmography," in Garcia, ed., p. 199.

8. Ibid., p. 202.

9. For a detailed history of the Disney animators' strike, see Michael Barrier's invaluable *Hollywood Cartoons: American Animation in Its Golden Age* (New York: Oxford University Press, 1999), pp. 279–85.

10. See Greg Ford, "'Cross-referred Media': Frank Tashlin's cartoon work," in Garcia, ed., p. 83.

11. Prouty, "Filmography," in Garcia, ed., p. 209.

12. All information on Tashlin's screenwriting career can be found in Prouty, "Filmography," in Garcia, ed., pp. 210–11.

13. Quoted in Prouty, "Chronology," in Garcia, ed., p. 191.

14. According to Prouty, Tashlin's "added scenes and retakes" amounted to 32.5 of 91 minutes, or 2,925 of 8,221 feet—just about 36 percent of the film. (Prouty, "Filmography," in Garcia, ed., p. 213.)

15. Prouty, "Chronology," in Garcia, ed., p. 191.

16. On the growing animosity between Martin and Lewis, see Nick Tosches, *Dino: Living High in the Dirty Business of Dreams* (New York: Dell, 1992), pp. 286–89.

17. Even at it limped toward collapse, the Martin and Lewis series produced a film just about every six months, a fact attested to by the release dates of the last three films: *Artists and Models*: November 7, 1955; *Pardners* (dir. Norman Taurog): July 25, 1956; *Hollywood or Bust*: December 6, 1956.

18. The Tashlin issue of *Positif* is 29, Fall 1958.

19. Jean-Luc Godard, review of *Hollywood or Bust*, *Cahiers du Cinéma* 73, July, 1957, p. 46. Translation appears in Jonathan Rosenbaum, "Tashlinesque," in Garcia, ed., p. 23.

20. Patron comment card for *The Glass Bottom Boat* preview at The Village Theater, Westwood, California, February 11, 1966. (On file in The Frank Tashlin Collection at The Margaret Herrick Library, Beverly Hills, CA)

21. Joe Dante, *Gremlins 2: The New Batch* DVD commentary track, Warner Home Video, 2001.

22. Bill Krohn, "The Outsider: Joe Dante on Tashlin," in Roger Garcia, ed., *Frank Tashlin* (London: British Film Institute Publishing, 1994), p. 135.

23. For the film's release on VHS, Dante shot and inserted a replacement scene, in which the tape appears to be faulty, a test pattern fills the screen, and the gremlins engage in video-specific antics. In this case, it is John Wayne who, from within archival footage, puts the miscreants in their place.

24. Krohn, "The Outsider," p. 137.

25. Peyton Reed's 2003 *Down with Love* contains various scattershot references to Tashlin, but most of these are made in the spirit of evoking a generalized 1960s pop-culture zeitgeist. The film's chief referent is the cycle of Doris Day/Rock Hudson (or James Garner, or Rod Taylor, as the case may be) movies made between 1959 and 1966.

26. A recent volume that addresses the complicated issues surrounding genre and American animation (and which contains an excerpt from the present book) is Daniel Goldmark and Charlie Keil, eds., *Funny Pictures: Animation and Comedy in Studio-Era Hollywood* (Berkeley: University of California Press, 2011).

27. Of Tashlin's (approximate) contemporaries, only Gregory La Cava moved between animation and live-action film. As an animator in the 1910s and early 1920s, he worked at the Raoul Barré studio and at William Randolph Hearst's International Film Service; as a live-action director, he made such comedies as *She Married Her Boss* (1935) and *My Man Godfrey* (1936), but did not work exclusively in this genre: La Cava also made numerous dramas, such as *Symphony of Six Million* (1932), *Gallant Lady* (1933),

and *Private Worlds* (1935). In more recent years, directors such as Tim Burton and Terry Gilliam have moved from animation to live action.

28. However, the Academy bestowed upon Lewis the 2009 Jean Hersholt Humanitarian Award (often viewed as something of a consolation Oscar) in recognition of his half-century of work with the Muscular Dystrophy Association. Like so many other facets of his career, the granting of this award carried with it a fair amount of controversy, as the familiar arguments about Lewis's objectification of "Jerry's Kids" once again resurfaced.

29. Noël Carroll, "Notes on the Sight Gag," in *Theorizing the Moving Image* (Cambridge: Cambridge University Press, 1996), p. 146.

30. Margaret A. Rose, *Parody: Ancient, Modern, and Post-modern* (Cambridge: Cambridge University Press, 1993), pp. 81–82.

31. I have made a similar distinction in my book *This Is Spinal Tap* (London: Wallflower Press, 2007).

32. Henry Jenkins, *What Made Pistachio Nuts?: Early Sound Comedy and the Vaudeville Aesthetic* (New York: Columbia University Press, 1992), pp. 281–82.

33. Tom Gunning, "Crazy Machines in the Garden of Forking Paths: Mischief Gags and The Origins of American Film Comedy"; Donald Crafton, "Pie and Chase: Gag, Spectacle and Narrative in Slapstick Comedy"; and Tom Gunning, "Response to 'Pie and Chase,'" in Kristine Brunovska Karnick and Henry Jenkins, eds., *Classical Hollywood Comedy* (New York: Routledge, 1995), pp. 87–105, 106–19, and 120–22, respectively.

34. See Gregory D. Black, *The Catholic Crusade against the Movies, 1940–1975* (Cambridge: Cambridge University Press, 1997), and Nina C. Leibman, *Living Room Lectures: The Fifties Family in Film & Television* (Austin: University of Texas Press, 1995), especially pp. 94–105.

1. TISH-TASH IN CARTOONLAND

1. Not counted in this tally are the approximately eight Disney cartoons on which Tashlin worked in some capacity between 1939 and 1941. As Howard Prouty puts it, this period in Tashlin's career is "definitely a subject for further inquiry." (Howard Prouty, "Filmography," in Roger Garcia, ed., *Frank Tashlin* [London: British Film Institute Publishing, 1994], p. 201.) The "Looney Tunes" DVDs have only recently amended the general unavailability of Tashlin's Warner Bros. cartoons; his Columbia cartoons, which many animators and animation scholars hold in high regard, have never been released on any form of video, and very rarely receive theatrical screenings, though they are occasionally aired on television. Tashlin's "one-off" cartoons have fared even worse, having very nearly joined the ranks of the forgotten.

2. I was able to see this rare film through the kind assistance of Jerry Beck and Mark Kausler.

3. Michael Barrier, *Hollywood Cartoons: American Animation in Its Golden Age* (New York: Oxford University Press, 1999), p. 74.

4. Leonard Maltin, *Of Mice and Magic: A History of American Animated Cartoons*, revised edition (New York: Plume Books, 1987), pp. 239–40.

5. Ibid.

6. Directors at the Schlesinger Unit were known as "supervisors," meaning that, in addition to their filmmaking duties, they oversaw the work of a small group of animators, in-betweeners, and writers.

7. For a much fuller account of this crucial moment in American animation history, see, especially, Barrier, *Hollywood Cartoons*.

8. Greg Ford, "'Cross-referred Media': Frank Tashlin's cartoon work," in Garcia, ed., p. 81.

9. Ibid., pp. 79–80.

10. Of course, there are no camera movements or high-angle shots per se in animation: such effects are simulated by the animator's hand. Throughout this volume, for the sake of clarity, all such devices are understood to be, in animation, simulated, though they are discussed using the same terms as their live-action analogues.

11. To be clear, Ford does not argue for the nonexistence of these techniques in pre-Tashlin animation; he may be correct that they were unusual. Still, they *do* occur in pre-1936 American animation. A single 1933 Popeye film, *Blow Me Down*, to take one isolated example, includes a high-angle shot of Popeye leaping up a saloon stairway, as well as an example of simulated camera movement: Popeye dispatches with a couple of dozen thugs in quick succession, and the camera "cranes" around the saloon to show us the locations in which Popeye's mighty punches deposit seven of them. (I thank Rachel Walls for calling this film to my attention.)

12. Leonard Maltin, *Of Mice and Magic*, pp. 231 and 234.

13. There are many such examples in Tashlin's animated *oeuvre*; one nearly identical such gag occurs in *Porky in the North Woods*, in which a sprightly beaver's swiftness is emphasized not once but three times with a repeated series of seven quickly cut shots.

14. Relevant here is a brief summary of the differences between Warners' two cartoon series, Merrie Melodies and Looney Tunes. Though now "Looney Tunes" is used as a catch-all term for Warner Bros. animation, the two series were, for years, distinct. Merrie Melodies, as their name shamelessly suggests, were designed to emulate the successful formula of Disney's Silly Symphonies, which were plotless cartoons designed around a piece of well-recognized music: characters would "act out" the lyrics to the song. Merrie Melodies were designed to exploit the vast Warner Bros. music cata-

log. At first, Looney Tunes were different only in name from Merrie Melodies, as they also were designed to showcase the songs of Warners' music library. In the mid-1930s, however, Looney Tunes became the Schlesinger Unit's forum for experimentation with recurring characters and more narrative-driven cartoons, while Merrie Melodies remained music-focused.

Speaking of the Weather, Have You Got Any Castles?, and You're an Education were all made under the Merrie Melodies banner, meaning that Tashlin is only partly responsible for their plotlessness. It was by studio decree that these and other Merrie Melodies are compendia of disconnected gags: they were never intended to present stories, but to promote pieces of popular music. All of Tashlin's Porky Pig films, however, are Looney Tunes. (See Barrier, *Hollywood Cartoons*, pp. 158–161, and Maltin, *Of Mice and Magic*, pp. 226–29.)

15. Of note is the film's framing device, in which a caricature of Alexander Woollcott, as the Town Crier (his popular radio character), provides a brief prologue and epilogue. The two Woollcott scenes—which total about eighty seconds—were trimmed from the film for its 1946 "Blue Ribbon" rerelease, and restored for the film's 2004 DVD release. (See Prouty, "Filmography," in Garcia, ed., p. 200.)

16. The film's title refers to the Warner Bros. feature *The Case of the Stuttering Bishop*, a 1937 Perry Mason mystery starring Donald Woods and Ann Dvorak.

17. In *Porky at the Crocadero*, Tashlin contorts Porky to have him impersonate Rudy Vallee, Paul Whiteman, and Cab Calloway; Howard Prouty calls this "Tashlin's most overt rebellion against the limitations of Porky's character. 'I hated him,' he said later—but no other director ever gave him a better showcase." (Prouty, "Filmography," in Garcia, ed., p. 200.)

18. Barrier, *Hollywood Cartoons*, p. 363.

19. Maltin, *Of Mice and Magic*, p. 236.

20. For a good, concise overview of the changes to Porky's appearance, see Jerry Beck, *Looney Tunes: The Ultimate Visual Guide* (New York: Dorling Kindersley Ltd., 2003), pp. 32–35.

21. Donald Crafton, "Performance in and of Animation," *Society for Animation Studies Newsletter* 1: 16, p. 10.

22. Ibid.

23. Ed Hooks, *Acting for Animators: A Complete Guide to Performance Animation* (Portsmouth, N.H.: Heinemann, 2000). See especially the Introduction and Chapter One.

24. Richard Williams, *The Animator's Survival Kit: A Manual of Methods, Principles and Formulas for Classical, Computer, Games, Stop Motion and Internet Animators* (London: Faber and Faber, 2001), p. 315. (Emphasis in original.)

25. Prouty, "Filmography," in Garcia, ed., pp. 206–7; Prouty, "Chronology," in Garcia, ed., pp. 188–89. Tashlin did direct three more Porky Pig films: *Porky Pig's Feat* (1943), *The Swooner Crooner* (1944), and *Brother Brat* (1944). For a thorough Warner Bros. animation filmography, see Maltin, *Of Mice and Magic*, pp. 421–23.

26. For overviews of the casting process in studio-era Hollywood, see Cathy Klaprat, "The Star as Market Strategy: Bette Davis in Another Light," in Tino Balio, ed., *The American Film Industry*, revised edition (Madison: The University of Wisconsin Press, 1985), pp. 351–76), and Ethan de Seife, "What's Sarong with This Picture?: The Development of the Star Image of Dorothy Lamour," http://archive.sensesofcinema.com/contents/02/22/lamour.html (last visited 3 August 2011).

27. Steve Schneider, *That's All Folks! The Art of Warner Bros. Animation* (New York: Henry Holt and Co., 1988), p. 143.

28. Ibid., p. 144.

29. For more on the evolution of Porky's appearance, see Barrier, *Hollywood Cartoons*, pp. 329–33.

30. See Maltin, *Of Mice and Magic*, p. 240, and Barrier, *Hollywood Cartoons*, p. 258.

31. Michael Barrier, "Bob Clampett: An Interview with a Master Cartoon Maker and Puppeteer," *Funnyworld* 12 (Summer 1970), p. 16.

32. Quoted in Maltin, *Of Mice and Magic*, p. 218.

33. Prouty, "Chronology," in Garcia, ed., p. 189.

34. Prouty, "Filmography," in Garcia, ed., p. 202.

35. In some cases, Tashlin, like many comic artists, simply stole his own jokes: a gag about William Powell (he is toothpick-skinny: a play on the *Thin Man* series), which Tashlin used in both *Speaking of the Weather* and *Have You Got Any Castles?*, shows up again in *A Hollywood Detour*.

36. Maltin, *Of Mice and Magic*, p. 246.

37. Michael Barrier writes that Bugs "may have been added to the cast" of *Elmer's Candid Camera* as a result of "early exhibitor and public enthusiasm" for the character in *Hare-um Scare-um* (1939). (Barrier, *Hollywood Cartoons*, p. 361.)

38. Ibid.

39. Schneider, *That's All Folks! The Art of Warner Bros. Animation*, p. 71.

40. Barrier, *Hollywood Cartoons*, p. 352.

41. Ibid., p. 441.

42. Ibid., p. 442.

43. The studio made 25 SNAFU cartoons (three were made by other studios), of which Tashlin directed four; Jones, eleven; Freleng, eight; and Clampett, two.

44. Greg Ford, "Cross-referred media," in Garcia, ed., p. 81.

45. See Maltin, *Of Mice and Magic*, pp. 426–29. One hundred and thirty-eight car-

toons in total were produced by the Schlesinger Unit during this period. In addition to those referred to above, Norman McCabe made ten; Robert McKimson, five; Tex Avery, two; and Arthur Davis, one.

46. Donald Crafton, "The View from Termite Terrace: Caricature and Parody in Warner Bros. Animation," in Kevin S. Sandler, ed., *Reading the Rabbit* (New Brunswick, N.J.: Rutgers University Press, 1998), p. 107.

47. Tashlin used this particular silly walk in a previous cartoon, *The Major Lied 'Til Dawn* (1938).

48. I am extremely grateful to Mark Kausler and Jerry Beck for showing me this rare film. Since the time I first saw it, *The Way of Peace* has been digitized and uploaded to the website of the Evangelical Lutheran Church in America: http://archive.elca.org/archives/film/wayofpeace.html (last visited 3 August 2011).

49. See Prouty, "Filmography," in Garcia, ed., p. 210, for details about the film's production.

50. In contrast to *The Way of Peace* stands Tashlin's book *The World That Isn't*, whose subject matter is similar but whose tone is radically different. (See Introduction.)

2. TASHLIN, COMEDY, AND THE "LIVE-ACTION CARTOON"

1. Brian Henderson, "Cartoon and Narrative in the Films of Frank Tashlin and Preston Sturges," in Andrew S. Horton, ed., *Comedy/Cinema/Theory* (Berkeley: University of California Press, 1991), p. 154.

2. See IMDB, "Biography for Frank Tashlin," http://www.imdb.com/name/nm0850895/bio (last visited 3 August 2011).

3. Dewey McGuire, "Well, what do you know? The little light: It stays on!," APATOONS 121, August 2002, p. 1.

This impulse receives its *reductio ad absurdum* in Jon Lewis's 2008 textbook *American Film*: "[Tashlin] was himself a cartoonishly large man — 6 feet 2 inches and 300 pounds — and he seemed particularly sensitive to the grotesque and the ridiculous." Jon Lewis, *American Film: A History* (New York: W.W. Norton, 2008), p. 266.

4. See Donald Crafton, "The View from Termite Terrace: Caricature and Parody in Warner Bros. Animation," in Kevin S. Sandler, ed., *Reading the Rabbit: Explorations in Warner Bros. Animation* (New Brunswick, N.J.: Rutgers University Press, 1998).

5. See Henry Jenkins, *What Made Pistachio Nuts? Early Sound Comedy and the Vaudeville Aesthetic* (New York: Columbia University Press, 1992), especially Chapter 3.

6. Frank Tashlin, quoted in Peter Bogdanovich, "Mr. Lewis Is a Pussycat," in Peter Bogdanovich, *Pieces of Time: Peter Bogdanovich on the Movies, 1961–1985* (New York: Arbor House, 1985), p. 58.

7. I thank Joe Dante for making this observation during an interview.

8. See http://www.michaelbarrier.com/Interviews/Tashlin/tashlin_interview.htm for an unedited transcript of Barrier's 1971 interview with Tashlin, in which the director discusses his working relationship with Stalling. (Last visited 3 August 2011.)

9. Joe Laurie, Jr., *Vaudeville: From the Honky-Tonks to the Palace* (New York: Henry Holt, 1953), p. 61.

10. Ibid., pp. 63–67.

11. Greg Ford, "'Cross-referred Media': Frank Tashlin's Cartoon Work," in Roger Garcia, ed., *Frank Tashlin* (London: British Film Institute Publishing, 1994), p. 81.

12. See Jonathan Rosenbaum, "Tashlinesque," in Garcia, ed., pp. 23–27, and J. Hoberman, "Frank Tashlin: vulgar modernist," in Garcia, ed., pp. 89–93.

13. Michael Barrier, *Hollywood Cartoons: American Animation in Its Golden Age* (New York: Oxford University Press, 1999), p. 435. "From [this point] on," Barrier writes, "there was no real difference between Looney Tunes and Merrie Melodies."

14. In point of fact, the economic factors behind a studio's decision to make a film in black and white or in color were complex, especially in the late 1950s and early 1960s—far more complex than may be addressed here. Gorham Kindem, in his excellent article on this subject, writes that, in the 1950s and 1960s, the distribution costs for black-and-white film were lower than those for color film, but that theatrical markets favored color films. So it was for complicated economic reasons—concerning production costs and the studios' main ancillary market, television—that a Tashlin film such as *The Man from the Diner's Club* (1963) was shot in black and white at a time when color was on the upswing. For a detailed look at this complex situation, see Gorham Kindem, "Hollywood's Conversion to Color: The Technological, Aesthetic, and Economic Factors," *Journal of the University Film Association* 2: 31 (Spring 1979), especially pp. 29 and 34–35.

15. Michael Barrier, "Interview with Frank Tashlin," in Roger Garcia, ed., *Frank Tashlin* (London: British Film Institute Publishing, 1994), pp. 156–57.

16. Interview with Chuck Jones by Greg Ford and Richard Thompson, in "Chuck Jones," *Film Comment* 1: 11, January-February 1975, pp. 25 and 36.

17. Interview with Tex Avery by Joe Adamson, *Tex Avery: King of Cartoons* (New York: Popular Library, 1975), p. 173.

18. Tashlin's one war-themed Columbia film, *Song of Victory*, is not especially comical: beyond some easy caricatures (e.g., Mussolini as a dumb, lumbering gorilla), the film is actually quite a serious take on Allied resistance.

19. Tashlin's VistaVision features are *Artists and Models, Hollywood or Bust, Rock-a-Bye Baby, The Geisha Boy*, and *Cinderfella*; his CinemaScope films are *The Lieutenant Wore Skirts, The Girl Can't Help It, Will Success Spoil Rock Hunter?, Say One for Me, Bachelor Flat*, and *Caprice*; *The Glass Bottom Boat* was filmed in Panavision.

20. David Bordwell, "Widescreen Processes and Stereophonic Sound," in David Bordwell, Janet Staiger, and Kristin Thompson, *The Classical Hollywood Cinema: Film Style and Mode of Production to 1960* (New York: Columbia University Press, 1985), pp. 360–62.

21. Gregory D. Black, *The Catholic Crusade against the Movies, 1940–1975* (Cambridge: Cambridge University Press, 1997), p. 5.

22. Untitled letter from Geoffrey Shurlock to Frank McCarthy, December 10, 1958. On file at the Margaret Herrick Library, Beverly Hills, CA.

23. Untitled letter from Geoffrey Shurlock to Frank McCarthy, April 1, 1958. On file at the Margaret Herrick Library, Beverly Hills, CA.

24. "Say One for Me," letter from Frank McCarthy to Frank Tashlin, December 12, 1958. On file at the Margaret Herrick Library, Beverly Hills, CA. An "A-1" rating indicated full approval from the powerful Catholic Legion of Decency,

25. "'Say One for Me'—Script," letter from John Trevelyan to J. Pattinson, Esq., December 19, 1958. On file at the Margaret Herrick Library, Beverly Hills, CA.

26. Frank Tashlin to Peter Bogdanovich, quoted in Prouty, "Filmography," in Garcia, ed., pp. 220–21. (The first two bracketed comments are mine; the third is Prouty's.)

3. "HURRY UP! THIS IS IMPOSSIBLE!": TASHLIN'S EARLY FEATURE FILMS

1. For Prouty's very detailed breakdown of Tashlin's contributions to *The Lemon Drop Kid*, see Harold Prouty, "Filmography," in Roger Garcia, ed., *Frank Tashlin* (London: British Film Institute Publishing, 1994), pp. 212–13.

2. Harold Prouty, "Chronology," in Garcia, p. 191.

3. Ibid.

4. Bill Krohn, "*The First Time*," in "Film Notes," in Garcia, ed., p. 164.

5. Today, and perhaps even in 1952, Joe's complaints come across as horribly sexist: Betsey is a failure at balancing housework and childcare, and she does not look as presentable as other women. It is difficult to determine if Joe's words are genuinely misogynist or if they are an attempt to satirize the cardboard machismo and sexual possessiveness of the American male; since other Tashlin films employ sexual/sexist humor that allows for each of these possible readings, both are viable. In fact, this ambivalence about gender is itself a hallmark of Tashlin's style. Still, this scene, viewed sixty years on, is somewhat difficult to decipher.

6. Untitled letter from Joseph I. Breen to Harry Cohn, May 4, 1951, p. 1. On file at the Margaret Herrick Library, Beverly Hills, CA.

7. Ibid.

8. Bob Hope and Bob Thomas, *The Road to Hollywood: My 40-Year Love Affair with the Movies* (Garden City, NY: Doubleday, 1977), p. 76.

9. Ibid., pp. 76–77.

10. Henry Jenkins, *What Made Pistachio Nuts?: Early Sound Comedy and the Vaudeville Aesthetic* (New York: Columbia University Press, 1992), pp. 60–62.

11. Ibid., p. 68.

12. Eddie Cantor, as told to David Freedman, *My Life Is in Your Hands* (New York: Blue Ribbon Books, 1932), p. 122.

13. See Jenkins, pp. 78–81, "'No Time for Plot': The Structure of the Vaudeville Act."

14. Joseph Laurie, *Vaudeville: From the Honky-Tonks to the Palace* (New York: Henry Holt, 1953), pp. 81, 83, 88, 93, 286.

15. John Lahr, "The C.E.O. of Comedy," *The New Yorker*, December 21, 1998, pp. 62–72.

16. Timothy White offers another quick sketch of Hope's "carefully casual screen personas—the crowing coward, the aspiring ladies' man and the stingy, shifty smart-ass with a repertoire of vague reassurances." (Timothy White, "The Road Not Taken: Bob Hope Without Laughter," *Rolling Stone*, March 20, 1980.)

17. A nearly identical gag appears in one of Tashlin's scenes in *The Lemon Drop Kid*.

18. The most thorough exploration of the homosexual elements of Hope's persona is surely that in Steven Cohan's essay "Queering the Deal: On the Road with Hope and Crosby," in Ellis Hanson, ed., *Out Takes: Essays on Queer Theory and Film* (Durham, NC: Duke University Press, 1999), pp. 23–45. Cohan's and Lahr's (and my own) observations about Hope's multifaceted sexual persona are essentially the same.

19. Though Tashlin contributed gags to the climactic swordfight scene in *Monsieur Beaucaire*, the above examples predate the Tashlin/Hope films. The sexual elements of Hope's persona were firmly established when Tashlin first directed him. (Tashlin mentions his contributions to this film in two interviews: Mike Barrier, "Interview with Frank Tashlin," in Garcia, ed., pp. 159–160, and Robert Benayoun, "The Raymond Chandler of Slapstick," in Garcia, ed., p. 126. He does not describe the gags in detail, but none of the scene's jokes are sexual in nature.)

20. Lahr, pp. 66, 73. The author does not cite the source of this joke, but it apparently aired in a 1940 radio show.

21. Hope appeared in several comic short-subject films between 1934 and 1936; see IMDb, "Bob Hope," http://imdb.com/name/nm0001362/ (last visited 3 August 2011).

22. Joe Morella, Edward Z. Epstein, and Eleanor Clark, *The Amazing Careers of Bob Hope* (New Rochelle, NY: Arlington House, 1973), pp. 98, 101.

23. Hope and Thomas, *Road to Hollywood*, p. 31.

24. This account does not consider Hope's vaudeville and radio personae, which had been established for some time. Initially, his shift to motion pictures seems to have "reset" his persona.

25. Eileen S. Quigley, ed., *2004 International Motion Picture Almanac, 75th Edition* (Groton, MA: Quigley Publishing, 2004), p. 20. Hope's complete rankings for this period are: 1941—four; 1942—five; 1943—two; 1944—three; 1945—seven; 1946—five; 1947—six; 1948—five; 1949—one; 1950—two; 1951—six; 1952—five; 1953—eight. These rankings represent the results of an annual survey of cinema owners.

26. Throughout this volume, "performance style" refers, simply, to an actor's method and techniques of acting, whereas "persona" refers to the combination of traits that adds up to his or her public image.

27. *Caught in the Draft* has not been chosen at random. The idea was to select a film with which Tashlin had nothing to do, and in which Hope's mature persona is on display (i.e., one made after *The Cat and the Canary*). Comparing *Son of Paleface* to an earlier Hope film, such as *College Swing* (1938), would surely highlight major differences in Hope's performance style, but it would be extremely difficult to attribute these differences with any certainty to Tashlin's influence, to the natural evolution of Hope's star image, or to any other single factor. In comparing *Caught in the Draft* and *Son of Paleface*, with the exception of the presence/absence of Tashlin, all other considerations are, for these purposes, roughly equal.

28. Quoted in Hope and Thomas, *Road to Hollywood*, p. 122. (Source not given.) The quotation is found in the section "Hope on Film," which Thomas appears to have written without Hope's help. "Healy" is also often spelled "Healey."

29. The fact that Hope's (often voluptuous) female costars commonly have male character names is another factor that complicates his own characters' sexualities.

30. Frank Tashlin, Robert Welch, Joe Quillan, *Son of Paleface*, Revised Final White version, dated August 7, 1951, p. 56. On file at the Margaret Herrick Library, Beverly Hills, CA. Production on this film began on August 7, 1951: this version of the script was approved at the beginning of the shoot. (See Prouty, "Filmography," in Garcia, ed., p. 213, for information on shooting dates.)

31. Quoted in Prouty, "Filmography," p. 214.

32. Of the seven "Road" films, five (*Road to Singapore* [1940], *Road to Zanzibar* [1941], *Road to Morocco* [1942], *Road to Utopia* [1946], and *Road to Rio* [1947]) were made before *Son of Paleface* commenced production.

33. Untitled letters from Joseph I. Breen to Luigi Luraschi, July 26 and August 9, 1951. On file at the Margaret Herrick Library, Beverly Hills, CA.

34. Robert Welch and Joseph Quillan, the film's cowriters, should also be credited with this decision.

35. See Thomas Schatz, "The Western," in Wes D. Gehring, ed., *Handbook of American Film Genres* (New York: Greenwood Press, 1988), pp. 29–31.

36. Ibid., p. 27.

4. THE ARTIST AND HIS MODEL: TASHLIN AND JERRY LEWIS IN THE 1950S

1. Peter Bogdanovich, "Mr. Lewis Is a Pussycat," in Roger Garcia, ed., *Frank Tashlin* (London: British Film Institute Publishing, 1994), p. 133. Lewis's character in his 1961 film *The Errand Boy* is named not Tishman but Tashman.

2. Robert Kass, "Jerry Lewis Analyzed: His Antics Are Reflections of Some of the Untoward Aspects of Our Time," *Films in Review* 3: 4, March, 1954, p. 119. Lewis is also very well represented in Steve Seidman, *Comedian Comedy: A Tradition in Hollywood Film* (Ann Arbor, MI: UMI Research Press, 1981).

3. Shawn Levy, *King of Comedy: The Life and Art of Jerry Lewis* (New York: St. Martin's Press, 1996), p. 104.

4. Ibid., p. 99.

5. Ibid., pp. 99–100.

6. Screenwriter Ed Simmons, quoted in Levy, p. 104.

7. Joey Adams with Henry Tobias, *The Borscht Belt* (New York: Bobbs-Merrill, 1966), pp. 179–80.

8. Stefan Kanfer, *A Summer World: The Attempt to Build a Jewish Eden in the Catskills, from the Days of the Ghetto to the Rise and Decline of the Borscht Belt* (New York: Farrar Straus Giroux, 1989), p. 106.

9. John Russell Taylor, "Jerry Lewis," *Sight and Sound* 2: 34, Spring 1965, p. 85.

10. Murray Pomerance, "Introduction," in Murray Pomerance, ed., *Enfant Terrible!: Jerry Lewis in American Film* (New York: New York University Press, 2002), pp. 3–4.

11. *You're Never Too Young* was filmed between October 18 and December 27, 1954, and *Artists and Models* was filmed between February 28 and May 3, 1955. (See IMDb, "Box Office/Business for *You're Never Too Young*," http://www.imdb.com/title/tt0048822/business, and IMDb, "Box Office/Business for *Artists and Models*," http://www.imdb.com/title/tt0047840/business, last visited 3 August 2011.)

12. Presumably the egg is part of some kind of protein-rich hair treatment; this is the kind of thing lost on modern viewers.

13. See Levy, pp. 194–207, for an account of the deterioration of the relationship between Martin and Lewis.

14. Memo from associate producer Paul Nathan to producer Hal Wallis, 18 April 1956. On file at the Margaret Herrick Library, Beverly Hills, CA.

15. Memo from William C. Davidson (presumably a studio doctor) to producer Hal

Wallis, 18 May 1956. (Results of the EKG administered to Lewis indicated "too much activity, overeating, or too many cigarettes.") On file at the Margaret Herrick Library, Beverly Hills, CA.

16. Memo from Nathan to Wallis, 18 April 1956. On file at the Margaret Herrick Library, Beverly Hills, CA.

17. Memo from Nathan to Wallis, 21 May 1956. On file at the Margaret Herrick Library, Beverly Hills, CA.

18. *Artists and Models* was released on 7 November 1955; *Hollywood or Bust* on 6 December 1956. (Between these two films, *Pardners*, directed by Norman Taurog, was released on 1 August 1956: for most of their ten-year screen partnership, a Martin and Lewis film was released roughly every six months.)

19. Memo from Geoffrey Shurlock to Hal Wallis, 12 April 1956. This memo, the only portion of the film's PCA dossier on file in an archive, refers to an "incomplete final script dated April 2, 1956." (On file at the Margaret Herrick Library, Beverly Hills, CA.)

20. The TV panel scene is a direct response to *The Seduction of the Innocent*, Frederic Wertham's infamous 1954 book about the corrupting influence of comic books.

21. Tashlin also makes a joke about Hollywood narration in the film's brief denouement. The four leads take the stage at the Artists and Models Ball in their everyday clothes. Tashlin pans to a prop churchbell tolling—cleverly hiding a cut—then pans back to show the actors in tuxedoes and wedding gowns. The actors make humorous reference to this impossible sartorial switch by looking down at their clothing in surprise, then up at the camera. The joke calls attention to the pat Hollywood ending in that even the characters are surprised by its suddenness.

22. As numerous critics have noted, Tashlin steals this joke from his own 1944 cartoon *I Got Plenty of Mutton*.

23. Untitled letter from Geoffrey M. Shurlock to Hal Wallis, January 20, 1955, pp. 1–4. On file at the Margaret Herrick Library, Beverly Hills, CA.

24. See untitled letters from Geoffrey M. Shurlock to Hal Wallis, January 20, January 25, February 9, and March 2, 1955. On file at the Margaret Herrick Library, Beverly Hills, CA.

25. Information on shooting and screening dates are from Howard Prouty, "Filmography," p. 215, in Garcia, ed.

26. Actually, this shot has a secondary purpose. In the background, beyond Sonia and Eugene, lurk three Communist spies in a doorway: this is the first time we learn that these men are in the house. (See Figure 4.9.) Tashlin could have argued for the shot's necessity on the grounds that it informs us of the presence of these narratively important characters. However, Sonia's association with the spies has already been clearly established in previous scenes, and we know that she is trying to ensnare

Eugene—that the henchmen are present is a given. Still, we may safely assume that Tashlin used this very argument during the censorship negotiations.

27. Undated memo, Paul Nathan to Hal Wallis, in the *Artists and Models* file at the Margaret Herrick Library, Beverly Hills, CA.

28. See, for instance, Frank Miller, *Censored Hollywood: Sex, Sin & Violence on Screen* (Atlanta: Turner Publishing, 1994), pp. 168–81, and Leonard J. Leff and Jerold L. Simmons, *The Dame in the Kimono: Hollywood, Censorship, and the Production Code from the 1920s to the 1960s* (New York: Grove Weidenfeld, 1990), Chapter Nine.

29. Gregory D. Black, *The Catholic Crusade against the Movies, 1940–1975* (Cambridge: Cambridge University Press, 1997), p. 149.

30. Quoted in Black, *Catholic Crusade*, pp. 154–55.

31. See Black, *Catholic Crusade*, p. 155. "Sexual perversion" was PCA argot for "homosexuality."

5. THE DIRECTOR AND THE BOMBSHELL: TASHLIN AND JAYNE MANSFIELD

1. *Time*, for instance, says that *Will Success Spoil Rock Hunter?* "easily slides home as the year's most hilarious movie" (unattributed review, "The New Pictures," *Time* 8: 78 [August 18, 1957], p. 78). Tashlin, in an interview with Robert Benayoun, refers to his Mansfield films as the best of his career. (Robert Benayoun, "The Raymond Chandler of Slapstick," in Roger Garcia, ed., *Frank Tashlin* [London: British Film Institute Publishing, 1994], p. 128).

2. Martha Saxton, *Jayne Mansfield and the American Fifties* (Boston: Houghton Mifflin, 1975), pp. 40–43.

3. Quoted in Saxton, *Jayne Mansfield*, p. 45.

4. Ibid., p. 52.

5. *Variety* at this time looked only at box-office estimates for certain American and Canadian cities, and the two films appear to have had different distribution patterns.

6. Interview with the author, New York City, July 2003.

7. The PCA files for *The Girl Can't Help It* are fairly nonspecific and unrevealing—a surprising situation, considering its many visual jokes about Jayne Mansfield's body.

8. Prouty lists the shooting dates of *Will Success Spoil Rock Hunter?* as March 19 through May 2, 1957. (Prouty, "Filmography," in Garcia, ed., p. 218.) See also untitled letters from Geoffrey Shurlock to Frank McCarthy, February 7 and March 13, 1957. On file at the Margaret Herrick Library, Beverly Hills, CA.

9. Frank Tashlin, untitled letter to Frank McCarthy, March 18, 1957. In the Frank Tashlin Collection at the Margaret Herrick Library, Beverly Hills, CA. (Emphasis in original.)

10. Lea Jacobs, *The Wages of Sin: Censorship and the Fallen Woman Film, 1928–1942* (Berkeley: University of California Press, 1995), p. 35.

11. Untitled letter from Frank McCarthy to Frank Tashlin, March 13, 1957. On file at the Margaret Herrick Library, Beverly Hills, CA.

12. Tashlin, untitled letter to Frank McCarthy, March 18, 1957. In the Frank Tashlin Collection at the Margaret Herrick Library, Beverly Hills, CA. (Bobo's surname had not yet been changed to "Branigansky.")

13. Emphasis mine.

14. Shurlock, untitled letter to Frank McCarthy, March 13, 1957. On file at the Margaret Herrick Library, Beverly Hills, CA.

15. Tashlin, untitled letter to Frank McCarthy, March 18, 1957. In the Frank Tashlin Collection at the Margaret Herrick Library, Beverly Hills, CA. (Emphasis in original.)

16. Shurlock, untitled letter to Frank McCarthy, March 13, 1957, p. 2. On file at the Margaret Herrick Library, Beverly Hills, CA.

17. Tashlin, untitled letter to Frank McCarthy, March 18, 1957. In the Frank Tashlin Collection at the Margaret Herrick Library, Beverly Hills, CA.

18. Untitled memo from Frank McCarthy to Buddy Adler, Frank Tashlin et al., June 4, 1957. On file at the Margaret Herrick Library, Beverly Hills, CA.

19. There are two important exceptions to the claim that the musical numbers are unintegrated with the flow of narrative information. The first is Eddie Cochran's number, "Twenty-Flight Rock," which Miller, Jerri, and Fats watch on television. Cochran's performance is crucial to the narrative: Fats, upon seeing it, insists to Miller that Jerri, even if she does not have a "trained voice," still has star potential—Cochran, after all, is a huge success in spite of his stuttering delivery and herky-jerky stage presence. Miller is forced to admit that Fats is right, and, against both Jerri's and his own better judgment, resumes rehearsals. This scene is discussed in greater detail later in this chapter.

The second key exception comes in the film's climactic scene, in which Jerri headlines a concert that also features Fats Domino, The Platters, and other acts. Slated to sing her hit "Rock around the Rockpile," Jerri has the conductor, Ray Anthony, switch tempos and back her up on a sad song, "Ev'rytime." Jerri handles the song beautifully, to the surprise of Miller, Fats, and the audience: until this point, we have only heard her lightbulb-shattering wail. Jerri explains her singing ability to Miller in a subsequent scene: she had feigned an inability to sing in order to free herself from her obligation to Fats. The "Ev'rytime" number is not only an instance of the integration of performance and narrative, but it is *the* key moment in the resolution of all of the film's narrative concerns. "Ev'rytime" is also the only musical number performed by one of the story's central figures (if we discount Jerri's "performance" of "Rock around the Rockpile" in the recording studio), a fact that instantly makes it more narratively vital than, for instance, Abbey Lincoln's fine rendition of "Spread the Word."

20. Tashlin makes a very ambiguous joke about the song's racial origins. While Tom and Jerri watch Cochran with mild befuddlement, Jerri's black maid, Hilda (Juanita Moore), demonstrates her enjoyment of the song by dancing around Jerri's living room. When Miller looks at her questioningly, Hilda makes a smiling gesture of dismissal and leaves the room, still dancing.

The scene's stance on racial matters is uncertain. Hilda, the only black person in the scene, seems to have a "deeper connection" to the music—arguably a version of the stereotype about the hypersexuality and "natural rhythm" of black people. But Hilda is also the only character to connect to the music on an authentic level: the song was made to be danced to, and she enjoys dancing to it. Jerri and Tom—both of whom are involved in the music industry—don't know what to make of the song. For them, Cochran's style is nothing more than a successful business model. This is precisely the kind of challenging, ambiguous cultural satire that Tashlin favors, as it reinforces the notion that rock music is *both* debased and authentic—a dynamic that was and is undeniably relevant to the American music industry.

21. This cameo role was originally intended for Jerry Lewis. See Prouty, "Filmography," in Garcia, ed., p. 218.

22. See Henry Jenkins, *What Made Pistachio Nuts? Early Sound Comedy and the Vaudeville Aesthetic* (New York: Columbia University Press, 1992), pp. 131–37.

23. Prouty, "Filmography," in Garcia, p. 218.

6. DISORDERLY CONDUCT: TASHLIN IN THE 1960S

1. See Ed Sikov, *Laughing Hysterically: American Screen Comedy of the 1950s* (New York: Columbia University Press, 1994), pp. 179–245; Dirk Lauwaert, "A fluttering Icarus," in Roger Garcia, ed., *Frank Tashlin* (London: British Film Institute Publishing, 1994), pp. 63–64; Robert Sklar, "Taking Tashlin seriously," in Garcia, ed., pp. 97–102. Sikov, in particular, makes a very strong case for the affinity between Tashlin and the decade of the 1950s.

2. The scene does, however, foreshadow a later event of very minor narrative value: the unexpected appearance of the Count Basie Orchestra at the climactic scene at the ball.

3. See Shawn Levy, *King of Comedy: The Life and Art of Jerry Lewis* (New York: St. Martin's Press, 1996), especially pp. 29, 59, and the photos at the center of the book.

4. Frank Krutnik, *Inventing Jerry Lewis* (Washington, D.C.: Smithsonian Institution Press, 2000), pp. 95–96.

5. Quoted in Levy, *King of Comedy*, p. 164.

6. Krutnik, *Inventing Jerry Lewis*, p. 94.

7. Levy, *King of Comedy*, p. 226.

8. "Whit.," review of *The Delicate Delinquent*, *Variety*, May 26, 1957.

9. Bosley Crowther, review of *The Delicate Delinquent*, *The New York Times*, July 4, 1957.

10. Lewis, quoted in Levy, p. 69. Lewis has always taken credit for this apt coinage.

11. Arthur Marx, *Everybody Loves Somebody Sometime (Especially Himself): The Story of Dean Martin and Jerry Lewis* (London: W.H. Allen, 1975), p. 205.

12. Krutnik, *Inventing Jerry Lewis*, p. 105.

13. Disregarding cameos, Lewis also made four other films in the transitional period 1957–1960: *The Sad Sack* (1957, George Marshall), *Don't Give Up the Ship*, (1959, Norman Taurog), *Visit to a Small Planet* (1960, Taurog), and *The Bellboy* (Lewis, 1960).

14. That sentiment is important to the film is supported by its studio publicity, which downplays the wacky aspects of the Lewis persona to emphasize the film's sentimental qualities. One of the film's taglines reads, "Jerry Lewis gets inside of you . . . halfway between your funnybone and your heart as CinderFella." (*Cinderfella* pressbook, Paramount Pictures, 1960. From the *Cinderfella* folder, University of Southern California Cinema/Television Library.) And the image on the film's poster was painted by Norman Rockwell!

15. Howard Prouty, "Filmography," in Garcia, ed., p. 221. Lewis gives this same account on the commentary track of the DVD of *The Bellboy*.

16. Claire Johnston and Paul Willemen, "Chronology," in Claire Johnston and Paul Willemen, *Frank Tashlin* (Colchester: Vineyard Press, 1973), p. 143.

17. David Ehrenstein, "Frank Tashlin and Jerry Lewis," in Garcia, ed., p. 45.

18. Ibid., p. 47.

19. Jerry Lewis with Herb Gluck, *Jerry Lewis in Person* (New York: Atheneum, 1982), p. 200.

20. Andrew Sarris, *The American Cinema: Directors and Directions, 1929–1968* (New York: E.P. Dutton, 1968), pp. 140–41. Sarris notes that much of the book's piece on Tashlin, including the above quotation, comes from an uncited piece he wrote in 1963.

21. Ibid., pp. 140–41.

22. Ibid., p. 241. Lewis's company in this section is W. C. Fields, Harold Lloyd, The Marx Brothers, and Mae West.

23. Though he rails against advertising in several films, Tashlin was not immune to the forces of product placement. In fact, *Who's Minding the Store?*, the film Tashlin and Lewis made immediately before *The Disorderly Orderly*, so noticeably places several products that *The New York Times* saw fit to run an article on the subject. (John

M. Lee, "Advertising: Tie-ins with Movies Increase," *The New York Times*, January 12, 1964, p. F12.)

24. Untitled memo from Geoffrey Shurlock to Paramount producer Edward Schellhorn, September 16, 1964. On file at the Margaret Herrick Library, Beverly Hills, CA.

25. The one slight exception may be the moment, during the beach chase, in which Bruce, in leaping over the participants of a seaside weenie roast, accidentally impales a hot dog on the pointed end of his ever-present umbrella. The phallic imagery is inescapable, and the gag represents one of the film's few moments of gag/narrative integration: Bruce, by chasing these women, effects his own emasculation.

26. *Say One for Me*, made in 1959 between *The Geisha Boy* and *Cinderfella*, is an exceptional film in many regards, and is discussed in detail in Chapter Two.

27. Joey Adams, for instance, writes, "Danny Kaye still retains the undisputed title 'King of the Catskills' for his versatility." (Joey Adams with Henry Tobias, *The Borscht Belt* [New York: Bobbs-Merrill, 1959], p. 6.)

28. Terry-Thomas with Terry Daum, *Terry-Thomas Tells Tales: An Autobiography* (London: Robson Books, 1990), p. 1. (All ellipses in original.)

29. Ibid., p. 100.

30. Ephraim Katz, *The Film Encyclopedia*, Third Edition (New York: HarperPerennial, 1998), p. 340.

31. Day does appear in one shot that features a small sexual sight gag. In a scene in which Jennifer (Day) pretends to seduce Zack (Dick Martin), Tashlin places an "erect" rocket-shaped decoration on a nearby table. (The setting is a party at the home of a NASA astrophysicist.) Given the narrative situation, and knowing Tashlin's fondness for such gags, it is difficult not to see this item as a phallic symbol. (Figure 6.9d)

32. Compounding the joke was the open secret that Lynde was gay.

33. A similar gag occurs in the Tashlin-Lewis film *The Geisha Boy*; the (or an) antecedent for both may well be a gag that appears in *Wackiki Wabbit*, a 1943 Bugs Bunny film by Tashlin's erstwhile Looney Tunes compatriot, Chuck Jones.

7. THE MAN IN THE MIDDLE:
TASHLIN, AUTEURS, AND PROGRAMMERS

1. For a nuanced survey of the differences between the various tiers of studio production, see Lea Jacobs, "The B Film and the Problem of Cultural Distinction," *Screen*, Vol. 33, No. 1 (Spring 1992).

2. Hawks's comedies during this period are *Monkey Business* (1952), *Gentlemen Prefer Blondes* (1953), and *Man's Favorite Sport?* (1964); Wilder's are *Sabrina* (1954), *The Seven Year Itch* (1955), *Love in the Afternoon* (1957), *Some Like It Hot* (1959), *The Apart-*

ment (1960), *One, Two, Three* (1961), *Kiss Me, Stupid* (1964), and *The Fortune Cookie* (1966).

3. Joseph McBride, *Hawks on Hawks* (Berkeley: University of California Press, 1982), p. 1.

4. See Brian Taves, "The B Film: Hollywood's Other Half," in Tino Balio, *Grand Design: Hollywood as a Modern Business Enterprise, 1930–1939* (Berkeley: University of California Press, 1995), pp. 317–19.

5. A more recent work, Denise Mann's *Hollywood Independents: The Postwar Talent Takeover*, categorizes Hollywood's output during this time in a different but parallel manner. Mann's key distinction is between the blockbuster (costly, star-studded, heavily promoted films) and the "art film." The latter term Mann uses unconventionally: it refers here not to the works of Godard, Antonioni, and Bergman et al., but to smaller-budget "A" pictures that aspired, in one way or another, to social, critical, or aesthetic importance. Mann identifies five subtypes of art films, and notes that these subtypes overlap. The categories Mann identifies that are significant to this chapter are the blockbuster itself (this is where she slots Howard Hawks's *Gentlemen Prefer Blondes*, a film discussed below) and one of the subtypes of art film that is defined by the "director-auteurs" who helmed them, as well as by the fact that they were "singled out by the international press . . . [as] demonstrat[ing] a unique visual style, compelling theses, and distinctive sensibilities." It is into this category that Mann slots films by Wilder, Huston, Hitchcock, Ray, Ford, and Tashlin, naming *Some Like It Hot*, *The Apartment*, and *Will Success Spoil Rock Hunter?* as exemplars (Denise Mann, *Hollywood Independents: The Postwar Talent Takeover* [Minneapolis: University of Minnesota Press, 2008], pp. 12–13). Program pictures are somewhat outside the book's purview, but Mann acknowledges that, in spite of the many industrial changes that transpired in Hollywood during the years that her book analyzes, the program picture "survived in the form of medium-budget 'genre' pictures," an apt description for the works of Taurog, McLeod, Walker et al. (Mann, p. 4).

6. Walker's comedies include (* indicates a Jerry Lewis film; † indicates a Bob Hope film): †*Road to Utopia* (1946), **My Friend Irma Goes West* (1950), **At War with the Army* (1950), **That's My Boy* (1951), **Sailor Beware* (1952), and †*Road to Bali* (1952). McLeod's comedies include *The Secret Life of Walter Mitty* (1947), †*Road to Rio* (1947), †*The Paleface* (1948), †*My Favorite Spy* (1951), *Never Wave at a WAC* (1952), †*Casanova's Big Night* (1954), *Public Pigeon No. One* (1957), and †*Alias Jesse James* (1959). Taurog's comedies include **Jumping Jacks* (1952), **The Stooge* (1953), **The Caddy* (1953), **Living It Up* (1954), **You're Never Too Young* (1955), **Pardners* (1956), *Onionhead* (1958), **Don't Give up the Ship* (1959), **Visit to a Small Planet* (1960), and no fewer than nine Elvis Presley films made between 1960–1968.

7. This accounting does not include Hawks's *Only Angels Have Wings* (1939) or Wilder's *Irma la Douce* (1963), which star Grant and Lemmon, respectively, but are not strictly comedies (though this is arguable in the case of *Irma la Douce*).

8. Mann, pp. 114–115.

9. Somewhat incredibly, there is no mention of this line in the extant Production Code Administration files on the film at the Margaret Herrick Library, Beverly Hills, CA. This joke does *not* appear in the text of the play on which the film is based. (See Steve Fisher and Alex Gottlieb, *Susan Slept Here* [New York: Samuel French, Inc., 1956].)

10. See Steve Seidman, *Comedian Comedy: A Tradition in Hollywood Film* (Ann Arbor, MI: UMI Research Press, 1981), especially the Introduction and Chapter One.

11. According to Joseph McBride, this is, in fact, Howard Hawks's voice. (Joseph McBride, *Hawks on Hawks* [Berkeley: University of California Press, 1982], p. 174.)

12. See Mann, pp. 118–120, for a consideration of Wilder's and Tashlin's films. Mann finds Wilder and Tashlin closer in comic temperament than I do.

13. For a typology of the ways in which performance is integrated into Hollywood comedies, see Henry Jenkins, *What Made Pistachio Nuts?: Early Sound Comedy and the Vaudeville Aesthetic* (New York: Columbia University Press, 1992), Chapters 4 and 5.

14. For further discussion of this scene, see Noël Carroll, "Notes on the Sight Gag," in Noël Carroll, *Theorizing the Moving Image* (Cambridge: University of Cambridge Press, 1996), pp. 146–157.

15. For an incisive, detailed study of the rise of independent Hollywood production, see, again, Mann's *Hollywood Independents: The Postwar Talent Takeover*, which addresses in detail this very phenomenon.

16. Curiously, Tashlin did establish The Frank Tashlin Co., Inc., in 1953, but its express purpose was the production of works for television. It produced only two shows: "Oops, It's Daisy" (1953) and "The Great Gildersleeve" (1954). (See Howard Prouty, "Chronology," in Garcia, ed., pp. 191–192, and "Filmography," in Garcia, ed., pp. 226–227.)

17. See Prouty, "Chronology," in Garcia, ed., *Frank Tashlin*, pp. 187–195, and Prouty, "Filmography," in Garcia, ed., pp. 198–226.

8: WHO'S MINDING THE STORE?: TASHLIN'S INFLUENCE

1. Quoted in Emanuel Levy, "Viva Pedro! Almodovar's Desire to Desire," available at http://www.emanuellevy.com/article.php?articleID=3086, last visited August 3, 2011.

2. Paul Julian Smith, *Desire Unlimited: The Cinema of Pedro Almodóvar*, second edition (London: Verso, 2000), p. 97. (Smith's "much has been made" refers to Bruce Babington and Peter W. Evans, *Affairs to Remember: The Hollywood Comedy of the Sexes*.)

3. Vito Russo, "Pedro Almodóvar on the Verge . . . Man of La Mania," in Paula

Willoquet-Maricondi, *Pedro Almodóvar Interviews* (Jackson: University of Mississippi Press, 2004), pp. 64–65.

4. Levy, "Viva Pedro!"

5. Russo, "Pedro Almondóvar on the Verge," p. 64.

6. For present purposes, I have considered as Godard's "early period" his fifteen features from *Breathless* (1959) to *Weekend* (1967), with *Le Gai savoir* (1968) serving as the definitive break with his New Wave period. Earlier films, like *Les Carabiniers* or *La Chinoise*, are of course political in content, but this is not the place to make such distinctions. Godard's career is too long and diverse to study in full here; the 1959–1967 films will suffice for present purposes, though I believe a more extensive comparison would be revealing.

7. Jean-Luc Godard, "Mirliflores et Bécassines," *Cahiers du Cinéma* 62 (August-September 1956), p. 46.

8. See http://www.toonopedia.com/loopy.htm for further information on this largely forgotten character. (Last visited 3 August 2011.)

9. See Lenny Borger, "A *Made in U.S.A.* Concordance" (Rialto Pictures, 2009), available online at http://www.filmforum.org/films/made.html (last visited 3 August 2011).

10. Though I cannot prove it, I harbor the suspicion that *Hollywood or Bust*, a road movie for which Godard had immense praise (his "Tashlinesque" remark, cited in the Introduction, originates from his review of this film), is a major influence on *Weekend*, which is, ultimately, a road movie just as episodic and as marginally unified as Martin and Lewis's last film. There are plenty of other road movies from which Godard may (or may not) have derived some inspiration, but it seems to me that the "anarchic" comedy of *Hollywood or Bust* would need only the slightest provocation to edge into the genuinely anarchic violence of *Weekend*.

11. See Jacques Rivette, "Notes sur une révolution," *Cahiers du Cinéma* 54, Christmas 1955, in Jim Hillier, ed., *Cahiers du Cinéma: The 1950s: Neo-Realism, Hollywood, New Wave* (Cambridge: Harvard University Press, 1985), p. 94.

12. Eric Rohmer, "Rediscovering America," in Hillier, *Cahiers du Cinéma*, p. 89. Translated by Liz Heron.

13. Bernard Eisenschitz, "Pardon My French," in Roger Garcia, ed., *Frank Tashlin* (London: British Film Institute Publishing, 1994), p. 105.

14. Amy Taubin, "Surface Tension," *The Village Voice*, 2 January 2001. Available online at http://www.villagevoice.com/film/0052,162620,21135,20.html, last visited 3 August 2011.

15. Dante's familiarity with the vaudeville idiom is also clear in "French Ventriloquist's Dummy," a segment deleted from the film but available on its DVD. The sketch

is about a Las Vegas ventriloquist who, due to a mix-up, must perform his act with a French dummy, who, of course, speaks only in French. Though an "interpreter dummy" (!), the French dummy at one point haughtily declaims that he does not do "cheap vaudeville jokes," but, rather, works in higher forms of performative art—a complaint suspiciously similar to one voiced by Jerry Lewis at the beginning of his film career.

16. This attempt was largely unsuccessful. According to Box Office Mojo, this $80 million film made only $20.9 million domestically, for a worldwide total of $68.5 million. (See Box Office Mojo, "Looney Tunes Back in Action," http://boxofficemojo.com/movies/?id=looneytunesbackinaction.htm (last visited 3 August 2011).

17. Interview with the author, 22 June 2004, West Hollywood, CA.

18. Interestingly, *Looney Tunes: Back in Action* is just as Godardian as it is Tashlinian, at least in its freewheeling combination of both "high" and "low" art, a tendency epitomized in a scene in which Bugs, Daffy, and Elmer Fudd rampage through The Louvre. Taking a page from the old Termite Terrace jokebook, Dante has the characters step "into" such paintings as Edvard Munch's *The Scream*, Salvador Dalí's *The Persistence of Memory*, and Georges-Pierre Seurat's *A Sunday Afternoon on the Island of la Grande Jatte*. (Never mind that the Louvre houses none of these paintings.) As Bugs and Daffy run through these paintings, their forms are reconfigured to match: they ooze through Dalí's surrealist landscape and, when inside Munch's painting, are rendered in bold, Expressionist brushstrokes. The topper to this extended set piece occurs when Elmer steps out of Seurat's painting still in microdotted form, at which point Bugs reads from an art-history textbook the definition of pointillism, and then proceeds to dispatch Elmer with a swift gust from a hair dryer. This gleeful combination of popular art and High Art echoes Godard's bouillabaise of referentiality, in which William Faulkner, Loopy de Loop, Mozart, Humphrey Bogart, Fritz Lang, and countless others attain equivalent cultural status. Indeed, inasmuch as Godard employs anarchic Hollywood comedy, we should not be surprised to find many other similarities between his and Dante's films.

19. Interestingly, none of the three admitted Tashlin acolytes discussed here seems to have drawn particularly heavily on one of the elements of Tashlin's style that has, over the years, attracted much critical attention: his risqué humor. It is not that these directors' works contain no elements of sexuality; far from it, as the topic is a central concern for Almodóvar and Godard (but not for Dante), both of whom seem no less than preoccupied with inter- and/or intragender relations. Rather, these directors are interested in sexuality but, unlike Tashlin, are not generally interested in presenting it within a context of ribald humor.

Tashlin is not an especially widely known director today, but many of those who *do* know his work are familiar with his blue humor. Several recent articles focus on Tashlin's ribaldry; for instance, the website for a Tashlin series in Berkeley remarks, "Tashlin gave new meaning to the phrase 'broad comedy'"; an article in the *East Bay Express* notes, "Sex in a Tashlin movie has the prurient, eye-popping brazenness of a teenage boy's pinup come to life"; and a review in *The Onion* of the Jayne Mansfield Collection DVD set can't resist the phrase "boob tube." For all of Tashlin's popular identity as a purveyor of saucy humor, none of the directors whose films most closely resemble Tashlin's seem especially interested in continuing along these particular Tashlinian lines. (See, respectively, Juliet Clark, "American Nonsense: Frank Tashlin," at http://www.bampfa.berkeley.edu/filmseries/tashlin2008; Kelly Vance, "The Guy Can't Help It," *East Bay Express*, 9 April 2008, at http://www.eastbayexpress.com/movies/the_guy_can_t_help_it/Content?oid=678907; and Nathan Rabin, "Jayne Mansfield Collection," *The Onion A.V. Club*, 16 August 2006, at http://www.avclub.com/content/node/51722 [all sites last visited 3 August 2011].)

20. Dante recently completed his first theatrical release since *Looney Tunes: Back in Action*. This film, *The Hole*, is a seemingly noncomic horror film designed to take advantage of the current wave of enthusiasm for 3-D technology. At the time of this writing, the film has not been picked up by an American distributor and has been shown only at festivals; it also won the top prize at the first Venice 3D Film Festival. (See Nick Vivarelli, "'Hole' wins Venice 3-D film prize," *Variety*, 14 September 2009. Available online at http://www.variety.com/article/VR1118008567.html?categoryid=13&cs=1&nid=2562; last visited 3 August 2011.)

INDEX

Adams, Joey, 96
Alias Jesse James (1959) (McLeod), 179
Almodóvar, Pedro, 187–90, 198
The Alphabet Murders (1966) (Tashlin), 170, 171, 172
Amazon Women on the Moon (1989) (Dante), 199–200
The American Cinema (Sarris), 151
anarchic comedy: Dante's use of, 7–8, 203–4; Godard's connections to, 195; and live-action/animation comparison, 55–56; Tashlin's legacy, 7–8, 198, 199, 201; vaudevillian roots of, 12–13. *See also* diegetic rupture; impossible comedy; reflexivity
animation: at Columbia/Screen Gems, 38–41; composition in, 17–18, 21–22, 28–29; editing pacing in, 21, 23–27, 53; identity of American, 52–53; introduction, 16–18; overview, 1–3; ubiquity of, xii–xiii; at Warner Bros., 1, 2–3, 18–30, 41–50, 56; *The Way of Peace* (1947), 50. *See also* live-action/animation relationship; Porky Pig
anticonsumerist satire: Dante's, 200, 201–2; Godard's, 195, 196–98; Tashlin's, 75, 140–42, 161–62, 179, 195, 204

Artists and Models (1955) (Tashlin): censorship issues, 114–18; vs. *Cinderfella*, 146, 150; vs. *The Disorderly Orderly*, 153–57, 161; as key work for Tashlin, 108, 110–18; vs. *You're Never Too Young*, 97–103
At War with the Army (1950) (Walker), 183
auteur directorial signature, Tashlin's claims to, 14–15, 174–80
authorship issue, 10, 147, 148–52
Average Shot Length (ASL), 23, 24, 64
Avery, Tex, 8, 17, 24, 41, 62
A Woman Is a Woman (1961) (Godard), 191–92, 194

Bachelor Flat (1962) (Tashlin), 6, 163–67, 168–69
Balaban, Barney, 76
Bande à part (1964) (Godard), 192, 194
Barrier, Michael, 31, 42
A Battle for a Bottle (1942) (Tashlin), 39
bawdy humor. *See* sexual humor
The Bear that Wasn't (Tashlin), 3
The Bellboy (1960) (Lewis), 150
Benny, Jack, 61–62
Black, Gregory D., 66–67, 117
blackout gags, 2, 11, 27, 28, 40–41, 150

Bob Hope films, 3, 4. *See also* Hope, Bob
Bogdanovich, Peter, 94
bombshell image, Mansfield's, 120–21, 125, 137
Booby Hatched (1944) (Tashlin), 48
Boom, Boom (1936) (King), 35, 36
Borscht Belt comedy, 96–97, 168
Bracken, Eddie, 3
breaking of the fourth wall, 56–57. *See also* diegetic rupture
Breen, Joseph I., 67, 72–73, 90
British Board of Film Censors, 67
Brown, Tregoweth, 58
Buddy's Beer Garden (1933), 18
Bugs Bunny, 41–42
The 'burbs (1989) (Dante), 204
Butler, David, 79
Byron, Jim, 120

The Caddy (Taurog), 179–80, 184
Cahiers du Cinéma, 5, 54, 191, 196
camera angles. *See* composition
Cantor, Eddie, 76–77
Caprice (1967) (Tashlin), 6, 169, 171, 172–73
Les Carabiniers (1963) (Godard), 191, 193
"cartooniness," 54–65
cartoons. *See* animation
Casanova's Big Night (McLeod), 179, 185
The Case of the Stuttering Pig (1937) (Tashlin), 30
The Cat and the Canary (1939), 78
Catholic Legion of Decency, 67, 108, 117
Caught in the Draft (1941) (Butler), 79–81, 84–86
Censored (1944) (Tashlin), 3
censorship: *Artists and Models*, 114–18; *The First Time*, 72–73, 74–75; *Hollywood or Bust*, 108; and lack of sexual humor in animation, 63; overview, 13; *Say One for Me*, 65–68; *Son of Paleface*, 89–90; taboo subjects, 117;

Tashlin as warrior against, 9–10, 13, 67–68, 74–75; *Will Success Spoil Rock Hunter?*, 128–32, 143
La Chinoise (Godard), 194, 195, 196
Cinderella Goes to a Party (1942) (Tashlin), 38, 40
Cinderfella (1960) (Tashlin), 6, 55, 64, 146–48, 149–50, 171–72
CinemaScope, 64
cinematography, live-action vs. animation, 53. *See also* composition
Clampett, Robert, 17, 34, 46
Cochran, Eddie, 139
Cohn, Harry, 72, 74
color-based comedy, Tashlin's lack of, 60–61, 188
Columbia Pictures, 2, 4, 6, 38–41. *See also The First Time*
comedian comedies, 12, 54, 56, 59, 175, 180. *See also* Hope, Bob; Lewis, Jerry
Comedian Comedy: A Tradition in Hollywood Film (Seidman), 12
comedy genre: and American animation, 52–53; increase in scholarly interest, xi–xii; and lack of respect in Hollywood, 208–9; and perils of working within a single genre, 14–15; Tashlin's contribution to, 14, 52. *See also* anarchic comedy; performative comedy
comic strip cartoons, 1, 61
composition: in animation, 17–18, 21–22, 28–29; camera movement as carrier of comedy, 26–27, 44–45; live-action/animation comparison, 53, 57–58; and widescreen space, 64, 135, 164, 194
Concerto in B-flat Minor (1942) (Tashlin), 39
consumer, satirizing of. *See* anticonsumerist satire
Contempt (Godard), 196
Cracked Ice (1938) (Tashlin), 27–28

Crafton, Donald, 14, 46
Crosby Bing, 6, 66, 91
Crowley, Patricia, 1
Cummings, Robert, 58–59, 71–74, 75, 176

"Daffy Ditties," 3
Daffy Duck, 46–47
Dalton, Timothy, 203
Dante, Joe, 7, 190, 191, 199–208
Day, Doris, 6, 167, 169
The Delicate Delinquent (1957) (McGuire), 148–50
DeLuise, Dom, 169, 170, 172
DeMille, Cecil B., 91
Desire Unlimited: The Cinema of Pedro Almodóvar (Smith), 188
diegetic rupture: in animation, 40; Dante's use of in *Looney Tunes*, 202–3; Godard's use of, 193–95, 197; live-action/animation comparison, 55–57; Mansfield films, 132, 134, 137–38, 142, 143; Martin and Lewis films, 103, 106, 111–12, 156; and program comedies, 180–81; *Son of Paleface*, 91–92; Tashlin's later films, 156, 158–59, 170–71
direct address to audience: Godard's use of, 194–95; Groucho Marx's use of, 143; in Tashlin's work, 132, 134, 142, 155, 156, 170; as vaudeville technique, 77, 96
directors of program comedies, 174–76, 178–81, 182–84
Disney, 2, 18
The Disorderly Orderly (1964) (Tashlin), 152–61, 197–98
Dog Meets Dog (1942) (Tashlin), 58
Domino, Fats, 139–40

"economy of gags," 32
editing: animation pacing, 21, 23–27, 53; in *The First Time*, 71; in *Hollywood or Bust*, 105; live-action/animation comparison, 53; vs. mise-en-scène for Tashlin, 12, 53, 65
Ehrenstein, David, 150
Eisenschitz, Bernard, 196
Elmer's Candid Camera (1940) (Jones), 41
The Errand Boy (1961) (Lewis), 152
Ewell, Tom, 126, 127, 132, 133, 135, *136*, 137
Explorers (1985) (Dante), 205–7

farce, 6, 163–67, 169, 171, 172
The First Time (1952) (Tashlin), 4, 69, 70–75, 90, 114, 176
Fleischer Animation, 1
Ford, Greg, 21, 43, 59
The Fox and the Grapes (1941) (Tashlin), 2, 40
frame-breaking, 8. See also diegetic rupture
France, critical acclaim in, 5
Frank Tashlin (Johnston and Willemen), 174
Fraser, Brendan, 203
Freleng, Friz, 17, 24, 31
frontal composition, 21–22, 57–58

gag/narrative integration: auteur of comedy and Tashlin's style, 181–82; defined, 13–14; *The Girl Can't Help It*, 135, 136, 137–38, 182; Lewis's avoidance of, 152–53; Porky Pig, 27–28; *Son of Paleface*, 90–92; Tashlin's later films, 145–48, 163–64; *Will Success Spoil Rock Hunter?*, 135, 137–38
gags: animation as crafting ground for, 55; defined, 10; staging and timing in animation vs. live-action, 64. See also specific types
gag writer, Tashlin as, 2, 3–4
The Geisha Boy (1958) (Tashlin), 57

The General (1927) (Keaton), 184
Gentlemen Prefer Blondes (1953) (Hawks), 182
The Ghost Breakers (1940), 78
The Girl Can't Help It (1956) (Tashlin): Dante and Tashlin's legacy, 206; vs. *The Disorderly Orderly*, 161; gag/narrative integration in, 135, 136, 137–38, 182; long-take comedy for plot summary, 65; Mansfield's performance in, 122–24; Mansfield's persona development, 119–20; satire in, 120, 126, 135, 138–41; sexual comedy in, 126–27; sight gags in, 60, 132, 133, 136
Give Me a Sailor (1938), 77
The Glass Bottom Boat (1966) (Tashlin), 6, 169, 170, 171, 172
Godard, Jean-Luc, 5, 54, 190–95, 204, 205
Gremlins 2: The New Batch (1990) (Dante), 7–8, 205
Gunning, Tom, 14

Hale, Barbara, 71–74, 75, 176
Hal Wallis Unit, 5
Have You Got Any Castles? (1938) (Tashlin), 27, 28
Hawks, Howard, 174, 176–77, 178, 180–81, 182
Hawks on Hawks (McBride), 174
Hellzapoppin' (1941), 8
Hoberman, J., 60
A Hollywood Detour (1942) (Tashlin), 38
"Hollywood ending," 133, 143, 179–80
Hollywood or Bust (1956) (Tashlin), 1, 103–8, 109
The Home Front (1943) (Tashlin), 42–44
Hook and Ladder Hokum (1933) (Tashlin), 1, 18
Hooks, Ed, 33
Hope, Bob: *Casanova's Big Night*, 179; *Caught in the Draft*, 79–81, 84–86; as comedian comic, 75; comedic persona of, 76–86, 96; performance style, 82–84; *The Private Navy of Sgt. O'Farrell*, 6–7, 168; *Road to Bali*, 176, 180; *Son of Paleface*, 82–86, 87, 88–89, 91, 92; and Tashlin, 70, 76, 81–82
How to Create Cartoons (Tashlin), 5
Hubley, John, 38

I Haven't Got a Hat (1936) (Freleng), 31–32
Illegal (1955), 121–22
impossible comedy: *Artists and Models*, 103, 112, 113; and cartooniness, 59; Dante's *Looney Tunes*, 201; *The Disorderly Orderly*, 158; *Gentlemen Prefer Blondes*, 182, 183; *The Girl Can't Help It*, 127; Godard's use of, 192; *Hollywood or Bust*, 105; *Son of Paleface*, 86, 87, 88, 89, 92, 93
improvisation, 76–77, 97
interruption. *See* diegetic rupture
intertextuality, 181, 192, 193
invisible style, 175
It's Only Money (1962) (Tashlin), 6, 161

Jenkins, Henry, 12, 32, 62, 76
Jerseyspeak, 101
Johnston, Claire, 150, 174
jokes. *See* gags
Jones, Chuck, 2, 17, 19, 24, 42, 62
Jumping Jacks (1952) (Taurog), 96

Kanfer, Stefan, 96
Kass, Robert, 94–95
Kaye, Danny, 6, 146, 147, 168
Keaton, Buster, 184
Keith circuit in vaudeville, 96
kettledrum gag, 89
King, Jack, 35
Krohn, Bill, 70
Krutnik, Frank, 148–49

The Lady Said No (1947) (Tashlin), x
Lahr, John, 77, 78
Lamour, Dorothy, 78, 79–81, 85
lampoon, 11, 75, 85, 91–92, 111, 134–35
Lanfield, Sidney, 4, 69
Laurie, Joseph, 58, 77
The Lemon Drop Kid (Lanfield), 4, 69, 70, 76, 79
Levy, Emanuel, 188
Levy, Shawn, 95, 149
Lewis, Jerry: *Artists and Models*, 97–103, 108, 110–14; authorship issue vs. Tashlin, 148–52; *Cinderfella*, 147–48, 149–50, 171–72; comic persona of, 94–96, 148–50, 161; dictation of camera style by, 57; *The Disorderly Orderly*, 152–61; *Hollywood or Bust*, 103–8; *It's Only Money*, 173; long-take comedy with, 64; overview of work with Tashlin, 5–6; performance style, 96–97, 98–101, 147; *You're Never Too Young*, 97–103
The Lieutenant Wore Skirts (1956) (Tashlin), 5, 177–78
Little Beau Porky (1936) (Tashlin), 19, 20
live-action/animation relationship: animated works influence on, 21–22; "cartooniness" in context, 54–65; introduction, 52–54; *Say One for Me* as exception to prove rule, 65–68
long-take comedy, 25–26, 46–47, 64–65
Looney Tunes, 1, 16, 42, 45–46
Looney Tunes: Back in Action (Dante), 200–201
Lord, Daniel, 67
Lynde, Paul, 169, 170

Made in U.S.A. (1966) (Godard), 192
Maltin, Leonard, 19, 23–24
The Man from the Diners' Club (1963) (Tashlin), 6, 145–46, 147

Mann, Denise, 176, 178
Mansfield, Jayne, 5, 59–60, 119–28, 136–38, 141–42, 143
Marry Me Again (1953) (Tashlin), 4, 58–59
Marshall, George, 95
Martin, Dean, 95–96, 98–99, 148, 149
Martin and Lewis films. *See* Lewis, Jerry
Marx, Groucho, 142, 143
Marx Brothers, 3
Masculin féminin (1966) (Godard), 192, 195, 196–97
McBride, Joseph, 174
McCarthy, Frank, 67, 128, 129
McGuire, Dewey, 54
McKimson, Robert, 31
McLeod, Norman Z., 4, 86, 175, 179, 185
Merrie Melodies, 1, 16, 18, 27–28
mise-en-scène: vs. editing in Tashlin's style, 12, 53, 65; live-action/animation comparison, 53–54, 58, 60; Tashlin's talent for, 9, 12, 53–54, 71, 132, 160
modular structure: Lewis's preference for, 149, 150–51, 152–53; live-action/animation comparison, 55; Tashlin's use of, 159–60, 162; vaudeville origins of, 77
Monkey Business (1952) (Hawks), 176–77, 180–81
Monsieur Beaucaire (1946) (Marshall), 3, 78
Morley, Robert, 171, 172
My Friend Irma Goes West (1950) (Walker), 95, 183

narrative. *See* gag/narrative integration; modular structure
Nasty Quacks (1945) (Tashlin), 46, 48
Nathan, Paul, 104, 116
New Wave criticism, 54
A Night in Casablanca (1946) (Mayo), 3

non-gags: in animation, 19, 20, 39; *Artists and Models*, 112–13; defined, 11; *The Disorderly Orderly*, 160; *The First Time*, 71; *Hollywood or Bust*, 105–6; importance for Tashlin, 12, 184–85; *Son of Paleface*, 88–89

offscreen space: in animation, 22–23, 45; *Artists and Models*, 113; *Cinderfella*, 171–72; *The Disorderly Orderly*, 155, 160; *Hollywood or Bust*, 105; *Son of Paleface*, 88–89; *Will Success Spoil Rock Hunter?*, 127–28
One, Two, Three (Wilder), 182

The Paleface (McLeod), 3, 4, 70
Paramount Pictures: and Hope, 70, 76, 79; and Lewis, 95, 152; Tashlin's contracts with, 3, 4, 5
parody, 11, 84–85, 111. *See also* satire; *Son of Paleface*
PCA (Production Code Administration), 9–10. *See also* censorship
performative comedy: animated characters, 33–38, 46–47; *The First Time*, 75; and frontal composition, 57–58; Hope's style, 82–84; Lewis's style, 96–97, 98–101, 147; Mansfield's style, 123–25; overview, 12–13
Le Petit Soldat (1963) (Godard), 194, 195
Petunia Pig, 2
Plane Daffy (1944) (Tashlin), 48, 49
Pomerance, Murray, 97
Porky at the Crocadero (1938) (Tashlin), 22
Porky in the North Woods (1936) (Tashlin), 22–23, 57
Porky Pig: composition and angles, 21–22; editing for humor, 23–27; gag/narrative integration, 27–28; and Mansfield's persona, 119; offscreen space, 22–23; personae and comic abilities, 56; and Tashlin's animated style, 19–20, 28–30; Tashlins development of, 2, 31–38
Porky Pig's Feat (1943) (Tashlin), 17, 44–45, 48, 58
Porky's Double Trouble (1937) (Tashlin), 27
Porky's Hare Hunt (1938), 41
Porky's Poultry Plant (1936) (Tashlin), 21, 22, 35
Porky's Railroad (1937) (Tashlin), 19–20
Porky's Road Race (1937) (Tashlin), 22, 23
Porky's Romance (1937) (Tashlin), 2, 22, 23, 32, 36–38, 58–59
Porky's Spring Planting (1938) (Tashlin), 24, 32, 57
Porky the Fireman (1938) (Tashlin), 23, 25, 64
Positif, 5, 54
The Private Navy of Sgt. O'Farrell (1968) (Tashlin), 6–7, 168, 171
"Private Snafu" series, 2–3, 42–43
producer, Tashlin as, 185
Production Code Administration (PCA), 9–10. *See also* censorship
program comedies, 174–76, 178–81, 182–84
Prouty, Howard, 69, 70, 143, 150
Puss 'n' Booty (1940) (Tashlin), 17, 45

quasi-diegetic breaks, 106, 140–41
Quigley, Martin, 68, 186

Randall, Tony: *The Alphabet Murders*, 170, 171, 172; *Will Success Spoil Rock Hunter?*, 121, 131, 132, 134, 137
rapid editing, 23–25, 26–27
reflexivity: Dante's *Looney Tunes*, 203; *The Disorderly Orderly*, 159; Godard's use of, 192, 193; *Hollywood or Bust*, 106; Tashlin's later films, 163, 171; vaudevillian roots, 12; Warner Bros. cartoons, 41, 47–48
"replacement" animation, 3

risqué humor. *See* sexual humor
Rivette, Jacques, 195–96
RKO, 4–5
Road to Bali (1952) (Walker), 176, 180
Road to Rio (1947) (McLeod), 86, 87
Rock-a-Bye Baby (1958) (Tashlin), 65, 161–62, 206
Rogers, Roy, 88, 90
Rohmer, Eric, 196
Rose, Margaret, 11
Rosenbaum, Jonathan, 60
running time and live-action/animation comparison, 64
Russell, Jane, 82–84, 85, 89
Russo, Vito, 189–90

Sarris, Andrew, 151–52
satire: *Artists and Models*, 111; auteurs of comedy, Tashlin's style vs., 178–80; Dante's, 200, 201–2, 204–6; defined, 11; *The First Time*, 75, 176; *The Girl Can't Help It*, 120, 126, 135, 138–41; Godard and Tashlin, 195–98; *Hollywood or Bust*, 108; live-action/animation comparison, 63–64; Tashlin's later films, 161–63; *Will Success Spoil Rock Hunter?*, 121, 134–35, 140–43
Say One for Me (1959) (Tashlin), 6, 65–68, 185–86
Scared Stiff (1953), 95
Schatz, Thomas, 92
Schlesinger, Leon, 1, 60
Schlesinger Unit, 2–3, 16–19, 34
Schneider, Steve, 34
SCOTArt system of illustration, 5
Screen Gems, 2, 38–41
The Second Civil War (1997) (Dante), 204–5
Seidman, Steve, 12, 56, 180
self-referentiality/self-reflexivity. *See* reflexivity
The Seven Little Foys (1955), 79

The Seven Year Itch (1955) (Wilder), 181–82
sexual humor: Almodóvar and Tashlin, 188–89; in animation, 17, 42–44, 63; and auteurs of comedy vs. Tashlin's style, 174–78; *Bachelor Flat*, 163–67; and censorship, 9–10, 72–73, 74, 90, 108, 114–16, 128–32, 143; downplaying of, 161; *The First Time*, 71, 72–74; in Hope films, 77–78, 89–90, 92, 114; in Lewis films, 96, 102–3, 107–8, 109, 113–18, 157, 161; live-action/animation comparison, 63; in Mansfield films, 126–32, 138, 142–44; overview, 13
showcase scene, 103, 146–47, 156–57
Shurlock, Geoffrey, 67, 115, 117, 128–31
sight gags: in animation, 32, 45–46; *Artists and Models*, 111–12; Dante's use of, 200; defined, 10–11; *The Disorderly Orderly*, 160; *The First Time*, 71; *The Girl Can't Help It*, 60, 132, 133, 136; Godard's use of, 191–92; *Hollywood or Bust*, 105, 106, 107–8; importance for Tashlin, 12, 185; live-action/animation comparison, 55, 64–65; *Son of Paleface*, 89; Tashlin's later films, 164–65, 171–72; *Will Success Spoil Rock Hunter?*, 132, 134–35, 143. *See also* non-gags
simulated camera movement, 26
Smith, Paul Julian, 188
Some Like It Hot (Wilder), 177
sonic humor: *Artists and Models*, 111, 113; *The First Time*, 71; *The Girl Can't Help It*, 123; Godard's use of, 194; *Hollywood or Bust*, 105; Lewis's vocalizations, 101–2; live-action/animation comparison, 58–59; *Son of Paleface*, 84, 89; in Tashlin's later films, 157, 172–73; *Wholly Smoke*, 29–30; *Will Success Spoil Rock Hunter?*, 142

Son of Paleface (1952) (Tashlin): vs. *Artists and Models*, 111; vs. *Caught in the Draft*, 79, 82–86; censorship issues, 89–90; as comedian comedy, 75; contract negotiations, 4, 70; gag/narrative integration, 90–92; impossible comedy in, 86, 87, 88, 89, 92, 93; lampooning of Hollywood narration, 92; sexual humor in, 114; various gags in, 88–89

Speaking of the Weather (1937) (Tashlin), 27

Stalling, Carl, 58

The Stooge (1953) (Taurog), 176

stop-motion animation, 3

studio system, 10, 12, 120, 174, 185–86, 196, 198, 208

Susan Slept Here (1954), 4–5, 57, 177

The Swooner Crooner (1944) (Tashlin), 46, 48

Tailleur, Roger, 54

Tashlin, Frank: and Almodóvar, 187–90; as auteur and program style director, 14–15, 174–80, 181, 182, 186; biographical sketch, 1–7; as censorship warrior, 9–10, 13, 67–68, 74–75; and Dante, 190, 199–208; and Godard, 190–98; hidden genius of, ix–x, 54; and Hope, 70, 76, 81–82; influence of, 7–10; legacy of, xiii, 7–8, 14, 52, 198, 199, 201, 208–9; and Lewis, 5–6, 57, 97–103, 148–52; live-action/animation relationship, 54–68; *mise-en-scène* talent of, 9, 12, 53–54, 71, 132, 160; and politics of studio system, 185–86; retrospective showings, xi; unique qualities of filmmaking style, 184–85; video availability of work, x; visual design talent of, 9, 17, 185. See also animation; *specific films and comedic techniques*

Tati, Jacques, 11, 19, 184

Taurog, Norman, 96, 97, 175, 176, 184

Taves, Brian, 175

Taylor, John Russell, 97

Termite Terrace, 1, 2, 19

Terry-Thomas, 6, 165–66, 168–69

"throwaway" gags, 104

"The Traffic Cop's Daughter" (still cartoon) (Tashlin), 61

Trevelyan, John, 67

Trigger, 89, 90

Twentieth Century-Fox, 5, 67, 120, 132, 134

Under the Shedding Chestnut Tree (1942) (Tashlin), 40

United Artists, 3, 6

Van Beuren animation studio, 1

"Van Boring" (comic strip), 1

Variety Girl (1947) (Marshall), 79

vaudeville: direct address to audience in, 77, 96; influence on Tashlin, 13; Lewis's Borscht Belt background, 96–97; live-action/animation comparison, 54, 56–57, 61–62; principal comic influences on, 54

visual design, Tashlin's talent for, 9, 17, 185. See also sight gags

Walker, Hal, 175, 176, 180, 183

Wallis, Hal, 95, 104, 115, 116

Walston, Ray, 66

Warner Bros., 1, 2–3, 18–30, 41–50, 56

The Way of Peace (1947) (Tashlin), x, 50–51

Weekend (1967) (Godard), 191, 192, 194, 197–98

Welch, Robert, 4, 70, 76

What Made Pistachio Nuts? (Jenkins), 12

The White Virgin of the Nile (movie-within-movie), 162

Wholly Smoke (1938) (Tashlin), 25–27, 28–30, 32
Who's Minding the Store? (1963) (Tashlin), 162
widescreen technology, 64, 135, 164, 194
Wilder, Billy, 174, 177, 178, 181–82
A Wild Hare (1940) (Avery), 41
Willemen, Paul, 150, 174
Williams, Richard, 33–34
Will Success Spoil Rock Hunter? (1957) (Tashlin): censorship challenges, 128–32, 143; vs. *Cinderfella*, 148; gag/narrative integration, 135, 137–38; and Godard's consumerist satire, 197–98; Mansfield's performance in, 124–26; Mansfield's persona development, 119–20; satire in, 121, 134–35, 140–43; sexual comedy in, 127–28, 143; sight gags in, 132, 134–35, 143
Wolf Chases Pigs (1942) (Tashlin), 40
Women on the Verge of a Nervous Breakdown (1988) (Almodóvar), 189–90
The World That Isn't (Tashlin), 4, 205

You're Never Too Young (1955) (Taurog), 97–98, 192

A SERIES FROM
WESLEYAN UNIVERSITY PRESS
Edited by Lisa Dombrowski
and Scott Higgins
originating editor: Jeanine Basinger

Anthony Mann
by Jeanine Basinger

It's the Pictures That Got Small
Hollywood Film Stars on 1950s Television
by Christine Becker

The South Korean Film Renaissance
Local Hitmakers, Global Provocateurs
by Jinhee Choi

Tashlinesque
The Hollywood Comedies of Frank Tashlin
by Ethan de Seife

The Films of Samuel Fuller
If You Die, I'll Kill You!
by Lisa Dombrowski

Kazan Revisited
edited by Lisa Dombrowski

Physical Evidence
Selected Film Criticism
by Kent Jones

The New Entrepreneurs
An Institutional History of
Television Anthology Writers
by Jon Kraszewski

Action Speaks Louder
Violence, Spectacle,
and the American Action Movie
by Eric Lichtenfeld

Hollywood Ambitions
Celebrity in the Movie Age
by Marsha Orgeron

Brutal Intimacy
Analyzing Contemporary French Cinema
by Tim Palmer

Soul Searching
Black-Themed Cinema from
the March on Washington
to the Rise of Blaxploitation
by Christopher Sieving

Paul on Mazursky
by Sam Wasson

A Splurch in the Kisser
The Movies of Blake Edwards
by Sam Wasson

ETHAN DE SEIFE is Assistant Professor of Film Studies at Hofstra University. He is the author of the book *This Is Spinal Tap*, and his articles have appeared in *Film International* and other journals. Visit his website, ethandeseife.wordpress.com, for further Tashliniana.